THE LIFE AND LETTERS
OF
JOHN DONNE

JOHN DONNE AT 18

THE LIFE AND LETTERS

OF

JOHN DONNE

DEAN OF ST. PAUL'S

NOW FOR THE FIRST TIME REVISED AND COLLECTED BY

EDMUND GOSSE

HON. M.A. OF TRINITY COLLEGE, CAMBRIDGE
HON. LL.D. OF THE UNIVERSITY OF ST. ANDREWS

WITH PORTRAITS, ETC.

IN TWO VOLUMES

VOL. I

WIPF & STOCK · Eugene, Oregon

Wipf and Stock Publishers
199 W 8th Ave, Suite 3
Eugene, OR 97401

The Life and Letters of John Donne, Vol I
Dean of St. Paul's
By Gosse, Edmund
ISBN 13: 978-1-5326-7810-3
Publication date 12/22/2018
Previously published by Dodd, Mead and Company, 1899

DEDICATION

to

The Right Honourable and Right Reverend MANDELL, LORD BISHOP *of* LONDON, D.D.

My Dear Lord Bishop,

By a strange coincidence, I was already deeply concerned in composing these volumes, when you, unaware of the fact, urged upon me the preparation of a Life and Letters of Donne as a work which, above all others dealing with Elizabethan and Jacobean Literature, now required to be performed. This was a most encouraging incident to me, and a fortunate omen. To offer you the completed work, however modestly and imperfectly wrought, is no more than common gratitude.

Yet even had this happy accident not occurred, I do not know to whom I could have offered my volumes so appropriately as to yourself. Not only would Donne, were he now alive, have you for his diocesan, but I conceive that since the death of John King in 1621, there has been no Bishop of London so capable of sympathising with Donne in all his fluctuations as you are. He trembled under Laud, your severe predecessor; and certainly not to Laud would any friend of Donne's have dared to dedicate a life which unveils the early frailties and the constitutional faults of the seraphical Dean of St. Paul's. But I have no fear that you will not be of the συνετοί. Of you it may be said, as Steele (we know) said of Hoadly:

> "*Virtue with so much ease on* BANGOR *sits,*
> *All faults he pardons, though he none commits.*"

As a poet, as a divine, as a metaphysician, as a humanist, and not least as a fragile and exquisite human being, Donne is certain of your sympathy.

More reasons for this dedication are needless, and yet I will add the gratification which it gives me to testify thus to our long personal friendship, and to my constant admiration of your genius and character.

Believe me to be,

My dear Lord Bishop,

Yours very faithfully,

EDMUND GOSSE.

PREFACE

THE work which I have here attempted to perform has been the occupation of many years, although it is but lately that I have had an opportunity of devoting myself to it consecutively. There may be one or two indulgent readers who recollect that so long ago as 1880 I announced, and then withdrew, a proposal to write the Life of Donne. It is more than I deserve, that, in these days of antiquarian and biographical activity, what is perhaps the most imposing task left to the student of Elizabethan and Jacobean literature should still be left hitherto unattempted. There is no lack of interest in the subject; there is no lack of material for the biographer; and yet this is the first time that a full life of Donne has been essayed.

The causes of this apparent neglect are not difficult to discover. In the first place, the exquisite eulogy of Izaak Walton is a little masterpiece of narration which no one of any judgment would hastily disturb. It has taken its place among our classics, and the attempt to patch it up and correct it, as often as it has been ventured upon, has merely led to critical disaster. The real Life of Donne must not be, what modern editors have made it, a more or less elaborate tinkering of Walton. In the second place, the material for a biography of Donne very largely consists of a collection of letters, printed in 1651, in a state of such confusion, such errors of the press, such an absence of dates in the majority of cases, such mistakes as to dates in the minority, that no biographer has hitherto ventured to unravel the knotted and twisted web. No one can have examined, even superficially, the *Letters* of 1651—which, even in these days of reprinting, remain in their single original issue—without perceiving that some intrepidity and a great deal of patience are needed to make them tell a consecutive and intelligible tale.

Walton's famous study appeared in its original form in 1640. What we read now is a recension of 1659, greatly expanded, corrected, and, in some degree, diverted from its original purpose. It is not sufficiently remembered that the original title of the narrative was: "The Life and Death of Dr. Donne, late Dean of St. Paul's, London." The words "and Death" disappeared from the enlarged edition, but it is well that we should bear them in mind. They indicate Walton's attitude in approaching his theme, the central feature of which was the dignified and even slightly scenic decease of the Dean, in the midst of pious and admiring friends. The keynote of Donne's life, in Walton's mind, was its preparation for his death; and so he hurries over the circumstances of forty years in a very few pages, that he may concentrate our attention on some forty months. In the days of Walton, of course, what we now call conscientious biography was unknown. The object of the author was not solely or mainly to tell in exact sequence the events of a career, but to paint a portrait in which all that was rugged or unseemly should be melted into a dignified gloom. He had to consider the morality of the reader; he dared not neglect the hortatory or the educational attitude. It is said that the late George Richmond, R.A., on being accused of not telling the truth in his delicate portraiture, replied with heat: "I do tell the truth, but I tell it in love." The ideal of the seventeenth-century biography was to tell the truth in love.

When Walton's "Lives" began to regain the great position which they are now never likely to lose, it was perceived that they were too rose-coloured and too inexact for scientific uses. In 1796 they were edited by Dr. Thomas Zouch, who returned to the task of annotation several times during his long life (1737–1815). The researches of Zouch, who was a useful and industrious antiquary, cleared away various obstructions in the text of Walton, but it did not dawn upon Zouch, as it has scarcely been evident to any later editor, that the discrepancies in the narrative were so

PREFACE

many and so important, as to be beyond the power of an annotator to remove. Meanwhile, in 1805, the Clarendon Press at Oxford issued an unannotated text, in two volumes. Zouch's text was re-issued in 1807, with a few additional notes; this has remained the foundation of all subsequent reprints of the "Lives," and mistakes of his are reproduced in the very latest issue which has left the press. One modern edition, however, is independent of Zouch, or rather substantially extends his labours. It is that which was published without a date (but I believe in July 1852), and without an editor's name (but under the care of Henry Kent Causton), in a cheap and obscure form as the opening volume of a projected "Contemplative Man's Library for the Thinking Few." Thinkers proved to be few indeed, and this modest little volume has become extremely rare. It contains, however, with a great deal that is inexact and fortuitous, genuine and valuable contributions to our knowledge of Donne.

Serious attention to the bibliography of the Poems of Donne was first called by Sir John Simeon in the treatise, founded on a rather late MS., which he printed for the Philobiblion Society in 1856. In 1872, the late Dr. A. B. Grosart exemplified the neglect which was still paid to the Dean of St. Paul's, by prefacing his edition of the Poetical Works, in two volumes, with the words, "I do not hide from myself that it needs courage to edit and print the poetry of Dr. John Donne in our day." His own issue, though not the happiest of his adventures, increased our knowledge of the poet, and tended to explode any prejudice existing against him. Twenty years more passed, however, without producing a really masterly text of Donne's poems. Dr. Brinsley Nicholson had long intended to prepare one, when he died in 1891. The responsibility was transferred to Mr. E. K. Chambers, who produced in 1896 an edition of Donne's poetical works in two volumes, which for all practical purposes leaves nothing to be desired. Donne as a poet is not likely ever to be better edited than by Mr. E. K. Chambers, although in later editions he will probably revise some of his conjectures.

The prose works remain in a very different condition. It is as painful as it is unbecoming to speak ill of one's predecessors, but I strive in vain to find a palliating word to say for what Henry Alford, afterwards Dean of Canterbury, issued as the "Works of John Donne, D.D.," in six volumes, in 1839. Alford was very young, was unaccustomed to the work he undertook, and had formed no standard of editorial excellence. I have been told that in later life he bitterly lamented the publication of this edition. If so, we must share his mortification; these pretended Works contain neither the *Pseudo-Martyr*, nor *Biathanatos*, nor *Ignatius his Conclave*, nor the *Miscellanies*, all of which remain unreprinted to the present day. Alford professed to give the poems, but "pruned, some may be disposed to think, unsparingly." He promised the *bonne bouche* of "valuable notes by the late Mr. S. T. Coleridge," which did not appear. But, worse than all this, Alford was so little acquainted with the difficulties of press-reading and collation, that his text absolutely swarms with errors. His notes are few, but they are almost always glaringly inaccurate. In short, this edition of the Works of Donne, which is the only one which has ever been attempted, is (it is distressing to have to say) no better than so much paper wasted.

The first man, indeed, who really saw that what was wanted was not a patched-up revision of Donne but a totally new Life, was Dr. Augustus Jessopp. More than fifty years ago, when he was an undergraduate at Cambridge, he began to make collections illustrative of the character and writings of Donne. He could find no publisher to undertake such an enterprise, which the production of Alford seemed to render impossible—an excellent example of the way in which a bad book may spoil the market for a good one. In 1855 Dr. Jessopp brought out a reprint of the *Essays in Divinity*, with copious and learned notes, which were little valued by the reviewers of forty years ago, but which now prove how eminently well Dr. Jessopp was fitted to illuminate the theological characteristics of the great Dean of St. Paul's. After that, until 1897, the general public had no means of knowing how persistent was Dr. Jessopp's interest in everything connected with Donne, except through his excellent article in the "Dictionary of National Biography."

Many years have passed since, by a mere accident, I discovered how lively was still the enthusiasm felt for the Dean by our admirable historian of East Anglia. I, also, had been making collections for the biography, and my first impulse was to place them unreservedly in Dr. Jessopp's hands. To this day, echoing the famous tirade of Young to Pope, I find myself saying—

> " O had he press'd his theme, pursu'd the track, . . .
> O had he, mounted on his wing of fire,
> Soar'd where I sink, and sung immortal [Donne],
> How it had bless'd mankind, and rescu'd me ! "

He claimed, however, that I should join him in the delightful labour. We soon found, however, a great difficulty in the road of our collaboration. In his own words, Dr. Jessopp "has never been able to feel much enthusiasm for Donne as a poet," whereas to me, even to his last seraphical hour in his bedchamber at St. Paul's, Donne is quintessentially a poet. This difference of view offered so great a drawback to conjoint study that, although, for some years, we continued to speak of our united work, it made no practical progress. I had, indeed, well-nigh abandoned the idea of completing my share of the undertaking.

Suddenly, in 1897, in terms of unexampled generosity, and in a mode which left me helpless to resist, Dr. Jessopp transferred the whole responsibility to my shoulders. My first intimation of his change of mind was received by reading the preface to a charming little life of Donne as a Theologian which he contributed to Mr. Beeching's series of "Leaders of Religion." In this he repeated his indifference to the poetry of Donne, and he declared that it was from me only that any adequate and elaborate biography of Donne was to be looked for. These printed words—in which sympathy and generosity, for once, I fear, may have betrayed my ardent friend to some error of judgment—were accompanied by a private letter, in which he placed all his material at my disposal, and offered me the inestimable advantage of his revision. This was a summons which it would have been churlish to disobey, and I immediately threw myself into a task which has been no holiday effort, and which I conclude at last with a thousand apprehensions. My severest and most learned critic, however, is silenced by his own declaration; however imperfect my work may prove, Dr. Jessopp cannot blame that of which he is the "onlie begetter."

The materials on which this life is founded must now be stated. Izaak Walton is, of course, the basis; the two versions or recensions of his narrative have been very closely examined, with a view to appreciating their spirit as well as their letter. It becomes obvious that Walton's personal knowledge of Donne was confined to the very close of his career. For some months (as I conjecture), in 1629 and 1630, he contrived to enjoy the Dean's intimacy, and beyond question to take notes of his conversation. We do not begin to understand what the early part of Walton's "Life of Donne" is until it occurs to us that it is largely Donne's own report of the incidents of his career. Replying to the enthusiastic curiosity of Walton, Donne would recount events the exact sequence of which had escaped his memory, would pass over in silence facts which seemed immaterial, and errors which he regretted, and would place his conduct in a light distinctly edifying to his listener. In short, without being in the least degree conscious that he was doing so, Donne would give a picture of his own life which was neither quite accurate nor perfectly candid. Whatever the great Dean said, Walton joyfully accepted; it would take too long to illustrate here, what the judicious reader will well understand, the necessity of treating Walton's narrative with the utmost sensitiveness, as a thread to be held tightly at some points and at others to be thrown resolutely away, in our progress through the labyrinth of Donne's career.

I would venture to deprecate the multiplication of annotated editions of Walton's "Life of Donne." They

PREFACE

are disrespectful to Walton, and they merely darken counsel with regard to Donne's career. Walton's treatment of the central years of his subject's life is a tangle quite inextricable by any number of notes. The "Life" is an exquisite work, which must stand alone, on the score of its sweet amenity and the beauty of its style. I yield to no one in my admiration of it, and I share to the full the opinion of Mr. Austin Dobson (expressed in an unpublished poem from which I have the indiscretion to quote) when he speaks of

> "old Izaak's phrase
> That glows with energy of praise,
> Old Izaak's ambling un-pretence
> That flames with untaught eloquence."

And the general impression the "Life of Donne" gives is, no doubt, as faithful as it is beautiful. As a compendium of dry consecutive facts about the career of the poet, however, it is absolutely misleading.

The correspondence of Donne, which is now for the first time collected, has been my main source of additional information. We are very richly supplied with letters from Donne, who seems to have enjoyed a wide reputation as a writer of epistles, and many of whose letters were kept, not on account of their intrinsic interest, but as models of epistolary deportment. Of these, one hundred and twenty-nine were published by John Donne the younger in 1651, and are now for the first time reprinted.[1] These letters, as has already been remarked, offer an extreme perplexity. No more tantalising set of documents can be imagined. They are printed with complete disregard to chronology; only twenty-two of the whole number are fully dated, and of these several are found to be dated wrongly; even the names of the persons to whom the letters are addressed are not always supplied, nor always correctly. These conditions make the *Letters* of 1651 far more difficult to deal with than any original MSS. are likely to be, for we have no data to go upon but what the careless original editor has

---

[1] The so-called second edition of 1654 is nothing but old sheets bound up with a new title-page, and Alford's attempt I take into no account.

chosen to give us, and we can never appeal to the author himself. In the few occasions where the originals of these letters have been preserved, the discrepancies between MS. and printed text are rather startling.

This neglected mass of correspondence is, notwithstanding, of extreme value. In the present work I have attempted no less arduous a task than to break up this inert mass of dateless letters, and re-arrange its component parts in consecutive illustration of the narrative. In this I have received inestimable help from Dr. Jessopp; it would be more just, indeed, to say that it is I who have supplemented his unpublished labours. If, however, in this huge enterprise, which is simply beset with pitfalls, I have fallen into error, I would take upon myself the full responsibility.

This re-arrangement and dating of the *Letters* of 1651 is the portion of the work which has given Dr. Jessopp and myself the most extended labour. Even now, we are not entirely at one with regard to the value of certain indications of internal evidence. It will, nevertheless, be denied by no candid reader that the determination to force Donne's correspondence to illustrate his biography had become a necessary one; and even if the minute critic does not always agree with the order selected here, there is a large majority of instances in which it is impossible that he should not admit its correctness and value. For the practical purposes of biography these *Letters* of 1651 have hitherto been almost of as little service as though they had never been printed.

Another neglected source of information about Donne is the little volume entitled *A Collection of Letters made by Sr. Tobie Mathews, Kt.*, and printed in 1660. Tobie Matthew (or Mathews), whose name frequently recurs in the following pages, was an acquaintance, although never a friend of Donne. He made a collection of holographs, which fell into the hands of John Donne the younger. The latter published them with a dedication to Lucy, Countess of Carlisle, the aged widow of his father's friend, James Hay, Viscount Doncaster and Earl of Carlisle, who had died nearly a quarter of a century before. Into this collection he shredded or flung some thirty letters written

PREFACE

by his father, but not included (with one or two exceptions) in the *Letters* of 1651. But if that publication was irregular, the Tobie Matthew collection is absolutely chaotic. The editor says of it, "it begins wheresoever you open it, and it ends wheresoever you see." A large number of the Donne letters have neither address nor signature, and are discoverable purely by internal evidence. Nevertheless, these are among the most valuable, because the most personal, which I have been able to discover. The volume of 1660 has never been reprinted or described. Besides the letters by Donne, it contains no small mass of highly important correspondence addressed to him.

Materials hitherto unpublished have been secured from the Domestic State Papers, the Manuscript Departments of the British Museum and the Bodleian Libraries, the Registers of Lincoln's Inn, the Registers of Wills at Somerset House, and the Library of Dulwich College. Various sources, such as the University Library at Cambridge, Sion College Library, and the Registers of St. Dunstan's-in-the-West, have been searched with no or disappointingly slight results. Mr. Horatio F. Brown has been so kind as to search the archives at Venice for me, but unhappily without success. Several very important letters have been copied from the collections of private owners, who were kind enough to permit them to be transcribed.

In printing Donne's letters, I have modernised the spelling, which has no philological value, and is often so eccentric as to annoy and repel the general reader. I do not think that "to join with you to move his Lordship to withdraw it" is made more luminous by printing it, "to joyne wth yo^w to moue hys Lp to wthdrawe ytt." In the same spirit, I have ventured throughout to give the dates in new style, as seems to me the only rational thing to do in the course of a modern narrative; and in this I have on my side the example of most of our reputed historians.

It is a great disappointment to me that so very little is still known about the incidents of Donne's early life. I am inclined to fear that we never shall discover anything precise about the wandering years of his youth. But even here we know quite as much about Donne as about Shakespeare or Spenser. From 1600 onwards until the death of his wife in 1617, that is to say, through the entire central portion of his life, our knowledge of his emotions and movements becomes so precise, in the light of the documents published in these volumes, that we may now claim to follow Donne's career more minutely than that of any other Elizabethan or Jacobean man of letters, except, perhaps, Bacon.

My object has not been confined to the collection of all the documents which I could find which illustrated the biography of Donne. I have desired, also, to present a portrait of him as a man and an author. As, therefore, his prose works are rare, and in most cases are inaccessible to the general reader, I have dwelt on their characteristics as well as on those of the poems. In short, what I have essayed to present, is a biographical and critical monograph on Donne in his full complexity.

It will be observed that I have not attempted to annotate the Letters, which would be a labour quite apart from my present object; but wherever names are quoted as those of men and women with whom Donne was brought into personal relations, I have endeavoured to say enough about them to render each reference of this kind intelligible. The amplification of this sort of information might be extended much further, but I have forced myself to recollect that my subject is a biography of Donne, and not the Life and Times of James I. Hence I have avoided being led aside into a consideration of the historical points raised in the news-letters.

Already so much has been said, and will be repeated, of my debt to Dr. Jessopp, that I may be silent regarding it here. I have to thank the Bishop of London for kind encouragement and some valuable suggestions. The Rev. William Hunt has most generously placed at my service his great knowledge of ecclesiastical history, and has read the proofs to their constant advantage. I have to thank Lord Kenyon for opening to me his remarkable ecclesiastical library at Gredington, and thus enabling me to enrich the chapter which deals with the recusant controversy. Suggestive ideas regarding the biographical value of the Poems I owe to the Hon. Maurice Baring. I am indebted to Mr. James Fitzmaurice-Kelly, the learned historian of Spanish literature, for valuable hints as to the nature and extent of Donne's Spanish studies. Professor Edward Dowden has lent me some important MSS. I am obliged to Dr. Norman Moore for a very curious diagnosis of the state of Donne's health and of the probable cause of his death, which I print as an appendix. I must not fail to acknowledge the prompt and careful secretarial services of Miss M. B. Curran. Without making him responsible for any errors into which I may have fallen, I would say that for my historical background I have gone to the various writings of Dr. Samuel Rawson Gardiner.

CONTENTS

OF VOLUME I

	PAGE
PREFACE	vii

CHAPTER I
CHILDHOOD (1573–1589) 1

CHAPTER II
YOUTH (1590–1597) 21

CHAPTER III
THE LYRICAL POEMS 53

CHAPTER IV
MARRIAGE (1597–1604) 85

CHAPTER V
THE PROGRESS OF THE SOUL 129

CHAPTER VI
LIFE AT MITCHAM (1605–1608) 143

CONTENTS

CHAPTER VII
TWICKENHAM (1608–1610) 205

CHAPTER VIII
CONTROVERSIAL WORKS—DIVINE POEMS . . . 243

CHAPTER IX
DRURY HOUSE AND PARIS (1610–1612) . . . 271

ILLUSTRATIONS

OF VOLUME I

	PAGE
PORTRAIT OF DONNE . . . . . . *Frontispiece.*	
Painted in 1591, *and engraved by* W. MARSHALL.	
FACSIMILE OF LETTER FROM DONNE TO SIR ROBERT COTTON *To face page*	108
TITLE-PAGE OF "PSEUDO-MARTYR" OF 1610, WITH DONNE'S HANDWRITING . . . . . ,,	248
PORTRAIT OF ELIZABETH DRURY AT HAWSTED . . ,,	272
PORTRAIT OF DONNE . . . . ,,	304
From a drawing made by G. CLINT, A.R.A., *after an original painting.*	

CHILDHOOD
1573–1589

CHAPTER I

CHILDHOOD

1573-1589

HISTORY presents us with no instance of a man of letters more obviously led up to by the experience and character of his ancestors than was John Donne. As we have him revealed to us, he is what a genealogist might wish him to be. Every salient feature in his mind and temperament is foreshadowed by the general trend of his family, or by the idiosyncrasy of some individual member of it. On both sides he was sprung from Catholics of the staunch old stock, animated by a settled horror of reform and by a determination to oppose it. For these views, held, apparently without exception, by all his maternal relations since the early days of Henry VIII., there were no sacrifices which were not to be made cheerfully, promptly. "No family," says Donne himself in 1610, "which is not of far larger extent and greater branches, hath endured and suffered more in their persons and fortunes for obeying the teachers of Roman doctrine." This habitual stress and tension had given to the members of this class—men and women of exceptional cultivation—an independence of opinion which bordered upon eccentricity, a contempt for English standards of religion and literature, a habit of looking to the Continent for intellectual stimulus, a manner of life superficially silken to excess, but tantalisingly abrupt and inscrutable in its movements. We see these characteristics in the Rastells and the Heywoods, but we find them superlatively in that illustrious descendant of theirs who is the subject of these pages.

What has just been said of the heritage of Donne from

his ancestors is mainly and obviously true of those on the maternal side. Nothing leads us to question that it was disturbed by anything on the paternal side; but here we are left to conjecture. Of the parentage of the poet's father nothing whatever is known. His name was John. As he possessed two maiden aunts—one a Dawson, the other a Cooper—his father (whose Christian name is unknown) must have married twice. He had a married brother, who left an orphan daughter, Alice Donne, who was still a child in 1576, and who is heard of no more. There were in Oxford some Dawsons with whom he kept up relations, and therefore the Dawson wife was probably the elder John Donne's mother. It seems possible that Edward Dawson, the Jesuit of Louvain, was a relative. Two cousins, Edward Dawson and his sister, Grace Dawson, were "decayed" and "aged persons" when the Dean of St. Paul's made his will in 1630. Another cousin, Jane Kent, had long lived with his mother as her maid. With these facts our extremely scanty knowledge of the poet's paternal forebears ceases, except that we know them to have been Catholics.

It is pure conjecture that John Donne was sprung from the ancient family of the Dwnns of Dwynn, in Radnorshire. There is one circumstance which favours the theory that he descended from the Duns or Dwnns of Kidwelly, in Caermarthenshire, namely, that their arms, *a wolf salient, and a chief argent*, were borne by Donne when he was Dean of St. Paul's. But if he had believed that he was able to prove himself to have been of knightly family, he would doubtless have done so. And it is noticeable that he never claims relationship with his prominent contemporary, Sir Daniel Donne, the Master of Requests, nor with John Donne of St. Martins-in-the-Fields, who was Gentleman of the Privy Chamber to James I. The fact, doubtless, was that Donne's father made his own way in trade, and had no ostensible claim to any mark of gentility. The name—variously spelt Donne, Don, Done, Dun, Dunne, Dwnne, and Dwynne—was a much commoner one in the sixteenth century than it has been since. A John Donne or Dwwnn, of Welsh descent, who was killed fighting in Flanders in 1576, may, conceivably, have been the poet's uncle. But, on the whole, we must take the statement of Walton that "the reader may be pleased to know that the poet's father was masculinely and lineally descended from a very ancient family in Wales" as breathing no more than a pious wish. For practical purposes the Donnes were reputable Catholics of the middle class, trading in the city of London.

It was very different on the maternal side. Here the child was hemmed in by a cloud of intense and distinguished witnesses to the faith of their fathers, persons who had suffered and striven, who had achieved in no small measure the laurel as well as the palm. One can imagine nothing more stimulating to the imagination of such a lad as Donne than to walk in the light which

"Beat bright upon the burning faces"

of the martyrs, poets, scholars, and enthusiasts of his race down four generations. His mother's great-grandmother, who was born in 1482, had been Elizabeth, sister of the illustrious Sir Thomas More. Elizabeth More married a friend and fanatical follower of the great Chancellor, John Rastell, the printer and lawyer. He was a wealthy man, and expended money as well as energy in defending Catholic doctrine against the Reformers. In 1534 he supported Sir Thomas More in his opposition to the Act of Supremacy, and shared his ruin. When the Chancellor was beheaded on the 6th of July 1535, Rastell was still in captivity, and he died in prison in 1536. This man, John Rastell (or Rastall) the elder, was an impetuous controversialist, and like his more eminent grandson by marriage, John Heywood, took an interest in the infancy of the drama. Of his interludes, one at least survives.

In Holbein's group of the family of Sir Thomas More, a young woman, with an irregular, eager face, stands at the Chancellor's right hand, and impulsively points out to him a passage in a book with her extended finger. Her animation is oddly contrasted with the passive modesty of her companions, the daughters of More. This was Margaret

Giggs, another direct ancestress of Donne's. She was a kinswoman of the Mores, possibly an orphan, who was adopted by the Chancellor and brought up with his daughters. Margaret Giggs was what we call "a character," and Holbein no doubt appreciated her individuality. She became a famous blue-stocking, one of the most learned women of her time, and a miracle of intellectual accomplishments. She was a passionate admirer of her adoptive-father, and when his daughter Margaret Roper was permitted to remove his body from the chapel of the Tower, the shirt in which he had been executed passed into the possession of Margaret Giggs, who made an heirloom of it. She was twenty-seven when the tragical event occurred, and had probably been for some years married to Dr. John Clements (or Clement), another distinguished ancestor of Donne.

John Clements was one of the most successful doctors of his time, and rose to be President of the College of Physicians. In his youth he was presented to Sir Thomas More, who made him tutor to his children. He thus met Margaret Giggs, whom he may have married about ten years after Wolsey, who was his patron, had made him Reader in Rhetoric to the University of Oxford. It would seem that the Clements escaped the general ruin of the More interests in 1535, but upon the accession of Edward VI. in 1547 they felt it advisable to emigrate. They settled at Louvain. Meanwhile two threads of family history had been pleasantly joined by the marriage of their daughter Winifred to William Rastell, the distinguished jurist, who was the son of John Rastell and Elizabeth More. He was a staunch Catholic, who was threatened with disabilities at the close of Henry VIII.'s reign. The Rastells accompanied the Clements in their flight to Louvain, and settled there through the reign of Edward VI. John Rastell the younger, afterwards a prominent Jesuit, also retired to Louvain; he was a brother or a cousin of William.

We descend another generation. Elizabeth Rastell, the daughter of William and Winifred, married the famous John Heywood, and these were the grandparents of Donne.

CHILDHOOD

John Heywood, who is supposed to have been born in 1497, was of the same stubborn Catholic fibre as the rest of the family. He was a singer and a "player on the virginal" to Henry VIII. in his boyhood, and after 1520 he developed a dramatic talent, which placed him easily at the head of the primitive theatre of his age. His interludes, of which the most remarkable are *The Pardoner and the Frere* and *The Four P.P.*, led the way directly to the foundation of English comedy. He was a jocose and laughter-loving man, but of immovable fidelity to his religion, and he fell from his comfortable place at Court in 1544, when he was accused of denying the royal supremacy. Heywood, however, was not of the stuff of martyrs, and he escaped execution by publicly recanting at St. Paul's Cross. Through the remainder of the reign, and until the close of the next, John Heywood was probably at Louvain or Malines.

John and Elizabeth Heywood had three children—Elizæus (commonly called Ellis), Jasper, and Elizabeth, the mother of our poet. Elizæus was born in London in 1530, went early to Oxford, and was elected to a Fellowship at All Souls' in 1548. Jasper, who was five years younger, after having been page of honour to the Princess Elizabeth, went to Oxford at the age of twelve, and eventually became Fellow of Merton in 1554. The brothers seem to have lived quietly at the university through the reign of Edward VI., though persisting in their Catholic faith. Their sister, Elizabeth, may have been born as late as 1540, and probably shared her parents' vicissitudes. She outlived every member of her own generation and of the next, surviving the latest of her children and dying in 1632, when she cannot have been less than ninety-two or three, and was probably more. Had it occurred to Walton to question this aged lady, or had her memory survived in extreme years, she would have thrown light on much that is now obscure in the early life of her illustrious son.

At the accession of Queen Mary the dew covered the fleece once more. The ancestors of the poet, in company with other distressed co-religionists, came hastening back from the Low Countries. John Heywood sat under a vine at the coronation of Mary, as Stow informs us, and congratulated her in a Latin discourse. His interludes and his epigrams, his ballads and his jests, were alike to the Queen's taste; to please her he indited and published in 1556 his elaborate allegorical poem of *The Spider and the Fly*, in which the cruel destroyer was the Protestant, swept away, before it could suck the juices of the pious fly, by the firm domestic hand of Mary. All through her reign John Heywood basked in the Queen's unbroken favour, and when she sank into her final dejection, he is said to have been brought to her bedside to divert her with his jokes.

The Rastells, too, returned from Louvain, and William, abandoning the printing-press, regained his prominent position in the law. He was active in the councils of Lincoln's Inn; in 1555 he was made a Puisne Judge. The family seems to have kept up an establishment at Louvain, where William's wife, Winifred, Donne's great-grandmother, died in 1553. His brother (or cousin), John Rastell the younger, returned thither on the accession of Elizabeth; but William struggled on in London until 1563, when he lost his judgeship, and withdrew to the Low Countries in disgrace. During the period of his favour at court he obtained permission to publish, in 1557, the Works of Sir Thomas More, the great family heirloom. William Rastell died in banishment in 1565, and in 1568 John left Louvain and settled in Rome, where he became a Jesuit, and lived on into the poet's childhood. Dr. Clements accompanied the Rastells back to England when Mary came to the throne, and he practised as a physician until the Queen died. At this event he and his wife retired to Malines. These persons—the great-great-grandparents of Donne—lived to be old people, and died, he on the 1st of July 1572, and she on the 6th of July 1570, both buried at Malines. They had been accompanied thither in 1558 by John Heywood, who was threatened, as a contumacious Catholic, with the loss of his lands, and who presented to his daughter Elizabeth, Donne's mother, an estate, probably in Kent, which had belonged to her mother, and which he was afraid might be forfeited.

The uncles of Donne suffered no less than the rest of the family by the death of Mary and the accession of Elizabeth. Elizæus Heywood threw up his Fellowship at All Souls' and went to Rome; Cardinal Pole became his patron, and, as the secretary of that statesman, it is possible that he visited England, but Florence was his residence. His brother Jasper resigned his Fellowship at Merton in May 1558 to avoid expulsion; but it could not have been, as has been supposed, for religion, as the Queen did not die till November 14. He was recommended to stay at Oxford by Cardinal Pole, who sought to obtain for him a Foundation Fellowship at Trinity, although without success. But late in 1558 Jasper Heywood secured a Fellowship at All Souls', perhaps the very one which Elizæus was resigning. From 1559 to 1561 Jasper was publishing his contributions to the grotesque joint-translation then being made of the tragedies attributed to " the most grave and prudent author Lucius Annæus Seneca," in verse of the " ugsome bugs " kind which has made the names of the translators ludicrous. He seems to have found it hopeless to withstand the new flood of Protestantism, and he soon withdrew to Rome, where he became a Jesuit in 1562. He was made a D.D. and appointed to the Chair of Moral Theology at the important training college of Dillingen, in Bavaria, in 1564, and thither his brother Elizæus came two years later, becoming himself a Jesuit there. In 1570 Jasper was appointed Father of the Society in Dillingen, and Elizæus was made the Head of the Jesuits in Antwerp.

Although it is not possible to point to a series of ancestors so active and distinguished as these on Donne's paternal side, yet there is evidence of the staunchness of the Catholics among whom his father was brought up. John Donne the elder, who was probably born about 1530, served his apprenticeship to James (afterwards Sir James) Harvey, Alderman of London. His interests were with the Ironmongers' Company, into whose freedom he was admitted in the reign of Mary. A wealthy ironmonger, Thomas Lewin, died childless in 1557, and we find John Donne immediately afterwards managing the affairs of the widow. By his will, dated 20th April 1555, Lewin bequeathed all his property in London and Bucks, which was very considerable, to his widow for her life, and after her death he directed that it should pass to the Master, Warden, and Company of "the mystery or occupation of the Ironmongers of the city of London and their successors, to hold the same until such time as a new monastery be erected at Sawtrey, in the county of Huntingdon, of the same order of monks as were then in the old monastery before its suppression, charged with the maintenance of a mass priest in the Church of St. Nicholas aforesaid, to pray and preach therein, and prepare other services as set out. . . . The said Master and Wardens are further enjoined to pay yearly to the Friars Observants within the realm of England the sum of five pounds; and a like sum to two poor scholars, one to be of Oxford and the other at Cambridge, towards their maintenance. . . . Immediately after the rebuilding of a monastery at Sawtrey, the said Master and Wardens are to pay to the abbot or prior the money previously devoted to the mass priest, . . . and shall cause a mass daily to be said, and four sermons yearly to be preached within the said monastery for the good of his soul."

Dr. Jessopp remarks that, "As far as I know, this is the first and last important bequest made after the plunder of the monasteries by Henry VIII. for the restoration of a suppressed religious house; and as the widow did not die till the 26th October 1562, when Queen Elizabeth had been on the throne nearly four years, Alderman Lewin's intentions, so far as the rebuilding of this Cistercian abbey was concerned, were never carried into effect, and the bulk of the property is still held, I believe, by the Ironmongers' Company, subject only to the charges for maintaining the two scholars at Oxford and Cambridge down to the present time."

We may conjecture that the elder John Donne married

Elizabeth Heywood a few years after the death of Mrs. Lewin, who left him handsomely rewarded for his services to her estate. But all particulars of his family life are unhappily lost, nor are they likely to be recovered, since the records of the parish in which he lived were destroyed in the Great Fire of London. He is thought to have had six children, but he neglects to mention their names in his will, a document which offers little to satisfy genealogical curiosity.[1] It does, however, bear testimony to a character of great generosity and amiability, and suggests to us that the father of the poet was a man of humane and estimable qualities.

JOHN DONNE, destined to become a celebrated poet and the greatest preacher of his age, was born in 1573 in the parish of St. Nicholas Olave, in the city of London, and probably in that "great messuage, with a garden attached," opening into Bread Street, which Mrs. Lewin had bequeathed to his father, and in which his parents resided. This house was destroyed in 1666. Of the childhood of Donne it is to be regretted that we know nothing. It is certain, however, that it opened in opulence. In 1574 his father became Warden of the Company of Ironmongers; and he was not only very prosperous, but had already amassed a fortune. He was taken ill, however, in the winter of 1575, and on the 16th of January following he made his will, being "sick in body, but of good and perfect mind and remembrance." This document is an admirable specimen of what the will of a "citizen and ironmonger of London" should be. The property is to be divided into three parts—one-third for his wife, one-third for his children, one-third for debts and legacies, the residue of this third to be equally divided among wife and children. Of the latter, if any die before reaching due age, the property of each is to be divided among the others. Two notable ironmongers, Francis Sandbach and Edmund Adamson, are appointed trustees, and after small legacies to the young cousin, Alice Donne, to the maiden aunts and to the Dawsons at Oxford, con-

[1] See *Appendix A*.

spicuous benefactions are made to the poor of the city of London. These include gifts to all the prisons of London and its suburbs, and to three hospitals. Mr. Sayward, the parson of the parish, is gracefully remembered.

The death of John Donne the elder must have occurred shortly after the drawing up of the will, which was proved by the widow on the 8th of February 1576. The poet was therefore left fatherless in his third year. Of his sisters, three died in infancy; and there survived, besides himself, a younger brother, Henry, and a sister, Anne, who was probably the eldest of the family, since in 1586 she married into a staunch family of Yorkshire Catholics and became Mrs. Avery Copley. Her husband soon died, and in 1594 she married again, this time a William Lyly of London, gentleman. Whether he belonged to that family of Lyly, gentlemen, who resided at that time in the parish of St. Bartholomew the Less, and of whom the author of *Euphues* was one, cannot be discovered. Mrs. Lyly died about 1616.

The boy may have been just able to observe and reflect when fresh persecutions fell upon his family. His grandfather, John Heywood, who is mentioned for a small legacy in the will of the elder Donne, was in 1577 included among Catholic fugitives whose lands were manipulated by a Royal Commission. There were troubles, too, in the Low Countries, which now proved to these fugitives less safe an asylum than they had hoped. Donne's uncle, Elizæus Heywood, was driven out of his house at Antwerp by a fanatical mob, and though he contrived to evade their actual violence and to reach his relations in Louvain, he did not recover from the shock, and died there on the 2nd of October 1578. John Rastell the younger died also at Louvain some months earlier. The old generation was passing away, all the leaders of it in banishment. The weary old playwright and epigrammatist, John Heywood himself, died, probably at Malines, somewhere about 1580. It is not unlikely that Donne saw this his illustrious grandfather in the flesh, for the absolute silence preserved with regard to his early education is best explained if we suppose that he was sent over to his own people at Malines or Louvain in earliest childhood. Later on "a private tutor had the care of him until the tenth year of his age," Walton says; but as Walton supposed that his father lived on until about 1589, his evidence is to be received with caution.

An exciting event in the family must have been the appearance of the boy's uncle, Father Jasper Heywood, on a mission to England from Rome. He arrived in the summer of 1581, when Donne was eight years old, in company with Father William Holt. The severity with which the Heywoods had been used had always been somewhat relaxed in the case of Jasper, who was understood not to belong to the extreme party. He was allowed to leave Dillingen, and became Superior of the English Jesuits in succession to Parsons. He must have been a quaint, fantastic person. He appeared to have had no sense of the delicacy of his position in England. He assumed the perilous airs of a Papal Legate, and was positively accused of a parade of wealth and pomp in his private life in London. He had lax views of discipline, and quarrelled with the austerer section of his co-religionists to such an extent that he was recalled by Rome in 1583, after having outraged the commonest prudence by summoning a Council under the style of Provincial of the Jesuits in England. The Government had its eye upon him, but he was permitted to set sail in peace. Unfortunately, the ship was unable to land at Dieppe, and was driven back by winds on the Sussex coast, where Jasper Heywood was arrested and brought in chains to the Clink Prison, in Southwark.

The winter of 1583–84 saw a fresh outbreak of Catholic persecution, but Jasper Heywood was again treated with special consideration. Urgent efforts were made to convert him; it is said that he was offered a bishopric if he would become an Anglican. On the 5th of February 1584 he was arraigned, with five other priests, in Westminster Hall; all six were condemned, and five were executed; but again a mysterious good fortune attended Jasper

Heywood, who was taken back to prison, where he languished until the summer of 1585. During his imprisonment, by special favour "he was permitted to receive visits from his sister," Elizabeth Donne, who was able to bestow upon him some care and nursing. As Dr. Jessopp says, it is fair to conjecture that she may sometimes have been attended by her son, the future poet, then twelve years of age, and "with a good command both of the French and Latin tongue." While Jasper Heywood was out of prison, and probably living with his sister at the house in St. Nicholas Olave—the Government not having made up its mind what to do with him—his two young nephews were sent to Oxford.

John Donne's acquirements at this early age were more than remarkable. Some one, perhaps his uncle Jasper, said of him that "this age hath brought forth another Pico della Mirandola," of whom the story was that "he was rather born wise than made so by study." He was brought up with a tenderness unusual in that age of summary punishments. He remembered long afterwards that his nurse was not allowed to whip him for a fault, but only to report the offence to his mother. "My parents," he says, "would not give me over to a servant's correction." Under his mother's care his talents blossomed forth with a precocity which obliged her early to take his mental training into her particular consideration. The policy of the broader Catholics was to send their sons to the English universities so soon as they were able to matriculate, the object being "to give the lads the advantage of a university training and familiarity with English academic life before the oath of allegiance could be administered to them." Between 1581 and 1584 eighteen such Catholic boys went up to Oxford. John and Henry matriculated with success, and were entered at Hart Hall on the 23rd of October 1584, the former being eleven and the latter ten years of age at the time. This was early even for the close of the sixteenth century, although the admission of extremely young boys was hardly unusual. For instance, Robert, Earl of Essex, was entered at Trinity

CHILDHOOD

College, Cambridge, in the beginning of May 1577, when his age was only nine years and six months.

Hart Hall was an ancient hostel, named after a certain Elias de Hertford of the thirteenth century. In 1740 it was erected into a college of Hertford, which, in 1805, decaying and reverting to the Crown, was merged in Magdalen Hall. Of Donne's career at Hart Hall, Walton says that "having, for the advancement of his studies, tutors of several sciences to attend and instruct him, till time made him capable, and his learning, expressed in public exercises, declared him worthy to receive his first degree in the schools," he forbore to take it, "by advice from his friends, who, being for their religion of the Romish persuasion, were conscionably averse to some parts of the oath that is always tendered at those times, and not to be refused by those that expect the titulary honour of their studies." If Walton is correct in dating this recusant evasion of the oath to his fourteenth year, Donne left Hart Hall and Oxford in 1586, after only six terms.

The fate of his uncle Jasper Heywood cannot have been indifferent to him. That unfortunate man, on the 21st of January 1585, in company with twenty other Catholics, had been shipped to France under pain of death if they ever set foot in England again; they landed at Boulogne-sur-Mer. The movements of Jasper during the next few years are uncertain; in 1589 we find him settled in Rome. He moved on to Naples, where he died on the 9th of January 1598, never visiting his native country again. Walton would have us believe that Donne was meanwhile transferred from Oxford to Cambridge, where he stayed at Trinity for three years, that is to say, till the autumn of 1589. Winstanley, a gossip of the close of the seventeenth century, repeats this in a different form: "Like a laborious bee, desirous to gather from more flowers than one, he was translated from Oxford to Cambridge, our other renowned nursery of learning, where he much improved his studies." It is curious, however, that the only evidence of Donne's being at Cambridge, which has ever been discovered, is now to be produced for the first time.

It is necessary at this juncture to deal with a curious mare's nest, the collection of epigrams which Donne was long supposed to have written as a boy. In 1652 John Donne the younger published a volume of his father's miscellaneous early writings, in which is included "a sheaf of Miscellany Epigrams, written in Latin by J. D., translated by J. Main, D.D." These pieces are sixty in number; most of them are merely gross, but towards the close there appear a group of verses about an investiture of Duke's Wood, or Bois-le-Duc. It used to be thought that these referred to an engagement outside the walls of that place in the Low Countries in 1585, when Donne was twelve years old. However, Dr. Brinsley Nicholson and Dr. Grosart have abundantly proved that what seems to be a reference to Heyn's capture of the plate-fleet could not have been written before 1628. External and internal evidence unite to demonstrate that these verses could never have passed from the pen of the great Dean of St. Paul's. It may, however, be curious to discuss certain features of the fraud perpetrated in 1652, for fraud there certainly was.

In the first place, these epigrams are alleged to be translated from Donne's Latin by "J. Main, D.D.," and first printed in 1652. This was Jasper Mayne, the noted witty divine and author of that very successful comedy *The City Match*. He was celebrated for his mystifications and practical jokes, which he continued even after his death, with the unfeeling jest of the legacy of a red herring to his faithful servant. In 1652 he was in great poverty, having been ejected from his student's place at Christ Church; and although he nominally held a college living, in Yorkshire, he was probably ready to earn a guinea by any fooling. He must have connived at the fraud, or even have palmed off his verses as really genuine on the credulity of Donne's son. But perhaps the joke had been attempted earlier. The original (1633) edition of the *Juvenilia* of Donne does not contain these epigrams. But does the original form of this book exist? I have discovered among the State Papers a very curious document, in which, on the 14th of November 1632, Sir Henry Herbert is called upon to give account before the Board of the Star Chamber why he warranted the book of Dr. Donne's *Juvenilia* to be printed. This most unusual order of inquiry was delivered, at the King's command, by the Bishop of London. It is possible that Mayne's spurious epigrams had slipped through then, and were only discovered just in time to be suppressed. The two editions of 1633 are extremely odd-looking books; it looks to me as though a fragment, with no prefatory matter and the last sheet cut off, had been hurriedly printed. Donne certainly wrote "epigrammata mea Latina," but they are lost. He had evidently neither part nor lot in the Jasper Mayne mystification of 1652. There exist juvenile English epigrams which are undoubtedly his, some printed, some still in MS., and these probably belong to the years after 1591.

We can hardly be wrong in supposing that the preoccupation with the Spanish language and literature which was so marked a feature of Donne's mature career was a result of Oxford influences. That university was the centre of a remarkable movement in favour of Spanish thought at the very time of Donne's residence. It is to be regretted that we possess so little definite evidence with regard to this interesting subject. James Mabbe, afterwards the translator of *Calisto and Melibea*, born in 1572, matriculated at Magdalen one term before Donne left Hart Hall and Oxford for Cambridge; and there is no evidence that these men ever met, although their careers were in several respects closely parallel. Mabbe travelled in Spain, was attached to John Digby, Earl of Bristol, and appears to have taken orders in the English Church about the same time that Donne did. Another Oxford man was Leonard Digges, of University, "highly esteemed as a perfect understander of the Spanish." Mr. Fitzmaurice-Kelly, whose acquaintance with this matter is unrivalled, points out to me that for about a century from the date of Henry VIII.'s marriage with Katherine of Aragón, there seems to have been felt in England a curiosity about Spanish thought, which did not die away until after the Civil War, and of which Oxford was always the centre. This interest in the serious side of Spanish intelligence was greatly stimulated by Luis Vives, a reader and almost a tutor to Queen Katherine, through whose influence he was made Professor of Humanities at Oxford. In the opinion of many competent judges, Vives was a philosopher of great power. He wrote, it is true, in Latin and not in Spanish, but he impressed Oxford with the sentiment and thought of Spain. When Donne was at Hart Hall, it is pretty plain that the Spanish Mystics were already known in Oxford. We find Francis Meres translating Luis de Granada, and thus, perhaps, even weaving Shakespeare into the transcendental web. I feel little doubt that Donne became acquainted at the university with Granada's *Guía de Pecadores*, and other similar works, half mystical, half heretical, in which the Spanish genius was being developed in the manner which was to prove so irresistibly fascinating to Donne. We may note that the great Spanish mystics all died during Donne's boyhood, and while he was in close family connection with Rome—St. Teresa in 1582, Granada in 1588, St. John of the Cross in 1591.

Of Donne's boyish friendships at college we know next to nothing. He was acquainted with at least one member of the Cornwallis family, whose name will reappear in our narrative. According to Izaak Walton, the main friend that Donne made at Oxford was Henry Wotton. Walton makes no distinct mention of this boyish friendship in his *Life of Donne*, but in his vaguer *Life of Sir Henry Wotton* he says, " I must not omit the mention of a love that thus was begun [at Oxford] betwixt him and Dr. Donne, sometime Dean of St. Paul's, . . . being such a friendship as was generously elemented; and as it was begun in their youth, and in an university, and there maintained by correspondent inclinations and studies, so it lasted till age and death forced a separation." This is really all we know about a matter which has been expanded into something much more positive; and it is to be remarked that when Donne, at the age of twelve, was settled at Hart Hall, Wotton at New College had passed his seventeenth year. He afterwards, it is true, removed to Hart Hall, and we may safely believe that the acquaintance began about 1585. The discrepancy of age between a young man of eighteen and a boy of thirteen must, however, have prevented at this time any close correspondence of ideas. We shall see later how very difficult it is to believe that Donne and Wotton, through the whole remainder of their lives, met otherwise than on rare and distant occasions.

It has not hitherto been observed that the Registers of the University of Oxford offer no conclusive evidence that Donne proceeded to Cambridge. When, on the 17th of April 1610, he received at Oxford the honorary degree of M.A., it seems to have been unknown that he belonged to the sister university. But, in all probability, he himself mentioned the fact, since, on the following day (April 18), we find him entered as a M.A. of Cambridge, incorporated at Oxford. He shared this transference with his friend, John Pory, also a Cambridge graduate. It was at Cambridge, doubtless, that Donne formed the acquaintance of a family of the city of York named Brooke, several members of which, but particularly Christopher and Samuel, were afterwards closely identified with him.

YOUTH
1590–1597

CHAPTER II

YOUTH

1590-1597

ACCORDING to Walton, Donne was "removed to London" about 1590, and "then admitted into Lincoln's Inn with the intention to study the law." And now we meet with a sudden flash of positive evidence in the midst of so much floating conjecture. In the 1635 and 1639 editions of the poems there is found a portrait, engraved by William Marshall in his best style after a large miniature, the original of which is no longer known to exist, on which are inscribed the words "Anno Dni. 1591 ætatis suæ 18. Antes muerto que mudado." The painting was probably a bad one, but enough character was preserved in it to make Marshall's engraving a very precious relic. The expression and attitude of the alert head and clenched hand are animated to the point of arrogance. The large eyes, widely opened, the set lips, the puffed-out nostrils, the lines at the base of the rather coarse nose—all combine to give to the face a look of intensity and self-sufficiency not very agreeable in a lad of eighteen, but highly characteristic of what was likely to be apparent in such a youth as Donne. "O well for him whose will is strong," we murmur in front of this portrait—

> "He suffers, but he shall not suffer long,
> He suffers, but he shall not suffer wrong."

The figure, in an oval, and drawn to the waist, is dressed in a plain military dress, without ornament, and the right hand grasps a rapier just below the pommel.

From this interesting portrait we gain two little crumbs

of fact; namely, that in 1591 Donne could sit for his portrait dressed as a soldier, and that he had already developed his taste for proverbial tags of Spanish ("Before I am dead, how shall I be changed"). But to build on so slight a foundation any structure of conjectural biography seems to me rash. We meet him next on the 6th of May 1592, when he entered at Lincoln's Inn, where the following entry exists:—

"London. M. Johannes Donne generosus admissus est in societatem istius hospicii sexto die Maii Anno Reginæ Elizabethæ xxxiv. Post : memorandum quod nomina hic subscripta proposuit et solvit ad usum hospicii prædicti 31/s quia fuit de hospicio de Thavis Inna.

Mancupatores { CHRISTO: BROOKE.
                EDWARDE LOFTUS.
Admissus fuit
                            per ROKEBY."

Near by him, at Thavies Inn, his only surviving brother Henry, like himself a Catholic, had chambers. A prescribed Seminarist, named William Harrington, took refuge here, and was arrested in May 1593 in the lodgings of Henry Donne, who was committed to the Clink Prison for harbouring this dangerous person. Here, a few weeks later, Henry Donne died of fever. Born in the spring of 1574, he had recently completed his nineteenth year. Of the six children of the elder John Donne only two now survived, the subject of this memoir and his sister Anne. The point which now detains us is that, by the death of Henry, the six children, "for whose maintenance" my father "provided all that wealth which he left"—to quote a letter which the poet long afterwards addressed to his mother—had dwindled to two. Anne Copley had received her portion, Mrs. Donne was in enjoyment of the considerable Lewin property, and it is therefore probable that when he came of age in 1594 John Donne found himself in possession of an accumulated fortune. Walton mentions the sum of £3000 as "his portion in money," but leaves it uncertain whether this was the original or the inherited amount.

To this period in the young poet's life we may attribute that awakening of his religious curiosity of which Walton gives so interesting an account. Dr. Jessopp has ingeniously shown that Donne's study of Bellarmine could not have taken place "about the nineteenth year" of Donne's age, as Walton believed, because the work of that famous Cardinal was not available until the publication at Lyons, in 1593, of the three volumes of his *Disputationes de controversiis fidei adversus hujus temporis Hæreticos*.[1] It would, therefore, be safer to say that, about his twenty-first year Donne began to be led to examine with independent judgment the proscribed and half-secret faith of his fathers. His mother and her friends had been solicitous "to improve his knowledge, and to that end had appointed him tutors, both in the mathematics and in all the other liberal sciences, to attend him. But with these arts they were advised to instil into him particular principles of the Romish Church; of which these tutors professed, though secretly, themselves to be members." In 1594, however, all this must long have been at an end. Donne had already mingled eagerly with the world of London and with the Court. He was no longer to be held in leading-strings by a mother or a tutor; and to discover his attitude with regard to Romanism, we turn to the best authority, himself, and to some words in the *Pseudo-Martyr* of 1610, which have been insufficiently considered in this connection :—

"They," he says, "who have descended so low as to take knowledge of me, and to admit me into their consideration, know well that I used no inordinate haste nor precipitation in binding my conscience to any local religion. I had a longer work to do than many other men; for I was first to blot out certain impressions of the Roman religion, and to wrestle both against the examples and against the reasons by which some hold was taken and

---

[1] The curious reader may compare this with Lancelot Andrews' *Responsio*, published in 1610.

some anticipations early laid upon my conscience, both by persons who by nature had a power and superiority over my will, and others who by their learning and good life seemed to me justly to claim an interest for the guiding and rectifying of mine understanding in these matters."

These words are not the report half a century afterwards of the conversation of an elderly man, but the confessions of the man himself at the age of thirty-seven. It is necessary to interpolate this remark, because the passage in *Pseudo-Martyr* immediately proceeds:—

"And although I apprehended well enough that this irresolution not only retarded my fortune, but also bred some scandal and endangered my spiritual reputation by laying me open to many misinterpretations, yet all these respects did not transport me to any violent and sudden determination till I had, to the measure of my power and judgment, surveyed and digested the whole body of divinity, controverted between ours and the Roman Church. In which search and disquisition, that God, which awakened me then, and hath never forsaken me in that industry, as He is the author of that purpose, so is He a witness of this protestation, that I behaved myself and proceeded therein with humility and diffidence in myself; and by that which, by His grace, I take to be the ordinary means, which is frequent prayer and equal and indifferent affections."

This authoritative account, it is evident, gives an impression which is scarcely in accord with Walton's view, that with "moderate haste," in his twentieth year, Donne rejected the Catholic doctrines and embraced the Anglican communion. "He believed the Cardinal Bellarmine to be the best defender of the Roman cause, and therefore betook himself to the examination of his reasons. . . . About the twentieth year of his age [he] did show the Dean of Gloucester [Dr. Anthony Rudde] all the Cardinal's works marked with many weighty observations under his own hand; which works were bequeathed by him,[1] at his

---

[1] No doubt, in that "Schedule signde wth my hand," which seems to have been detached from Donne's Will and lost.

death, as a legacy to a most dear friend." Rudde ceased to be Dean of Gloucester early in 1594.

Such is the evidence; and we hold nothing more that is very definite, until, about the year 1603, we find Donne a convinced opponent of Romanism. It is hardly possible to doubt that to himself, in advancing years, the obsession of religious thoughts in his early youth appeared to have been greater than in truth it was. Without question, at all times and in all conditions John Donne was a man prepared for the enthusiastic study of divinity, but that in his passionate salad-days this was combined with any practical enthusiasm for piety, it is quite impossible to believe. The early writings of Donne are not those of a depraved or even of an immoral man, but they are reckless in language, sensuous in imagery, full of the pagan riot of the senses, and far indeed from any trace of the pietist or the precisian. Doubtless, all through his period of *Sturm und Drang*, Donne retained his intellectual interest in theological subtleties; there can be no reason to question the exactitude of Walton's story about the annotated copy of Bellarmine's *Disputationes;* but to Donne himself, in his later days of sanctification, it would be irresistible to exaggerate a little, and to antedate his earnestness of spiritual purpose. Walton has a luminous phrase, which is hardly in keeping with the rest of his deposition. He says that from 1591 onwards Donne "had betrothed himself to no religion that might give him any other denomination than a Christian. And reason and piety had both persuaded him, that there could be no such sin as Schism, if an adherence to some visible Church were not necessary." This seems to me to supply the key of the situation. As soon as Donne found himself free from his mother's tutelage, his attachment to the Catholic faith began to decline; presently his indifference to its practice, combined with an intellectual scepticism as to its tenets, led him away from any Christian communion, yet all the while he nourished a kind of dormant religiosity, ready to break forth into flame as soon as the tumult of the senses and the enraged curiosity of life had been somewhat assuaged by experience. Inwardly, the seed of the spiritual life was healthy, and was biding its time for expansion; externally, we may picture John Donne, from 1590 to 1600, as leading a life of fair propriety in action perhaps, but one in which religion and sanctity of purpose could not be suspected by the closest observer.

From conjecture and report, however, we are able to take refuge in an important and considerable body of poetical work. The *Satires* of Donne were not published, so far as we know, until after his death. As we at present possess them they are seven in number; of these the first five were printed in 1633, the sixth in 1635, and the seventh in 1669. By great good fortune we are not left in doubt as to the approximate date of their composition. To the Harleian manuscript of the first three in the British Museum (MS. Harl. 5110) the date 1593 is attached; the fourth, although it contains interpolations which seem to belong to 1597, is dated 1594 in the Hawthornden MS. The other three are later, and less interesting from a biographical point of view; but it is much to know that we have nearly six hundred lines of very independent and characteristic verse which we can confidently attribute to Donne's earliest manhood.

The choice which Donne made of a poetical medium testified to his high originality and carelessness for accepted opinion. The year 1593 may be taken as the central date of that luxuriant blossoming of lyrical and dramatic, pastoral and amatory, verse in England which has been the marvel and the bewilderment of critics. Edmund Spenser was in the heyday of his magnificent productiveness; the song and the sonnet were at the height of the fashion; this was the year of the murder of Marlowe, and of the escape, as if from some invisible bondage, of the fearless spirit of Shakespeare. It might have been supposed that a young man of Donne's energy and ambition would have begun with a pastoral romance, a sonnet in imitation of Sidney, or at least a madrigal for the theorbo. *Venus and Adonis* was in the press; Robert Greene, though lately deceased, was still posthumously vocal; Samuel

Daniel, with his classic graces, was still trying to divert the course of English poetry. Would not these examples of the æsthetic fervour of the age tempt the new poet to imitation, at least until the wings of his personal style were fully fledged? By no means; from the very first Donne was a rebel against the poetic canons and tendencies of the age.

In selecting Satire as the species of poetry in which to make his maiden essays, Donne obeyed an instinct which was moving simultaneously in several countries of Europe. During the Middle Ages, of course, satire had been universally distributed, usually taking the form of allegorical narrative. This had never died out, and the generation of Donne had the opportunity of reading a belated specimen of it in Spenser's *Mother Hubbard's Tale*; but as a distinct species of poetry, closely modelled on the three great Latin masters, satire belongs, throughout Europe, to the very close of the sixteenth century. Satire, in this precise and restricted sense, was an exclusively Latin product. Quintilian had warned off Greek pretension to a claim in it when he boasted, "Satira quidem tota nostra est." But the scholiasts of the Renaissance were not able to perceive this, and they became hopelessly bewildered in attempting to account for formal satire. In 1582 Isaac Casaubon was appointed, at the age of three-and-twenty, to the chair of Greek in the University of Geneva. For fourteen years he lectured there on Greek and Latin literature, presenting to the young minds of Europe a new and fertile conception of classical literature, not as a mass of unrelated texts, but as a living and developing imaginative entity. In the course of thus investigating and vivifying the authors of antiquity, Casaubon approached the Latin satirists, on whom his master, the elder Scaliger, had expended somewhat less than his usual acumen. Casaubon threw an entirely new light over the subject by his extraordinary lectures on Persius.

It is hardly too much to presume that the sudden interest in formal satire displayed by the poets of Western Europe was born in the class-room at Geneva. After 1596 it was most certainly stimulated in France by Casaubon's lectures at Montpellier and in Paris. His commentary on Persius, it is true, was not published until 1605, but it preserved the notes of lectures delivered in Geneva long before. These criticisms had produced a wide impression throughout learned Europe before they are known to have been published. Scaliger, who did not appreciate Persius, had declared that Casaubon's dissertation was better literature than its theme, "the sauce better than the fish." The view of the Genevese professor was, indeed, in the highest degree novel. Not only did he lift Persius, for the first time, to a level with Horace and Juvenal, but on many points he ventured to prefer him. As Casaubon's was the earliest elaborate and comparative criticism of the Latin satirists which had been attempted, and as it was carried out at a most timely moment with extraordinary brilliancy, it was not unnatural that it exercised a great influence. It is probably not too much to say that the criticisms of Casaubon created satire, in its exact sense as a poetic form, both in England and France. It is, at least, certainly the fact that they defined and settled the shape in which it was to be passed on to Dryden and Boileau.

Scarcely any attempt had been made to naturalise the Latin satirists in Elizabethan literature. Under the title of *A Medicinable Moral*, a certain Thomas Drant had endeavoured to versify the *Satires* of Horace, but the first English translation of Persius was that published by Barten Holiday in 1616, followed by fragments of Juvenal by W. B. (perhaps William Burton, the translator of Erasmus) in 1617. But a group of young English poets in the last decade of the sixteenth century had determined to introduce into the national repertory the biting, invective poem which had flourished so brilliantly in Rome. No movement in our literature is more clearly defined, or has been less closely studied. It did not begin until 1593, and the action of the Bishop of London in 1599 gave it its death-blow, yet during those six years enough satire of the formal Latin type was produced to make a definite mark on our poetical history. It is a curious fact that the English satirists, who were five in number, are not known to have held any communication with one another. Joseph Hall, when at length he published his *Virgidemiarum* in 1597, boldly assumed that he had no competitor. In the Prologue to the First Book of these "Toothless Satires" he says—

> "I first adventure, with foolhardy might,
> To tread the steps of perilous despite;
> I first adventure; follow me who list,
> And be the second English satirist."

But Hall was really, and in his own limited sense, not even the second, but at most the third.

The first collection of satires directly founded on Horace was contained in *A Fig for Momus*, published in 1595, by the delicate lyrist and prose writer of romances, Thomas Lodge. In these pieces, however—there are six of them in Lodge's miscellany — the soft, invertebrate prosody and the general want of definition of style deprive them of that virulent energy which is indispensable in satire, and which the other Elizabethan satirists clearly perceived to be necessary. Leaving Lodge, then, behind us, and Donne, as not published, being also postponed, Joseph Hall, who braved the dangers of publication in 1597, deserves some of the honours of innovation. He was a still younger man than Donne, having been born on the 1st of July 1574, a wild and witty fellow, afterwards to sober down and be commonly called, as Fuller tells us, the "English Seneca, for the pureness, plainness, and fulness of his style." He was to become Bishop, first of Exeter and finally of Norwich, and to die, a very old man and the last survivor of the early Elizabethans, in 1656. In 1597 his temper was not yet edifying, and his style, though full, neither pure nor plain. The vogue of his Satires was brilliant and brief; the first part of his celebrated *Virgidemiarum* was entered at Stationers' Hall in March 1597, the second part in March 1598, the completed work in June 1599, and a couple of months later, in company with the productions of other satirists, Hall's poems were suppressed and burned in the court of the Bishop of London.

These publications of Hall's are of striking interest to us in our present inquiry. The fact that Donne withdrew his *Satires* from the press deprives us of any expression of the contemporary attitude of his mind towards satire; but Hall speaks freely in his prefaces. In his "Postscript to the Reader," Hall makes a claim to be considered absolutely original as an imitator of Juvenal and Persius, to have arrived in English directly from the study of " my ancient Roman predecessors." He is eager to state that with the exception of the *Satires* of Ariosto " and one base French satire, I could never attain the view of any for my direction." Finally, closing what is really a very curious little critical essay on this untried theme, Hall characteristically boasts that he thinks that his poems have caught a resemblance to " the sour and crabbèd face of Juvenal's," and that his merit is enough " to stop the mouth of every accuser." He shows himself, in short, a daring and even impudent, but very original, young swash-buckler of poetry.

If in 1597 Hall could discover in the European literatures no direct precursor of his new kind of verse, except Ariosto and " one base French satire," Donne in 1593 could have found still less. The first French satirist, of the Latin type, was Vauguelin de la Fresnaye, but his *Satyres françoises*, which are not more vigorously written than those of Lodge, were not published until 1605. It is not to be doubted, I think, that the " base French " work of which Hall speaks so contemptuously was the famous *Satire Ménippée*, that extraordinary political treatise, in prose and verse, by many hands, which was first printed at Tours in 1594. By that time, however, Donne had entirely learned what lesson he chose to learn from Persius and Juvenal; the *Satire Ménippée* has no real resemblance to the Elizabethan satires. What has a very close and very curious resemblance is the work of Mathurin Regnier, who was born in 1573, the same year as Donne. Nothing would be more convenient than to account for the outburst of Elizabethan satire by saying that it was evidently the result of hasty imitation of Regnier. Unfortunately the

French poet did not begin to write satires until 1598, by which time the mushroom school of London satirists was already at the height of its vogue. Not less impossible is it to conceive that Donne and Hall could influence Regnier, and this is another of those curious occasions in literary history when an idea, dormant for centuries, simultaneously springs up to life in natures wholly unrelated.

Another of the young Elizabethans was John Marston. The son of an Italian and probably Catholic mother, at Oxford from 1591 to 1593, settled in London about 1594, and mixing either in friendship or in enmity with all the leading wits, Marston has been dimly conjectured to have been acquainted thus early with Donne; of this, however, I can find not the slightest evidence. Marston affected, no less than Hall, to be one who scourged the errors of Society; he liked to be known by the nickname of Kinsayer, as one who " kinsed" or docked the tails of wandering dogs and stray social abuses. His publications were *Pygmalion's Image and Satires* in May 1598, and *The Scourge of Villany* in September of the same year. His public career as a satirist, like Hall's, was cut short by the Bishop of London in 1599. So, no doubt, was that of Edward Guilpin, whose *Skialetheia* was printed early in 1598. This, the latest of our five first satirists, is the most shadowy of all; his book has come down to us in one perfect copy only, and of the life of the author we know nothing, save that he was a Cambridge man. I shall presently print an epistle of Donne's, hitherto unpublished, which possibly throws a faint light on Guilpin's career.

Such were the earliest English followers of Juvenal and Persius, among whom Donne might have taken precedence had he been anxious to share their reputation. To understand their aims and their historical position is indispensable to a comprehension of Donne's first essays in the art of poetry. They, with and, as it would appear, after him, though probably without conscious collusion, attempted to introduce into English poetry what had been so powerful an element in the Roman, the *Satura*—that "mixture" of social scandal and moral diatribe in a picturesque sort of realistic rhetoric which Lucilius had been the first to develop into a fine art. The reader of Mr. Mackail's brilliant summary of the genius of Lucilius may take it as a description, not of what Hall was—for he lacked the talent—but of what he wished to be. If his rivals and he failed to equal the rough founder of Roman satire, they were still less capable of reproducing the charm of Horace. Curiously enough, they do not seem to have perceived that in the *Second Book* of that poet they had, placed at their hand, the perfect model of what they wished to do. But if they missed Horace, whose vogue in England came later, they claimed as their direct and only masters the shades of Persius and Juvenal.

It is not difficult to comprehend the charm which these two poets of Rome exercised over young revolters from convention such as Donne and Hall. In Juvenal, the deep knowledge of life, the universal cynic savagery, the resolute and brutal determination to haul Truth up out of her well, however roughly, were precisely the qualities to fascinate poetic youths in a state of rebellion against pastoral sweetnesses and the waxen ideals of the Cambridge school. They were attracted, doubtless, to Persius for opposite reasons, and less consciously. The sympathetic poet of Volterra had been, like themselves, led by the fierce imaginations of youth into those paths where the aged Juvenal walked, borne down by bitter experience of the world and of men. Donne and Hall would be drawn to Persius because, like him, they were young and bookish. They did not perceive that Persius imitates Horace; they took him for a Heaven-sent stoic, who scourged the age and died at twenty-six. Casaubon, quite alone among scholars, was exalting Persius even at the expense of Juvenal. To resemble Persius, to reproduce his manner, was evidently the devout aim of Marston and Donne, Hall and Guilpin alike.

But the first thing observable about Persius was that he was very difficult to understand. This charge was brought against his style by older scholars, and has been repeated since. He is still the type of obscurity, of the quality which makes a classic author awkward to construe and still more awkward to explain. But Casaubon had thrown out a new idea. Like Coleridge, two centuries later, he suggested that Persius was "not obscure, but hard"; and he elaborately defended his favourite satirist on this score. What he did not defend was the metre of Persius, which he seems to have found extremely daring and irregular. This has not been the habitual verdict of scholars, who have considered that the poet of Volterra paid a singular and almost affected attention to the form and execution of his verses; perhaps the very zeal with which Persius cultivated the ancient forms of Latin prosody may have seemed harsh to Casaubon. This is of no consequence, however, to us; it is enough to remember that, whether justly or unjustly, the versification of Persius was supposed, at the end of the sixteenth century, to be violent and rugged, and his style turbid and involved to an extreme degree.

This assumption then of the violence and darkness of the great Roman satirists entered into the idea which our young Elizabethans formed of what manly satire must be. Even in their own day those rough qualities which have made these writers a portent in English literature were recognised and widely objected to. Hall in 1597 confessed, "It is not for every one to relish a true and natural satire, being of itself, besides the native and inbred bitterness and tartness of particulars, both hard of conceit and harsh of style." This postulate of the self-evident necessity of satire to be obscure and elliptical, violent and "tart," was accepted at the end of the sixteenth century without inquiry. A man who should write satires must write like "angry Juvenal" and "crabbèd Persius." It was the complaint against Lodge's *Fig for Momus* that it was too smoothly versified for satire. Milton was the first of our critics to point out the error of this conception, and to show that nothing could be further from the arrogant pomp of Juvenal than the grotesque shrieks and contortions of his Elizabethan followers. In the *Apology for Smectymnus*, Milton reproves the triviality of this "presumptuous undertaking with weak and unexamined shoulders." He is mainly attacking Hall. But Marston, too, and Guilpin, and Donne perhaps most of all, might have remembered that "a Satire, as it was born out of a Tragedy, so ought to resemble his parentage, to strike high and adventure dangerously at the most eminent vices among the greatest persons, and not to creep into every blind tap-house that fears a constable more than a satire."

With these comparative observations on the rise of satire in England, we have placed ourselves in a position to examine more closely those specimens of it which are of the highest interest to us here—the *Satires* of Donne. The first four of these poems give us, in fewer than six hundred lines, our most definite occasion for studying the aims and peculiarities of this poet at his start in life. Those who read the *Virgidemiarum* are presented to a fuller gallery of portraits and a more conventionally elegant versification; Marston is more lucid, and sometimes more musical. Neither of these satirists, however, displays so bold an originality as Donne. Hall in particular keeps so close to the ancients, that his text is sometimes little more than a cento of paraphrased passages from Juvenal. From the very first Donne was independent. His isolation from the accepted models of style—that feature on which we shall have incessantly to insist—is apparent from the opening of his poetical career. The earliest verses from his pen which we know that we possess are those with which the First Satire opens—

"Away, thou changing motley humourist,
Leave me, and in this standing wooden chest,
Consorted with these few books, let me lie
In prison, and here be coffin'd when I die."

Thus, in 1593, with the verse of Spenser, Sidney, Peele, and Watson murmured around him, soft and voluptuous measures Italianating the rude tongues of the preceding generation—thus, with an accent not yet formed yet already his own, a native and individual accent founded on no English or foreign predecessor, the boy of twenty speaks to us.

The Satires of Donne are not general invectives as those of Hall are, nor fantastic libels against individuals like those of Marston, but a series of humorous and sardonic portraits of types. The edition of Theophrastus, which Casaubon was to revolutionise European *belles-lettres* by publishing in 1598, was still unknown, but Scaliger had more vaguely drawn attention to this class of ironic portraiture. Each of Donne's satires is woven about some such type as the Theophrastians a little later loved to define and describe. The hero of the First is a gossiping, volatile society-man, with whom the poet, in his stoic simplicity, proudly contrasts himself. The poem is a study of London life. The young Donne among his books loves to wander out into the streets and observe life, yet only, in disgust, to return to his lodging, well satisfied with his own "coarse attire," and glad to lock himself in and confer in silence with God and with the Muses. He says little that we can take to be autobiographical; we could wish that his pride had stooped to gossip about himself. We faintly divine him, a "subtle-witted, antic youth"—perhaps in "black feathers" and "musk-coloured hose," upon occasion—liable to fierce outbursts of dissipation and yet at all times master of himself, master of his tongue and brain, insolent and isolated among "the many-coloured peacocks" who, as he scornfully tells us, sought his company as one "of sort, of parts and qualities." The chatter and folly of such an one are merrily recounted at the close of the First Satire, when, incautiously leaving his chamber for the streets of London, Donne is pounced upon by a "fine, silken, painted fool," the typical society-man, who attaches himself to his arm, and sails along with his morose companion until, luckily,

> "At last his love he in a window sees,
> And, like light dew exhaled, he flings from me."

The Second Satire is enflamed with the scorn of London—

> "I thank God, I do hate
> All this town perfectly,"

and contains an ironic reference to Papists, "poor, disarm'd, not worth hate," which may have been inspired by the misfortunes of his brother Henry. In general, this satire is an attack on the Lawyer, as a type, and is by no means an attractive or lucid composition. One of the few personal touches which have been traced in Donne's *Satires* is found in this poem, where a contemptuous reference to "Coscus," a lawyer of offensive insolence, who is scarcely a poet, has been identified with Sir John Davies, afterwards Attorney-General for Ireland, and author of the celebrated philosophical poem *Nosce Teipsum*. The misfortune is that Davies, in 1593, was but a law-student, and had not published anything, although he had licensed, and apparently withdrawn, his *Orchestra*. All the efforts we make to define the friendships and associations of Donne in those earliest years seem to be frustrated by the stubbornness of dates. We are thrown back on a closer study of his own words, and we find him in this Second Satire pushing to a fresh extremity his newly-invented violence of prosody. Occasional groups of fine ringing lines there are—such as these travestying the volubility of the lawyers—

> "Words, words which would tear
> The tender labyrinth of a soft maid's ear,
> More, more than the Sclavonians scolding, more
> Than when winds in our ruin'd abbeys roar;"

but, as a rule, if the style is more matured, it is less poetical than in the First Satire, and the ugly parts of the poet's genius, its arrogance, its truculence, its immodesty, are disagreeably displayed.

The Third Satire is far more interesting. This is a diatribe against the extravagance and hypocrisy of the Religious Man. This was a dangerous topic in those angry days, and that this work lay unprinted for forty years need not surprise us. The theologian in Donne makes his first appearance in the Third Satire. An attitude of austere and vigilant scepticism is manifested throughout; Donne here occupies the position, not of one who sneers or ridicules, but who stands aside, trying the spirits whether they be of God. It would be deeply interesting, but it seems to be wholly beyond our knowledge, to decide whom the poet addresses in his fervid opening lines. We vaguely discover the son of a pious father, a fighter with or against the Dutch, an Arctic explorer, a traveller in the Tropics,

> "Whose countries limbecs to our bodies be."

The poet, looking around, surveys the weaknesses of that wild, fantastic world in which he had been born, and sees that religion is still the ruling passion of mankind. The valorous swashbuckler, who fears nothing else, must yet fear God. Then the satire becomes a sermon—the first that its author preached from any pulpit—

> " Know thy foes; the foul devil, he whom thou
> Strivest to please, for hate, not love, would allow
> Thee fain his whole realm to be quit; and, as
> The world's all parts wither away and pass,
> So the world's self, thy other lov'd foe, is
> In her decrepit wane, and thou, loving this,
> Dost love a wither'd and worn strumpet; last,
> Flesh, itself's death, and joys which flesh can taste,
> Thou lovest; and thy fair goodly soul, which doth
> Give this flesh power to taste joy, thou dost loathe."

The adult manner of Donne, as poet, as thinker, and as fantasist, is before us here. Then follows a tormented and obscure picture of the condition of the various branches of the Christian Church. Emancipated from his Catholic convictions thus early, Donne can ridicule his Mirreus for seeking true religion at Rome, simply because he knows that she was there a thousand years ago. But Crantz, who seeks her at Geneva, is even in more parlous case, making love to the new Calvinism—

> "Plain, simple, sullen, young,
> Contemptuous, yet unhandsome."

Graius prefers the Anglican Church, enamoured of her recent laws and present fashions, acquiescing in the acts of the Court of High Commission and that tyranny of the Bishops under which the last years of Elizabeth were groaning. In Phrygius, who abhors all forms of religious practice, and in Gracchus, who loves all alike, Donne sums up with what may possibly be allusions to the Puritans of the day, to those who, like the extreme Brownists, called for the extermination of the national church. But in 1593 it was dangerous, even in an unpublished paper, for a reactionary to note down thus boldly his views with regard to church discipline, and Donne is studiously vague. His own attitude is plainer and far more important to us. In lines where he drops the satirical attitude, and admits us to the motions of his own conscience, we may observe him with profit—

> "Though Truth and Falsehood be
> Near twins, yet Truth a little elder is.
> Be busy to seek her; believe me this,—
> He's not of none, nor worst, that seeks the best;
> To adore, or scorn an image, or protest,
> May all be bad. Doubt wisely; in strange way,
> To stand inquiring right, is not to stray;
> To sleep, or run wrong, is."

Precisely so, our nineteenth-century poet has assured us that—

> "There lives more faith in honest doubt,
> Believe me, than in half the creeds."

Donne proceeds, with one of those grand and virile images for which his style was to be prominent—

> "On a huge hill,
> Cragged and steep, Truth stands, and he that will
> Reach her, about must and about must go,
> And what the hill's suddenness resists, win so,
> Yet strive so, that before age, death's twilight,
> Thy soul rest, for none can work in that night."

This very remarkable poem is conducted in a darkness unusual even in the writings of Donne, but those who will adventure in it, and bring to it no more than they find—for glib conjecture is here all out of place

—will be rewarded by a strange passion of intellectual poetry.

The Fourth Satire is more than twice as long as either of its predecessors. It and the First Satire are found among the MSS. at Hawthornden, and are described as "after C. B.'s copy," that is, no doubt, copied by, or in agreement with a text prepared by, Christopher Brooke. The Fourth Satire is dated 1594 at Hawthornden; in the Ashmolean collection it is described as "A Satire against the Court, written by Doct. Dun in Queen Elizabeth's Reign." A reference to "the loss of Amiens," which was captured by the Spaniards in March 1597 and recovered by Henry IV. in September of the same year, has led Mr. Chambers to conjecture that the Hawthornden date is a mistake for 1597. But the looseness of texture in the poem suggests to myself the idea that it has been enlarged and patched, and it may well be that it was originally composed in 1594 and extended a few years later. An allusion to "Guiana's rarities" may remind us that the attention of Englishmen was first drawn to Guiana in 1594, when Raleigh sent Captain Jacob Whiddon on the earliest expedition to spy out that fabulous land of promise.

This Fourth Satire is furbished forth with an extraordinary array of learned allusions. The young poet is not averse to letting us remark how wide and curious his reading has been, nor to dazzling us with references to Calepine the lexicographer, and Surius the German historian. Jovius (Paolo Giovio) and Aretino are more familiar names to us, but a compliment to Theodore Beza, as being—with "some Jesuits and two reverend men of our two Academies"—the most learned of living linguists, is interesting for its actuality. In this satire, moreover, occur certain of the very rare Elizabethan references to Rabelais, to Dante, and to Albrecht Dürer.

One of the features which was to distinguish Donne from most of his illustrious contemporaries was to be his aggressive realism, his determination to substitute for classical and romantic metaphors images drawn from the life, science, and speculation of his own day. If we compare the texture of one of Spenser's *Complaints* or a romance of Greene's with any of these early satires of Donne, we shall be astonished at their unlikeness in this respect. The Fourth Satire is particularly rich in details of this realistic order, and is singularly, if tantalisingly, interesting to us by contrast, if we consider that it was written, doubtless in London, just when another and greater poet, who may have daily brushed the sleeve of Donne, was preparing for the composition of *Midsummer Night's Dream*. A figure whom the exploits of English travellers was beginning to make familiar in the streets of London was the Geographical Adventurer, half freebooter, half man of science, a man, as Lodge says in his *Rosalynde*, "rough, as hatched in the storms of the ocean, and feathered in the surges of many perilous seas." The exploits and death of Thomas Cavendish, the navigator whose "dismal and fated voyage," as Purchas calls it, had infuriated Spain and made the foreign policy of Elizabeth more difficult than ever, had filled the city with swashbucklers, bearded like the pard, all ready to tell the strangest tales of Patagonia or the Azores.

In the bosom of John Donne, though he was doomed to a life of little personal adventure, there leaped the heart of a circumnavigator. His portrait of one of these queer portents of travel is among the most picturesque which he has left—

"Towards me did run
A thing more strange, than on Nile's slime the sun
E'er bred, or all which into Noah's ark came;
A thing which would have posed Adam to name;
Stranger than some antiquaries' studies,
Than Afric's monsters, Guiana's rarities;
Stranger than strangers; one, who for a Dane,
In the Dane's massacre had sure been slain,
If he had lived then; and without help dies
When next the 'prentices 'gainst strangers rise;
One whom the watch, at noon, scarce lets go by.
 .   .   .   .   .   .
His clothes were strange, though coarse and black, though bare;
Sleeveless this jerkin was, and it had been
Velvet, but 'twas now—so much ground was seen—
Become tufftaffety, and our children shall
See it plain rash awhile, then nought at all.
The thing hath travell'd, and, faith, speaks all tongues."

Three more pieces are now appended to the *Satires* of Donne, and although they seem to be of a later date, they may be considered here and dismissed; they are of minor importance. The Fifth Satire is directed against the bribing of judges. It is attributed by Mr. E. K. Chambers to 1602-3, but I think it a little earlier in date. Some one who is Donne's master and the Queen's servant is busily engaged in attempting to root out that scandalous habit of the courts, and this is doubtless the Lord Keeper—

> "Greatest and fairest Empress, know you this?
> Alas! no more than Thames' calm head doth know
> Whose meads her arms drown, or whose corn o'erflow.
> You, sir, whose righteousness she loves, whom I
> By having leave to serve, am most richly
> For service paid, authoris'd, now begin
> To know and weed out this enormous sin."

Here the address is almost unquestionably to Lord Ellesmere, by this time become, as we shall see, Donne's principal patron. The Fifth Satire is a very bad poem, much of it spoiled to the ear by the terrible rattle of redundant feet in verse which it is hard to explain and impossible to justify. Every now and then, however, the laborious reader meets with a splendid phrase, which illuminates the dark mass, as when the poet, in the course of a metaphor indeed most strained and obscure, speaks of "the vast ravishing seas."

The Sixth Satire, which is addressed in the Harleian MSS. "to Sir Nicholas Smith," was first printed in 1635. It is a fragment of slight value, and, I think, of questionable authenticity. It is either not written by Donne, or it marks a strange and unfortunate caprice on his part to write in the smooth and conventional versification of the age. The prosody bears scarcely any trace of his peculiarities. This Satire, which is not to be distinguished from what Donne elsewhere calls an Epistle, is directed against an old man amorous, who wishes to marry the young and charming widowed daughter of a justice. Far more interest attaches to the Seventh and last Satire, which was not printed until 1669, but which is headed on a MS. copy,

"Satire 9th to Sir Nicho. Smith, 1602." Internal evidence points to the correctness of this date, especially in lines recording the intrepidity of William Epps, the Man of Kent, at the Siege of Ostend. The poem opens with a beautiful series of illustrations of Sleep's house, mystically built by Ariosto, Ovid, Spenser, and "many mōe." Donne confesses that he once spent his nights in London streets, in the company of "fighting and untruss'd gallants," habits which must go back at least five years from the date of this satire, which is also that of his marriage. A curious reference to Abraham Fraunce, with his full name, has baffled the commentators; but it is surely an allusion to that popular and sentimental work in English hexameters, *The Countess of Pembroke's Ivychurch*, completed in 1592—

> "O vile verse! and yet our Abraham Fraunce
> Writes thus and jests not."

In the *Ivychurch*, and still more in his version of the Psalms called *The Countess of Pembroke's Emanuel* (1591), Fraunce showed himself a belated and peculiarly unskilful hanger-on of the school of Gabriel Hervey and the other patrons of rhymeless, accentuated verse. The phrase "our Abraham" does not seem to me to betoken any personal friendship on the part of Donne, but merely to allude to a compilation of Fraunce's, *The Lawyer's Logic* (1588), a handbook to the practice of common law which was in vogue in Donne's younger days, and was doubtless familiarly used by him and by his fellow-students.

The Seventh Satire is evidently so much later than the first four in date of composition, that its autobiographical touches take us too far ahead for our present purpose; yet it is of importance to us to find Donne confessing that his soul at first had loved "that idle and she state" of being a courtier. The poem closes with an outburst of splenetic raillery against political personages in high places. Here is an extraordinary boldness of language about Essex and the Queen, who "was old before that she was dead"; and still more open sneers at James of Scotland and his troop of camp-followers, with sumpter-horses and packsaddles. His estimate of the King changed when he was brought, as we shall see, into personal relations with him; and the Seventh Satire merely breathes the petulant resentment of a young man, who had been devoted to Essex, and now saw threatened the introduction into his country of a tribe of foreigners and an exotic court.

Donne published nothing in prose or verse during these years of his youth. Had he desired to print, at the close of the century, some such miscellany as most of his contemporaries indulged in, the action of the Bishops in 1599 would have been enough to prevent it. On the 1st of June of that year John Whitgift, Archbishop of Canterbury, and Richard Bancroft, Bishop of London, issued an order "that no Satires or Epigrams be printed hereafter"; and it was almost a generation later before Wither, in his *Abuses Stript and Whipt*, ventured to resuscitate satire in a much milder form. Four days after the issue of the decree the poems of Marston were publicly burned, and a like fate seems to have befallen Hall and Guilpin. If Donne had been so rash as to print, the same prohibition and the same ignominious punishment would unquestionably have been doled out to him. It is probable that both would have taken a still more serious form, for there are few relics of the days of Elizabeth, not directly controversial, which strike us as so likely to scandalise and infuriate Archbishop Whitgift as the third of Donne's *Satires*.

At the age of twenty-three Donne engaged himself for foreign service under the Earl of Essex. The Government had at length determined to complete the work of crushing Spain, whose strength was already seriously impaired by the defeat of the Great Armada. Spain was threatening again. She had gained a footing in Brittany, and had taken Calais. England was in some danger, and the Queen was persuaded of the fact. She was, indeed, unusually liberal, and contributed seventeen ships and £50,000. In the month of April 1596 a commission was issued, empowering Essex and the Lord Admiral Howard to act with Sir Walter Raleigh and Lord Thomas Howard in offensive measures against Spain. Raleigh was appointed main purveyor of levies. On the 1st of June the fleet put to sea, amounting, with the Dutch allies, to about one hundred and fifty vessels, on one of which was sailing, with thoughts which we can but dimly conjecture, the subject of this memoir.

On this expedition, as well as on the subsequent one, Donne was attached to the person of Essex, and, as Walton says, "waited upon his lordship." He was therefore, in all probability, on board the *Repulse* on the eventful morning of June, when Raleigh, by dint of his impetuous rhetoric, persuaded Essex and the Lord Admiral that a fight by sea presented to our arms far greater advantages than a fight by land. It is not forbidden to us to be convinced that Donne was leaning over the side of the *Repulse* when Raleigh, flushed with hope and eagerness, returned from his visit of persuasion to Howard, and as he passed under the great ship, shouted up to Essex, "Intramus," with so magnetic a thrill in his voice, that Essex flung his hat far into the sea in an ecstasy of high spirits. Next morning broke the day of St. Barnabas the Bright,[1] with its magnificent victory by sea and land. It is to the morning after this great day that I attribute the composition of an epigram of Donne's, which I print here[2] for the first time.

Raleigh, severely wounded in the leg by a splinter, had been unable to join Essex in his land-attack on the city of Cadiz. On the morning of the 12th of June, hearing that a fleet of forty richly-laden carracks had fled down the Rio Puerto Real, with a view to escaping to the Indies, Raleigh communicated to Essex his desire promptly to pursue them even to the farther side of the world. This spirited proposal, before Essex could reply, had received its answer from the Duke of Medina Sidonia, who set the whole argosy on fire. But the matter must have been admiringly discussed on board the *Repulse*, and it must have been on the morning of the 12th of June 1596 that Donne addressed these lines to Raleigh—

---

[1] June 11, *N.S.*   [2] From the Westmoreland MS.

CALES [*i.e.* CADIZ] AND GUYANA.

"If you from spoil of the old world's farthest end
To the new world your kindled valours bend,
What brave examples then do prove it true
That one thing's end doth still begin a new!"

The naval power of Spain was finally shattered, and in the autumn of 1596 Essex returned victorious. On the return voyage he invaded Portugal, and the young Donne cannot but have been interested in the capture of the books of the Bishop of Algarve, which, brought in due time to Oxford, were given to the University Library. Before the ships of Essex returned to England, Raleigh had started for that third expedition to Guiana, to which Donne probably refers in the title of the epigram printed above.

A year later young Donne had a similar and still more striking experience of naval warfare. He was attached to that expedition into the Spanish parts of the Atlantic which is known as the Islands Voyage. Essex, as before in his famous ship the *Repulse*, set forth from Plymouth on the 10th of July 1597, hoping to arrive in about three weeks in the archipelago of the Azores. The object of the English and Dutch adventurers was to intercept the plate-ships on their annual flight from India with treasure for Spain. Before the fleets contrived to get away into the Atlantic they were confronted by a tempest of exceptional violence, which parted Raleigh's squadron from the rest, and has been picturesquely described by him in prose. The squadrons were shattered, and some ships lost; Raleigh, with the *Bonaventure*, put back to Plymouth, and Essex took refuge in Falmouth. It was from this port, in all probability, that Donne sent to London his poem of "The Storm." Meanwhile, still in heavy seas, the fleet collected its forces and started in the third week of August 1597, arriving early in September in sight of Terçeira in the Azores. On entering the Tropics Donne wrote his poem called "The Calm."

These two short pieces, which take a prominent place

in the poetical history of our author, and have even a considerable importance in the evolution of English verse, were sent as epistles to Mr. Christopher Brooke. This young man seems to have been one of Donne's earliest, as he certainly remained one of his closest and most loyal, friends. In their lodgings at Lincoln's Inn he was "chamber-fellow to Donne," that is to say, they leased chambers together. To his immediate contemporaries Christopher Brooke was an object of enthusiastic admiration and affection. He was evidently the most amiable of men, ready for every friendly office. His love of literature was keen, and he preferred the company of poets to that of lawyers. Anthony à Wood, enumerating the friends of Christopher Brooke, tells us that he was "known to and admired by Joh. Selden, Ben Jonson, Mich. Drayton, Will Browne, George Withers, and Joh. Davies of Hereford." His own gifts as a poet are warmly eulogised by his contemporary, but he was never induced to collect his verses into a volume, and those occasional "eclogues" or "epistles" which have come down to us, give a very disappointing impression of his talent. No doubt the man was far more attractive than his work; he strikes us as a centre of radiating influence. The great writers whom Wood names as his companions mainly belong to a later date than 1597, but Drayton and Ben Jonson were probably already personally known to Brooke and Donne. We shall presently meet other members of the Brooke family in the course of this narrative.

"The Storm" and "The Calm" have a considerable resemblance in style to the *Satires*, and are written in the same harshly cadenced heroic measure. They are exercises in deliberate description, pure *tours de force* of artisan's work in poetry. They exemplify some of the worst features which the literary production of Donne was to develop—its aridity and roughness. That these were wilfully introduced, in direct opposition to and appeal against the rosy Elizabethan sweetness, we cannot allow ourselves to doubt. These were attempts, without any reference to antique examples or far-fetched illustrations, to paint what the poet saw or thought he saw. Here is an example from "The Storm"—

> "Then, like two mighty kings which, dwelling far
> Asunder, meet against a third to war,
> The south and west winds joined, and, as they blew,
> Waves like a rolling trench before them threw.
> Sooner than you read this line, did the gale,
> Like shot not feared till felt, our sails assail,
> And what at first was called a gust, the same
> Hath now a storm's, anon a tempest's name."

In this strained verse there is little melody and a deliberate abeyance of fancy, but the effort to obtain a realistic effect is most curious. Here is the result of the wind's action on the maimed and shattered flotilla—

> "Then note they the ship's sicknesses, the mast
> Shaked with an ague, and the hold and waist
> With a salt dropsy clogged; all our tacklings
> Snapping like too-high-stretchèd treble-strings;
> And from our tattered sails rags drop down so
> As from one hanged in chains a year ago."

Here, at all events, is observation—the eye is upon the object. "The Calm," which was greatly admired by contemporaries, and won the difficult suffrages of Ben Jonson, is in the same manner, but displays a greater extravagance. The intense heat of the Tropics in August offers the poet a theme with which he plays like a conjurer with a set of balls. The sailors go mad with the "calenture" or mirage-fever of nostalgia; and every extravagant phenomenon of great heat is dwelt upon—

> "On the hatches, as on altars, lies
> Each one, his own priest, and own sacrifice.
> Who live, that miracle do multiply
> Where walkers in hot ovens do not die;
> If in despite of these we swim, that hath
> No more refreshing than a brimstone-bath;
> Back from the sea into the ship we turn
> Like parboiled wretches on the coals to burn."

These ingenuities were in an entirely new fashion, and those who were not repelled by their novelty were attracted by their "wit." Long afterwards, when visiting Drummond at Hawthornden, Jonson recited with strong commendation the lines from " The Calm "—

> " In one place lay
> Feathers and dust, to-day and yesterday;
> Earth's hollownesses, which the world's lungs are,
> Have no more wind than th' upper vault of air."

Here we find ourselves at the very start-point of a new spirit in literature, the love of precise notation of prosaic fact in the forms and languages of poetry. The exquisite Elizabethan idealism was undermined at last; here was the beginning of decadence; here opened the invasion of the Visigoths.

The Islands Voyage proved highly unsuccessful. Donne describes himself to Christopher Brooke as having volunteered for three reasons: firstly, in the hope of prize-money; secondly, in order to escape from amatory adventures, "the queasy pain of being beloved and loving"; and thirdly, to satisfy the adventurous "thirst of honour or fair death." That he enjoyed a few months of rest from the burden of too much loving seems to have been his principal gain. Essex mismanaged the expedition, and the English volunteers won neither wealth nor glory at Ferrol. In October 1597 the combined fleets returned to England with a great quarrel more than smouldering between their commanders.

References to his early travels are rather faintly suggested than defined in his later letters and poems. One phenomenon, however, deeply impressed Donne upon the Islands Voyage; the startling form of Teneriffe is several times referred to in his writings. In this connection I am privileged to quote from the letter of a friend who is deeply in sympathy with the poets of the seventeenth century. Lady Londonderry, herself on an Islands Voyage, writes of sailing past the Peak of Teneriffe: "After the sun had set, and the crimson, orange, and deep green were fading into a soft grey, we saw the crescent moon floating in the wake of the sun, and, like a luminous boat, striking, as it seemed, against the side of the Peak; in a moment it flashed across me how our Donne had written—

> 'Doth not a Tenarus or higher hill
> Rise so high like a rock, that one might think
> The floating moon would shipwreck there and sink.''

So, century after century, the miraculous vision recurs for those who have eyes to see it.

It is now necessary to give some words of Walton's upon which comment is difficult. After mentioning Donne's voyage to the Azores in 1597, Walton continues—

"But he returned not back into England till he had stayed some years first in Italy, and then in Spain, where he made many useful observations of those countries, their laws and manners of government, and returned perfect in their languages.

"The time that he spent in Spain was, at his first going into Italy, designed for travelling to the Holy Land, and for viewing Jerusalem and the Sepulchre of our Saviour. But at his being in the farthest parts of Italy, the disappointment of company, or of a safe convoy, or the uncertainty of returns of money into these remote parts, denied him that happiness, which he did often occasionally mention with a deploration."

In the Westmoreland MS.,—where twenty epigrams are given, instead of sixteen as in the printed editions,—several pieces have Italian titles, as "Caso d'un muro" for "Fall of a Wall," and "Zoppo" for "A Lame Beggar." Whether this indicates that they were composed in Italy it is hard to say. One unpublished epigram, very characteristic of Donne in its style and versification, may be printed here—

"Il Cavaliere Gio: Wingfield.

> "Beyond th' old Pillars many have travellèd
> Towards the Sun's cradle, and his throne, and bed.
> A fitter Pillar our Earl did bestow
> In that base Island; for he well did know
> Farther than Wingfield no man dares to go."

This is obscure, but not impenetrable. Sir John Wingfield, son of Richard Wingfield and Mary Hardwicke, was the only Englishman of note that perished in the capture of Cadiz. He served with his brothers, Sir Richard and Sir Edward Wingfield, and was quartermaster-general of the army. He was attached to the Earl of Essex, and doubtless was constantly brought into personal communication, up to the time of his death, with Donne. Sir John Wingfield, who married Susan Bertie, had been knighted in 1586. His death, probably under Donne's own eyes, at Cadiz in 1596, must have impressed the young poet, and produced, at a time when he was occupied with the Italian language, the epigram here printed.

Another epigram, which is not in the published collections, reflects on the evil cuisine with which Elizabethan travellers in Spain were afflicted—

> "Thou in the fields walk'st out thy supping hours,
> And yet thou swear'st thou hast supp'd like a king:
> Like Nebuchadnezzar, perchance! with grass and flowers,—
> A salad worse than Spanish dieting!"

Into the difficulties involved by the very interesting passage quoted above from Walton, we must enter in another chapter.

THE LYRICAL POEMS

CHAPTER III

THE LYRICAL POEMS

THE career of Donne between 1592, when he entered at Lincoln's Inn, and 1602, when he married, is shrouded in a mist, which is the more exasperating to the biographer in that just enough is revealed through it to show the value of what is hidden. It is, however, useless to dogmatise as to the exact sequence of the poet's interesting movements. We have two or three precise data, among which the most salient are that he went to Cadiz in June 1596, and returned from the Azores in the autumn of 1597. But at some period Donne saw military service, travelled widely in Europe, and became private secretary to Lord Ellesmere. He also wrote a great body of very singular and moving poetry, some part of which, at least, has been preserved to us, although it was not printed during its author's lifetime. The extreme importance to the student of Donne of all these particulars has tempted his successive biographers, and even Walton, into positive statements which can, by the nature of the evidence, be not treated as more than conjectural.

That Donne travelled in his youth is certain, but it is strangely difficult to make even a fair guess at the date. Walton, who has been speaking of 1592, says, "About a year following he resolved to travel," and "took the advantage" of the Earl of Essex going to Cadiz to carry out this resolve. But the Cadiz expedition took place in 1596, and here are four years unaccounted for. Again, after the Azores, Walton distinctly tells us that "Donne returned not back into England till he had stayed some years, first in Italy, and then in Spain." According to this account, his journeys began in October 1597 and occupied "some years." But in 1602 Donne had served the Lord Keeper as secretary for four years, and could not have been spending that time in prolonged foreign travel. We are almost forced to suppose that Walton was in error in making the Cadiz expedition the beginning of Donne's travels, and in suggesting that he proceeded to Italy in the autumn of 1597. We have the years 1592 to 1596 unoccupied, and on the whole, it seems the more reasonable conjecture to believe that these were Donne's years of foreign travel.

If we may venture to suppose Walton ill-informed on this point, the fact that Donne had made himself familiar with the Spanish language might account for the readiness with which Essex consented to take him on the two expeditions. Donne "waited on his lordship," and might well be accepted on having put forward the nature of his qualifications. When he was in Italy, and still more, perhaps, in Spain, he had made "many useful observations of those countries, their laws and manner of government, and returned perfect in their languages." With regard to the scope of Donne's travels, Izaak Walton, who is our only authority, had an indistinct impression. In 1633 he believed that Donne had in his youth gone "to see the blessed place of Christ's nativity." But by 1640 he had become otherwise informed, and more exactly stated that when Donne first went to Italy his design was to pass on into Palestine for the purpose of visiting Jerusalem and the Sepulchre of our Saviour. "But at his being in the farthest parts of Italy, the disappointment of company, or of a safe convoy, or the uncertainty of returns of money into those remote parts, denied him that happiness." Accordingly he turned back into Spain, and spent there the months which he had intended to dedicate to the Holy Land.

It is possible that the extent of time spent by Donne in his travels was unconsciously exaggerated by Walton, and that they simply occupied the space between the Cadiz and the Azores expeditions. Coryat, that garrulous traveller from Odcombe, in the county of Somerset, took only five months to "gobble up" his famous "Crudities" in half the countries of Europe. But the austerely distinguished Donne, a student both of literature and manners, was not likely to hurry over the ground in the way in which that absurd and macaronic personage disported himself. To Coryat, in 1611, Donne addressed two scornful epistles full of his own peculiar wit and magic; these might have given him opportunity for some luminous references to his personal journeyings, but, unhappily, he was obstinately reticent on that subject, and the satires on the "Crudities" might have been written by a man who had never strayed out of London city. In the general darkness which assails us, we are not able to decide even by what route Donne returned to England, nor whether he passed through Germany on this first occasion. It was a peculiarity of his nature to cultivate an extreme personal reserve through which he would occasionally flash a spark of confidence or confession which merely made the rest of the tissue darker and more impenetrable. If we know nothing definite of the early life of Donne, it is mainly, no doubt, that in later years he refused to vouchsafe particulars concerning it, even to his closest friends. We may conclude the series of our conjectures by suggesting that such journeys as Walton speaks of must have been a severe drain upon the young man's fortune, and may account in part for its dispersion.

During these years of turmoil and voluntary exile Donne was dissecting the anatomy of the world; he was tasting life and rolling it, a savoury morsel, upon his tongue. All his writings, whether early or late, assure us of this fact. Sacred or profane, they are not the outcome of a cloistered or a sequestered spirit, but of one that has moved widely in the confused mass of mankind, has rubbed shoulders with motley crowds, has tried without diffidence or excessive scruple all modes and manners of existence. More, probably, than any other poet of the Elizabethan age, Donne lived. His soul was thirsty with the consuming strain after experience, and it was in active movement and in personal contact with widely various types, that he discovered that relief which gentler spirits find in meditation and in the exercise of unfettered fancy. His mental and moral conditions in these years of his youth were turbulent and confused; his soul, still unsteadied and unrefined, poured forth a volume of muddy waters. Later on was to follow the serene and limpid majesty of a life directed by faith and duty. But in earlier days there was no tame, domestic stream to be sheltered from impurity by soft and grassy dykes. The youthful soul of Donne was in flood, and it raged whither it could, stormily, but downwards ever, towards a dimly-foreseen future of sanctity and repose.

What his occupations were in these years we may faintly perceive. In all this period Donne is dimly revealed to us as a sort of Elizabethan Goethe. His intellect glutted itself with knowledge, without inquiring whether that knowledge might be considered by precisians to be forbidden or dangerous. His nominal pursuit was law, in which, we are assured, his proficiency became universal; he "knew all laws." That theology occupied him strenuously, though probably feverishly and intermittently, he himself has told us in the remarkable preface to the *Pseudo-Martyr*. He mastered "the grounds and use of physic, but, because it was mercenary, waived it." His writings, both in prose and verse, testify to his eager curiosity in all branches of the science of his time, his "hydroptic immoderate desire of human learning." He scorned, in the gaping travellers of his age, that avid and shallow credulity which expended itself on "talk of Will Conqueror and Prester John." He went deeper; he endeavoured, without prejudice, an observer, to detect the true movement of thought, of speculation, of research in the principal European centres of that time. Perhaps, in his youth, he understood England less than he did Spain, Italy, or Germany. Something, at least, curiously exotic, curiously out of sympathy with insular habits of feeling, is to be detected in his early writings. In that florid and fiery age Donne too, and in a superlative degree, cultivated plants and flowers, but they were not of any recognisable home-grown varieties.

For we come now to what positively remains to us out of these crepuscular years of Donne's youth. From behind the smoke and twilight in which his movements are so tantalisingly concealed, one positive entity emerges, and that is his poetry. We have seen in the previous chapter that his *Satires*, those strange experiments of a precocious originality, are more or less distinctly dated. They existed in part, we know, so early as 1593. But of the lyrics and epistles which must now occupy our attention we can but say that external and internal evidences alike point to their having been, in by far the greater number of instances, composed before the close of the sixteenth century. Here Ben Jonson—coeval with Donne, and intimate with him in the latter's pre-clerical days—Jonson who admired Donne as warmly as it was possible for such "a contemner and scorner of others" to admire any one—told Drummond of Hawthornden that Donne wrote "all his best pieces ere he was twenty-five years old." This would bring us to 1598, or the date of Donne's return from the Azores. This date is anything rather than final, yet it may probably be taken to indicate that from 1593 to 1598 was Donne's blossoming period as a lyrical poet.

The independence of Donne's character and his want of sympathy with the trend of the English literature of his age are curiously exemplified in his persistence in keeping his verses unpublished. The Elizabethan anthologies, in which are found examples of almost every other poet of position, and of multitudes of versifiers who never attained reputation at all, know nothing of the splendid compositions of John Donne. Even *England's Helicon*, to which many of his acquaintances contribute, and which closes with an epithalamium by his most intimate friend, Christopher Brooke, offers us not one scrap of Donne. In the course of this biography the very rare instances in which he consented to print his poetry will in due succession be recorded. But if they were all taken together, they could hardly be eked out into a pamphlet. In spite of his genius and his fame Donne was practically a posthumous poet. What he wrote from 1593 onwards was not printed until 1633, and then without authority, and apparently without arrangement. Donne's attitude towards his verses was singularly human. He grew to consider them scandalous or trivial, and yet he could not bring himself to destroy them. In his letters he apologises for them; he deprecates, and yet confesses a weakness. He will not print them, yet he has no objection to seeing them circulate in manuscript. When they become objects of curiosity and mystery he affects to smile, but does nothing to destroy the illusion. We feel that no outrage on his memory was performed in the act of their posthumous publication, but that he had expected all along to be ultimately pushed up the slopes of Helicon, faintly resisting.

Yet it is always convenient for the reputation of poets that they should take pains to arrange and circulate their own works. This disdainful dropping of verses, as a hen lays eggs, in the hope that some one will eventually pick them up, brings with it serious disadvantages. To students of Donne it has brought a great number of annoyances. In the first place, the text of no other English classic is so dubious, so conjectural. Instead of receiving from the poet's own hand what he asserts to be his, we reach him across a wide margin of "dubious" and "attributed" pieces, fading away on its outer edge into what is more or less obviously spurious or borrowed. Again, we know not what is meant, nor by whom, in the existing arrangement of Donne's poems. They are presented to us in sections, entitled "Songs and Sonnets," "Epigrams," "Elegies," "Epithalamions," "Satires," "Letters," "Funeral Elegies," "Divine Poems," but how far these represent the poet's wishes cannot be conjectured. In 1650, John Donne the younger, writing to Lord Craven, remarked that in previous impressions of his father's poems "the kindness of the printer" had "added something too much, lest any spark of this sacred fire might perish undiscerned." But in his own later editions he left out scarcely anything, and this phrase is perhaps merely an apology for what might seem, though genuine, trifling.

It will be our business in the present biography to break up this inchoate mass of verses, and to redistribute it as carefully as possible, so as to let it illustrate the life of its author. We have, accordingly, already detached the "Satires." To the second period of Donne's life belong the "Songs and Sonnets" and the "Elegies." These two sections, in my opinion, should be treated as one. They appear, in the main, to belong to the same period, to deal with identical moods and passions, and to be distinguished simply by their structure, the "Songs and Sonnets" (there is not one real sonnet amongst them) being lyrics in stanzaic form, and the "Elegies" being amatory poems in heroic measure. It is to be noted that these early "elegies" have nothing funereal about them, but that the word is used by Donne exactly in the same sense as it is in the history of Latin poetry, as, for instance, to describe the poems in which Propertius narrates and analyses the story of his infatuation for Cynthia. With Donne the parallel was doubtless a conscious one, and he believed that his rhyming couplets reproduced the effect of the elegiac measure. When, therefore, we speak of the love-poetry of Donne we include, with the lyrics, the score or so of romantic personal pieces, mainly in heroic verse, which form a kind of commentary on the songs. Four-fifths of this body of highly original and curious poetry in all probability belong to the years from 1593 to 1600.

When we come to consider the relation of the early poetry of Donne to that which was being produced elsewhere in England, so abundantly, during the closing years of the sixteenth century, we shall have to dwell on its curious divergence from all the established literary traditions of the time. Among these traditions, that of taking an imaginary episode in love and embroidering fancies upon it was one of the most accepted. In the more favourable instances of a pretended revelation of amatory adventure in verse, such as the *Idea* of Drayton in 1593 and 1594, or the *Amoretti* of Spenser in 1595, it is almost impossible for the most ingenious reader to build on the shadowy and nebulous basis any superstructure of conjectural biography. At first sight it may seem that Donne offers the same intangibility; but there is this difference, that, after twenty readings, the story indicated by Spenser or Drayton in his sonnets continues as vague as ever, whereas the careful study of Donne, when the first obscure crust is broken, reveals a condition of mind and even a sequence of events so personal, that we hardly dare to take our legitimate advantage from it.

We read Donne, however, to little purpose if we do not perceive that he was, above all things, sincere. His writings, like his actions, were faulty, violent, a little morbid even, and abnormal. He was not, and did not attempt to be, an average man. But actions and writings alike, in their strangeness, their aloofness, were unadulterated by a tinge of affectation. Donne was Elizabethan in his absolute straightforwardness of character; it was left to his Caroline disciples to introduce into a mode of expression founded upon his a trick of pastiche, an alloy of literary pretence. Donne, in turbid and violent language—for, with all his genius, he lacked the last ornament of a perfect style, lucidity—expressed what he himself perceived, suffered, and desired. If, therefore, we can but comprehend what Donne is saying, and realise what his character is, if we can but appreciate the curious alternations of cautious reserve and bold confession in which he indulges, if we can but discover how to stand on his own level, there is hardly a piece of his genuine verse which, cryptic though it may seem, cannot be prevailed upon to deliver up some secret of his life and character.

The dangers of such a conjectural reconstruction of biography are obvious, yet I believe that in few cases in literary history is that method more legitimate than here. When Donne speaks of his personal experience, there is something so convincing in his accent, poignant and rude at once, that it is impossible not to believe it the accurate record of a genuine emotional event. I am not unaware that, in 1625, writing to Sir Robert Ker, he said, "You know my uttermost [in verse] when it was best, and even then I did best when I had least truth for my subjects." By truth he means here what, in the evolution of his taste, he had come to regard as an excess of realism; and beyond question, what he here describes as his "best" were those pieces of metaphysical extravagance, where he had "least truth for his subjects," but embroidered conceit after conceit upon a false or trivial first idea. The Second Elegy, with its extravagant ingenuity about the elements of a fair face, the "anagram" of beauty, is a capital example of what we now have come to detest as thoroughly bad art, but of what particularly dazzled the followers of Donne, and laid the foundation of his excessive fame as a wit. These are what Donne regarded with complacency as his "best," but to us they are little else than grotesque, the symptoms of a malady of the mind.

Very different, however, from these chains of "enormous and disgusting hyperboles," as Dr Johnson called them, are the numerous poems in which Donne, retaining of course the tortured manner natural to him, recounted the adventures of his body and his soul. In their consideration of these poems the biographers of Donne, misled by an amiable fallacy, have not chosen to give their true weight and meaning to words about the scope of which there can be no honest question. Walton, in his exquisite portrait of his friend, has nothing at all to say of the stormy and profane youth which led up to that holy maturity of faith and unction. He chose to ignore or to forget anything which might seem to dim the sacred lustre of the exemplary Dean of St. Paul's. Yet even Walton admitted that Donne "was by nature highly passionate," and doubtless he was well aware that below the sanctity of his age lay a youth scored with frailty and the injuries of instinct. Later biographers have had less excuse for attempting to conceal those tenebrous and fiery evidences, which but add a more splendid majesty to the career rising out of them into peace and light. To pretend that Donne was a saint in his youth is to nullify the very process of divine grace in the evolution of a complex soul, in the reduction of a magnificent rebel to a still more brilliant and powerful servant.

In the early poems of Donne, then, we observe three stages of experience. If in the following pages I define these with more exactitude than the text may seem to some readers to warrant, I do so merely for purposes of convenience. I am well aware of the danger of attempting to press the fluidity of an old lyric into the glass of a modern theory. Yet, although the frontiers of my divisions may be, and indeed must be, uncertain, my confidence in their general distribution increases every time that I read the poems. It will be remembered that there was no attempt at arrangement in the first collection of Donne's posthumous poems in 1633; but in 1635 the sections which have since been familiar to us were adopted, and the lyrical pieces known as "Songs and Sonnets" opened the volume. Though the text was constantly revised, this arrangement was retained, and can never again be disturbed. My impression, after close consideration of it, is that it represents, in a confused and inexact way, the arrangement of the author, or rather, that a vague indication of the relative dates of composition may, with the exercise of great caution, be obtained from it. I will, at all events, go so far as to say that I am persuaded that among the true *juvenilia* of Donne are to be placed the opening pages of the edition of 1635.

In this earliest series of his poems we find him a mere butterfly of the court, ostentatiously flitting from flower to flower, indulging his curiosity and his sensuousness wherever satisfaction is offered to him. "Women's Constancy" is the complete expression of his unattached condition of mind and body. In "Love's Usury," with the impertinence of the successful gallant, he promises to turn monogamous when he is old. In these early days his experiences are all of sensation and superficial emotion. He wanders wherever his desires attract him, rifles all blossoms for their honey, boasts—in the manner of impudent youth—his detachment from all chains of duty or reflection. He is the ideal light o' love; he will pluck the rose wherever he finds it, and he is confident that for the wise youth who knows how to nip the flower discreetly there can be no thorns. The tone of these earliest lyrics is one of sceptical, even contemptuous, arrogance. In "A Fever" the mistress of the moment is ill, but it only amuses the lover. The malady is an excuse for a *feu de joie* of conceits; she may die of it, for all he really cares. In these foppish, heartless lyrics Donne is most interesting when most frankly sensual. "The Good Morrow" is the perfectly contented and serene record of an illicit, and doubtless of an ephemeral, adventure. "The Sun Rising," perhaps the strongest of the early lyrics, gives no evidence of soul, but is a fine hymn of sturdy, virile satisfaction. What could be more spirited, in its boyish way, than the opening stanza—

> " Busy old fool, unruly Sun,
>   Why dost thou thus,
> Thro' windows and thro' curtains, call on us?
> Must to thy motions lovers' seasons run?
>   Saucy pedantic wretch, go chide
>   Late schoolboys and sour prentices;
> Go tell court-huntsmen that the king will ride,
>   Call country ants to harvest offices;
> Love, all alike, no season knows nor clime,[1]
> Nor hours, days, months, which are the rags of time."

From a young lover in this mood we need not be scandalised to receive such a poem as "The Flea," that extremely clever piece of impudent ribaldry, nor expect a deeper sense of the dignity of womanhood than is found in "The Indifferent," that uproarious claim to absolute freedom in love. Here Donne reminds us of a very different poet, of the nomadic Verlaine, with his "Es tu brune ou es tu blonde?—Je ne sais!" In "The Legacy," more seriously, and with an intuition of deeper feeling, Donne playfully upbraids his heart for its own too-flagrant infidelities. When he rips up his bosom to send his heart to the woman of the moment he is alarmed at first to find none there, and he suffers his first shudder, his earliest movement of conscience, in this instant, when the threatened impotency of genuine feeling suddenly chills the light tumult

---

[1] If, as I think likely, this was written about 1595, the "clime" was probably France, and "the king" Henry IV., a mighty hunter, our ally, and very popular in England. But there is no need to press a poet to this extremity of exact allusion.

of his love. But in another moment he recovers his composure: all is not lost—

> "Yet I found something like a heart,
> But colours it, and corners had;
> It was not good, it was not bad,
> It was entire to none, and few had part;
> As good as could be made by art
> It seemed, and therefore for our loss be sad.
> I meant to send that heart instead of mine,
> But O! no man could hold it, for 'twas thine."

Serious for a moment, with a presage of better things, the mood has changed before the stanza was over, and the lash of satire at feminine frailty leaps out. Of this arrogance of juvenile cynicism the mandrake song remains the most poetical expression—

> "If thou be'st born to strange sights,
> Things invisible to see,
> Ride ten thousand days and nights
> Till age snow white hairs on thee,
> Thou, when thou return'st, wilt tell me
> All strange wonders that befell thee,
> And swear
> Nowhere
> Lives a woman true and fair.
>
> If thou find'st one, let me know;
> Such a pilgrimage were sweet.
> Yet do not, I would not go,
> Though at next door we might meet.
> Tho' she were true when you met her,
> And last till you write your letter,
> Yet she
> Will be
> False, ere I come, to two or three."

A young gentleman of fashion, wit and fortune, intent upon pleasure, and flaunting these impudent colours in his cap, is the sure target for amorous misfortune, and Donne was now about to enter upon a very stormy and painful episode.

For various reasons, which will be presently enumerated, I am inclined to date the beginning of this deplorable but eventful liaison in the summer of 1596. The decline of it seems to have occupied Donne's most vivid and poignant thoughts between his return from Cadiz and his start for the Azores. If the evidence bears out this supposition, we have to reflect that Donne was now in the four-and-twentieth year of his life. He was independent in fortune, and singularly unfettered by family ties. At a very early age he had become his own master, not in the conventional sense only, but in religion, morals, speculation, and action. The piety of admirers has slurred over, but has not been able to erase, the fact that at this period Donne was a type of the Renaissance young man, avid for pleasure and for knowledge and experience, which were his highest expressions of pleasure; in a high degree, he must have been a law unto himself. His conscience was entirely emancipated; his religious sense was occupied exclusively with the scholastic skeleton of dogma. Above all, in his intense instinctive curiosity he had proclaimed himself cynically polygamous. He had asked—

> "Are sun, moon, or stars by law forbidden
> To smile where they list, or lend away their light?
> Are birds divorc'd, or are they chidden
> If they do leave their mates, or lie abroad at night?
> Beasts no jointures lose
> Though they no lovers choose,
> But we are made worse than those."

But to this impudent assertion of a mutual right to incessant change the heart itself suddenly proffers a reply. Donne was abruptly faced by a passion which has left upon his verse a deeper impress than any other event, and may be said to have made him what we know him as a poet. With that curious nonchalance of his, the progress of this liaison is scarcely veiled in the powerful verses which are called forth by the tragical events of this adventure. We can reconstruct the story almost without danger of a mistake.

Donne, after boasting of the independence of his heart, was suddenly subjugated by the beauty of a married lady. She was a woman of some social position; her husband was a rich man, in possession of a large house in which hospitality was dispensed. The poet had the entry of the Court, and it is almost certain that his mistress also had. We know, from several admissions, that he fell in love with her at first sight at a social gathering of persons—

> "I brought a heart into the room,
> But from the room I carried none with me."

His heart, hitherto whole and callous, was shattered into reflecting fragments like a mirror, was torn into rags like a garment. His passion completely overwhelmed him; for the first time, though he had loved so often, he felt the genuine tyranny of love. The lady offered no strong resistance to his suit, and his vanity was gratified, and his affection accordingly fortified, by his success in overcoming her scruples.

One of the earliest expressions of his accepted passion appears to me to be the very important lyric called "Love's War," which remained in MS. until 1802. Donne is dreading his departure for the Azores, and he confesses that—

> "Midas joys our Spanish journies give;
> We touch all gold, but find no food to live;
> And I shall be in that hot parching clime
> To dust and ashes turn'd before my time.
> To mew me in a ship is to enthral
> Me in a prison that were like to fall,
> Or in a cloister, save that there men dwell
> In a calm heaven, here in a swaying hell.
> Long voyages are long consumptions,
> And ships are carts for executions."

In this mood of depressed apprehension he almost decides to leave others to seek glory under "thrusts, pikes, stabs, yea bullets," and stay at home with the kind and comfortable mistress, who has just opened her arms to him. With "Love's War" may be connected the Fifth Elegy, which appears to date from the same time. He is starting for Spanish lands; he tells his mistress that he may be weather-beaten when he returns, torn with rude oars or tanned with the sun, his head turned grey, his body a sack of bones,

"And powder's blue stains scatter'd on my skin."

These may be the results of a defeat and capture of English sailors in the Atlantic, and for such reverses he is prepared in the melancholy moment of quitting England and his love. He leaves his picture with her that she may continue to remember him as he leaves her, "fair and delicate."

It was perhaps necessary that he should quit England for a while. His life since manhood had been haunted by all the phantoms of infidelity. He had been pursuing with frenzy an illusive chimera of pleasure. But in spite of all his impudent protests, the strong heart of John Donne could not be satisfied by these ephemeral captures. His passions were now dominant and his blood imperious. The instinct that drives vehement young men to acts of madness was violent in him. He had been looking around him for an adventure, for some liaison which could give him the measure of his own vital intensity. If the moralists will allow us to say so, his ethical ambition had risen a grade, from the pursuit of woman as a species to the selection of one who should present herself to his imagination as a symbol of the Feminine. We must remember, to comprehend the conditions depicted in the "Songs and Sonnets" and the "Elegies," that we have to do with no simple pastoral swain, but with one of the most headstrong and ingenious intellects of the century, now, for the time being, concentrating itself on the evolution of its own *vita sexualis*. And we must remember, too, that it was from these agonies and errors, bleeding as from rods with the wounds of passion, that Donne rose slowly to those spiritual heights in which he so glorified the grace of God.

But to such a nature, so roused even in the storm of illicit passion, there was but a short space for complete satisfaction. At first the crushing of "joy's grape," as Keats puts it, excluded every other sentiment, and Donne composed—we dare not allow ourselves to overlook the fact—some of the most sensual poetry written in the history of English literature by any poet of eminence. It was, perhaps, needful that he should go off to the Islands, since the liaison was carried on in the first instance with astonishing effrontery. The husband was a deformed man, and was stationary all day in a basket-chair. This gave the lovers confidence, but the lady, as Donne tells her in one of the later denunciatory pieces, was dull in speech and unready in mind. Their secret meetings, stolen correspondence, and artificial language were, no doubt, thoroughly after Donne's own ingenious heart, but they distracted and alarmed the lady. With singular complacency, alluding to her original want of cleverness, he says that he has "refined her into a blissful paradise." "The Apparition" shows that Donne did too well his work of awakening those slumbering faculties which the roughness and jealousy of her husband had crushed so long. On this subject the Seventh Elegy throws a curious light.

But when he returned from the Azores, and took up once more those vows of constancy which had been sealed during his absence by stealthy means—"we can love by letters still, and gifts"—there seems evidence of a change in the poet's sentiments. By a perverse ingenuity very characteristic of him, he reversed the process which had made the easy seduction of the lady grateful to his vanity, and in that very fact, no longer flattering to him, he sees a proof of her lack of stability and value. He discovers her to be less youthful than he thought her, and, in the reflex of his passion, her autumnal sensuality exasperates him. She overdoes the mysteries of their meetings, the alphabet of flowers, the secret messengers, the elaborate and needless subterfuges. The Thirteenth Elegy is, doubtless, the expression of this turn of the tide. She is still his "dove-like friend," still in profuse and burning couplets his love rages when he thinks upon her. Yet he upbraids the passion which he cannot resist, and even the lady he still worships—

> "Was't not enough that thou didst hazard us
> To paths in love so dark and dangerous,
> And those so ambush'd round with household spies,
> And over all thy husband's towering eyes?"

He begins to feel the horror and the ridicule of the intimate feast under the light of the family candlesticks, where the afflicted and jealous husband, daring not to complain openly in words, yet

> "Swollen and pamper'd with great fare,
> Sits down and snorts, caged in his basket-chair."

The poet's first revolt is a refusal to meet in the lady's own house—

> "Now I see many dangers; for it is
> His realm, his castle, and his diocese."

As yet, Donne still exults in the betrayal, but the Nemesis of his sin is falling upon him. They must part, make fewer meetings, run less risk; "she must go, and I must mourn." He permits the symptoms of a growing lassitude in himself to be perceived; there follow angry words, and those recriminations that are so surely the death of love. The Third Elegy marks a sense of her declining devotion to him, and characteristically, although he cools to her, his pride is exquisitely wounded at her becoming less ardent to him. In a note of mingled mockery and trepidation he recommends to her an "apostasy" that may confirm her love, and in a brilliant flash of caprice informs her that

> "Change is the nursery
> Of music, joy, life and eternity."

Does she take him at his word, or does he mistake her timorous withdrawal for the heart's act of treason? We cannot tell, but the sources of his forbidden joy are poisoned, and jealousy stings him at last to vehement and gross attack. There are no hate-poems in the language finer of their kind, filled with a stronger wind of vindictive passion, than those which now close this incident.

To distribute these lyrics according to the order of their composition would be preposterous. They possess a close similarity of style; they were probably written at short intervals, all possibly in the summer of 1597. "The Curse" is an expression of the angry lover's first rage; but he comforts himself that his mistress has been extremely discreet and secret, and that the open ridicule of defeat may be spared him. "The Message" breathes the same egotistical spirit, and denounces the forced fashions and false passions which have fooled him and destroyed him. He perversely parodies Marlowe's beautiful pastoral song to satirise those hands and eyes that, as he believes, have been his ruin—

> "Let others freeze with angling reeds,
>   And cut their legs with shells and weeds,
>   Or treach'rously poor fish beset,
>   With strangling snare or windowy net.
>
> Let coarse bold hands from slimy nest
> The bedded fish in banks out-wrest;
> Or curious traitors, sleeve-silk flies,
> Bewitch poor fishes' wandering eyes."

With all his rage, he feels himself still drawn to the false one, with agonising threads of desire; and "Love's Deity," with the enchanting melody of its opening couplet, gives expression to his torture—

> "I long to talk with some old lover's ghost,
>   Who died before the God of Love was born;
> I cannot think that he who, then, loved most,
>   Sunk so low as to love one which did scorn.
> But since this God produced a destiny,
> And that vice-nature, custom, lets it be,
> I must love her that loves not me."

Here the note is as the note of Catullus—

> "Odi et amo. Quare id faciam fortasse requiris.
>   Nescio, sed fieri sentio et excrucior."

To this period also we may assign the passionate wilfulness of "The Prohibition"—

> "Take heed of loving me;
> At least remember, I forbade it thee.
> Not that I shall repair my unthrifty waste
>   Of breath and blood upon thy sighs and tears,
> By being to me then what to me thou wast;
>   But so great joy our life at once outwears.
> Then, lest that love by my dearth frustrate be,
> If thou love me,—take heed of loving me."

THE LYRICAL POEMS

"The Will" carries us on a further step to acrid scorn and contemptuous satire. He will die, smitten by great Love, to whom, however, he prays for a moment's respite, that he may make some legacies. His codicils are burning ironies; he gives—

"My tongue to Fame; to ambassadors mine ears;
To women—or the sea—my tears."

Jealousy has now taken possession of him. He fancies that his mistress has had twenty lovers before him, that she entertains younger lovers now. In the midst of the boisterous cynicism of this poem there are touches which we like to note—

"My constancy I to the planets give;
My truth to them who at the court do live;
Mine ingenuity and openness
To Jesuits; to buffoons my pensiveness;
My silence to any, who abroad have been;
My money to a Capuchin;"

and this—

"To him for whom the passing-bell next tolls,
I give my physic-books; my written rolls
Of moral counsels I to Bedlam give;
My brazen medals unto them which live
In want of bread; to them which pass among
All foreigners, my English tongue."

Much more serious, indeed of a noble and resigned melancholy, is "The Funeral," in which he announces that he is "Love's martyr," and, by an image which had impressed his fancy so much that he repeats it in several poems, announces that when they come to enshroud his body, they will find

"That subtle wreath of hair, which crowns my arm,
The mystery, the sign you must not touch,"

all that remains to him now of one loved so passionately and proved to be so false. Since she will now have none of him, he will at least bury some of her, and at the Last Day, when the bodies stir, his arm will be seen to wave with "a bracelet of bright hair about the bone."

But all these poems of hatred and enforced resignation pale before "The Apparition," in which, as he tosses between sleep and waking, the horror of his situation, the vileness of the woman he has loved, and the whole squalor of the outworn liaison come upon him and overwhelm him. The fierce passion in this brief lyric, a "hate-poem" of the very first class, is closely akin to those flashes of lurid light in which the contemporary tragedians excelled, "steeping us," as Charles Lamb says, "in agonies infernal." Such error, however, as Donne had indulged in could be washed out in no less bitter waters. "The Apparition" is brief, and must be read complete to produce the terrific effect of its reluctant malediction—

> " When by thy scorn, O murderess, I am dead,
>   And that thou think'st thee free
>   From all solicitation from me,
> Then shall my ghost come to thy bed,
> And thee, feign'd vestal, in worse arms shall see;
> Then thy sick taper will begin to wink,
> And he, whose thou art then, being tired before,
> Will, if thou stir, or pinch to wake him, think
>   Thou call'st for more,
>   And, in false sleep, will from thee shrink:
> And then, poor aspen wretch, neglected thou,
> Bathed in a cold quicksilver sweat wilt lie
>   A verier ghost than I.
> *What I will say, I will not tell thee now,*
> Lest that preserve thee; and since my love is spent,
> I'd rather thou should'st painfully repent,
> Than by my threatenings rest still innocent."

This is the culmination of the incident, the flames of hatred now quickly subsiding into a heap of the ashes of indifference and satiety. This exhausted cynicism is interpreted by "Love's Alchemy," where the poet protests that all women are alike vile, and the elixir of happiness an imposture not to be discovered by any alchemist who "glorifies his pregnant pot," only to be fooled and disenchanted. So, also, in a most curious ode, the "Nocturnal upon St. Lucy's Day," amid fireworks of conceit, he calls his mistress dead, and protests that his hatred has grown calm at last. So this volcanic passion sinks back into its crater at length, leaving this series of astonishing poems to illustrate it, poems which, as Donne himself says, are "as all-confessing and through-shine" as glass itself. When he grew supine once more, he reflected, rather splenetically, on his want of common prudence in this revelation of the adventures of the soul. As he said to Rowland Woodward, he had shown these "love-song weeds and satiric thorns" to too many of his friends to be able to quench the incident in oblivion, and too many copies of them had been made by his private admirers to preclude their circulation.

Donne, in his own words, had "stained" his soul's "first white," but his conduct from this time forth seems to have given no scandal. One or two love-passages appear to have ruffled the tenour of the wave of life which was carrying him towards the bourne of matrimony. He sees and is the sudden victim of beauty again and again.

His sensitive heart is ingenious in self-torture, and to what extremities it still can fling him we read in "The Blossom." The lady of the moment has left him a week ago, and in three weeks more he is to meet her in London. In subtle, modulated verse his heart taunts and plagues him, for he no longer knows what he desires nor what he is. His previous adventures have made him cautious, even sceptical, and he will not frankly give way to this sweet, insidious hope. He apostrophises his own trembling heart, which knows not whether to bide with him or to follow the new and desired mistress—

> "Well then, stay here; but know,
> When thou hast stay'd and done thy most,
> *A naked thinking heart, that makes no show,*
> *Is to a woman but a kind of ghost;*
>   How shall she know my heart?"

To the same vague category of emotions which faintly stirred the poet between his great criminal liaison and his ultimate betrothal, I am inclined also to attribute, on internal and structural evidence, the Tenth Elegy, as well as, perhaps, the extremely fantastic lyric called "The Ecstasy," with its obsession on the word "violet"; this had, unquestionably, at the time of its composition an illuminating meaning which time has completely obscured. A few of the Epistles, too, may belong to this early period, and one of the most important of these, the second to Sir Henry Wotton, I am able for the first time to date. This poem is given in the Westmoreland MS., in my possession, with the heading, "To Mr. H. W. 20 July 1598. At Court." But the majority of the Letters in Verse, and probably all the Divine Poems, belong to a period subsequent to the poet's marriage.

To any date earlier than that of his own marriage may be assigned a poem which holds a somewhat unique position in the roll of Donne's undoubted writings. In the "Epithalamion made at Lincoln's Inn" he drops his accustomed manner and closely imitates the imagery, the prosody, and the tone of Spenser. His own peculiar individuality lies below the rich Spenserian embroidery, and the result has a mellifluous glow which we could wish to see more frequent in Donne. The occasion of this stately, sensuous ode is uncertain; all we know is that the bridegroom was one who was a member of the Inn, and not an assiduous one, for he combined "study" with "play" in it. So impersonal is the poem, so made to order, that we know not whether to indulge a guess that the nuptials of Christopher Brooke form its theme. If it were suggested that Donne's own secret marriage was here celebrated, we should be unable to reject the idea on any internal evidence. In this class of Elizabethan poem the best of men permitted themselves so fescennine a liberty, that it is difficult to give a specimen to modern readers; this stanza, however, represents the poem not unfairly—

"Daughters of London, you which be
  Our golden mines and furnish'd treasury,
You which are angels, yet still bring with you
Thousands of angels on your marriage days,
Help with your presence, and devise to praise
  These rites, which also unto you grow due;

> Conceitedly dress her, and be assign'd
> By you fit place for every flower and jewel;
> Make her for love fit fuel,
> As gay as Flora and as rich as Ind;
> So may she, fair and rich, in nothing lame,
> To-day put on perfection and a woman's name."

The pun about "angels"—the divine ministrants and the earthly coin—was a favourite one with Donne. In the Eleventh Elegy he plays upon it until we lose all patience with so much self-satisfied ingenuity—

> "*Angels*, which heaven commanded to provide
> All things to me, and be my faithful guide,
> To gain new friends, to appease great enemies,
> To comfort my soul, when I lie or rise";

or—

> "Twelve righteous *angels*, which as yet
> No leaven of vile solder did admit";

or—

> "Pity these *angels* yet; their dignities
> Pass Virtues, Powers, and Principalities."

The extravagance might be pardoned once, but its recurrence is more and more intolerable. Yet it was precisely this dross and slag of his genius which endeared Donne as a poet to his immediate followers.

We have here, therefore, a substantial body of poetry composed before 1600, not one fragment of which was printed then, or probably during the lifetime of the poet, whose few verse-publications were of much later date of composition. This refraining from the printing-press was very unusual in the reign of Elizabeth, although common enough through the troubled years of Charles I. If we seek for reasons for the refusal of Donne to court publicity in any form, we are faced by several plausible suppositions. One is, that he was by his interests isolated from other young men of letters of his time; another, that he was a Catholic; yet when such contemporaries as Southwell and Constable had printed their verses with impunity, there could be little danger for one so much more discreet than they, as Donne was. But to my own mind, the real source of Donne's unwillingness to publish what he had no disinclination to distribute in MS., lay in the fact that so large a part of his verses, and among them the most powerful and eloquent, were occupied with the discussion of a liaison which could not be confessed, and which he had yet described in terms which would have made it patent to every instructed reader. To have published the early poetry of Donne would have been to court an instant, and probably a very distressing, scandal. I have no belief whatever in the "now missing, privately printed" issues of Donne's poetry, which some enthusiasts are always hoping to discover. The existence of such collections is incompatible with Donne's direct statement to George Gerrard (April 14, 1612), in which he refuses to pardon himself for having at last "declined" to the weakness of printing "anything in verse," the reference being to *An Anatomy of the World* of 1611–12. In 1614, as we shall in due time discover, considerable pressure was put upon Donne to print his poems. His momentary intention was to do this, "not for much public view, but at my own cost, a few copies."

In later life there is no question that Donne declined to be, as he called it, "the rhapsodist of mine own rags," and blazon forth the verses of his youth. Ben Jonson went too far when he told Drummond of Hawthornden that Donne, after 1615, "repented highly, and sought to destroy all his Poems," but this was doubtless the general opinion. It is endorsed and enlarged by Walton in a passage, charmingly written, which it may be well to quote at this point, while expressing a warning against its being taken as a minutely accurate record:—

"The recreations of his youth were poetry, in which he was so happy, as if Nature and all her varieties had been made only to exercise his sharp wit and high fancy; and in those pieces which were facetiously composed and carelessly scattered (most of them being written before the twentieth year of his age), it may appear by his choice metaphors that both Nature and all the Arts joined to assist him with their utmost skill."

THE LYRICAL POEMS 79

The admiration for precocity which was so strongly marked at and after the Renaissance here leads Walton to attribute to his friend an early ripeness which we know was not existent. So, too, these lyrics, full of the profoundest passion, and written as with the heart's blood of the poet, are to Walton but facetious recreations, written to amuse his extreme youth and then carelessly scattered. Thus Montaigne has, until very lately, perplexed and successfully confounded bibliographers by pushing back into the very infancy of La Boétie, and treating as a mere lighthearted exercise, that humanist's mature treatise of *La Servitude Volontaire*. To attribute the great lyrics of Donne to a period closing in 1592 is an hypothesis offensive to historical and literary common-sense; and Walton's object in writing the passage just quoted was certainly twofold—he wished to glorify Donne by exaggerating his youthful cleverness, and at the same time to modify any scandal accruing from his early poems by describing them as facetious trifles, carelessly composed by the lightheartedness of a boy. Walton proceeds, speaking of that of which he had greater personal knowledge:—

"It is a truth, that in his penitential years, viewing some of those pieces that had been loosely (God knows too loosely) scattered in his youth, he wished they had been abortive, or so shortlived that his own eyes had witnessed their funerals; but though he was no friend to them, he was not so fallen out with heavenly poetry as to forsake that."

But we hardly know what Walton means by "forsake," since we possess no evidence that Donne began to write sacred verse until after he went to Mitcham in 1605. If there was a harvest of Catholic poetry in his youth, as some have conjectured, it has wholly disappeared.

His secular lyrical poetry, although it was not printed, soon began to be widely circulated. There must have been numerous MS. copies of it, not a few of which are still in existence, although none, perhaps, so early as 1600. In 1619 Donne himself gave such a MS. to Sir Robert Ker; the Westmoreland MS. is a similar collection, made about

the same time, and presented by the poet to Rowland
Woodward. The poetaster, Thomas Freeman, in his *Run
and a Great Cast*, published in 1614, refers to having read
Satires, "The Storm" and "The Calm" in a MS. of this
kind, and adds—

> "I prithee, Persius, write a bigger book."

Sir John Simeon's interesting find of MS. poems at
Swanley is probably a copy of a copy, for it is dated 1644.
In relation to Donne's habit of circulating his poems in
MS. only, and so making a mysterious matter of them,
Mr. E. K. Chambers very ingeniously points to a passage
in Drayton's *Of Poets and Poesy*, addressed to Henry
Reynolds, in which, having given a list of names of living
poets and having omitted Donne, he continues—

> "For such whose poems, be they ne'er so rare,
> In private chambers that encloister'd are,
> And by transcription daintily must go,
> As though the world unworthy were to know
> Their rich composures, let those men then keep
> Those wondrous relics in their judgment deep,
> And cry them up so, let such pieces be
> Spoke of by those that shall come after me.
> I pass not for them."

As Mr. Chambers amusingly remarks, Donne had evidently neglected to convey a copy to Drayton, who, indeed, besides being ten years older, was diametrically out of sympathy with Donne's temperament and genius.

Drayton has been named among the early friends of Donne, and he may have been an acquaintance, since he is said to have begun life as a page in the family at Polesworth, of which Donne's most intimate and constant friend, Sir Henry Goodyer, became the head. But Drayton was Donne's senior by ten years, and there is no evidence of their having met at Polesworth. It is usual to speak of Donne as forming part of the brilliant company which sparkled at the Mermaid Tavern, and as taking part in the wit-combats of that famous resort. For this I find no species of evidence, and it appears to me on the whole to be unlikely that Donne sought the company of these London wits, "so nimble and so full of subtle flame," in their familiar haunts. All that we really know on the subject is that he was familiar with the Brookes, and that he was acquainted with Ben Jonson. His other early friends, not a numerous band, were mostly private persons. He tells us that he had but a "short roll of friends writ in his heart," which the name of Mr. J. L. (or J. P., for this may be an error in transcription) "begins." Even of the few friends whom we can more distinctly trace, the majority are perhaps incorrectly attributed to a date earlier than 1600.

But of the sons of Robert Brooke, twice lord mayor of York, there is no question. Christopher Brooke was Donne's chamber-fellow at Lincoln's Inn from 1592 onwards; to him "The Calm" was addressed in 1597. Samuel Brooke, who was much younger, must have been a scholar at Cambridge when Donne first arrived in London, but he afterwards joined Christopher. With the part played by both brothers at the wedding of Donne, much will presently have to be said. To each of these men familiar verse-epistles are addressed, and two sonnets, which are evidently connected with the same order of incidents, are dedicated to a M. B. B. Dr. Grosart suggested that these were the initials of Sir Basil Brook, but that gentleman, who was a Shropshire man, educated at Oxford, and knighted in 1604, had nothing to do with the York Brookes, who were all closely identified with Cambridge. The address is no doubt to some obscurer member of the family of Robert Brooke, some Mr. B. Brooke whose identity is lost past probable recovery. The Brookes, and particularly Christopher, were intimate with many of the writers of their time. Besides Ben Jonson and Michael Drayton, Selden, Browne, John Davies of Hereford, and afterwards Wither, are associated with the name of the friendly and enthusiastic Christopher Brooke.

In the Westmoreland MS. there occurs an epistle from

Donne to Mr. E. G., which has never till now been printed, and which runs as follows :—

> "Even as lame things thirst their perfection, so
> The slimy rhymes bred in our vale below,
> Bearing with them much of my love and heart,
> Fly unto that Parnassus, where thou art.
> There thou o'erseest London. Here I have been
> By staying in London too much overseen.
> Now pleasure's dearth our City doth possess;
> Our theatres are filled with emptiness;
> As lank and thin is every street and way
> As a woman delivered yesterday.
> Nothing whereat to laugh my spleen essays
> But bear-baitings or law exercise.
> Therefore I'll leave it, and in the country strive
> Pleasure, now fled from London, to retrieve.
> Do thou so too; and fill not, like a bee,
> Thy thighs with honey, but as plenteously
> As Russian merchants, thyself's whole vessel load,
> And then at Winter retail it here abroad.
> Bless us with Suffolk's sweets; and, if it is
> Thy garden, make thy hive and warehouse this."

The only known denizen of Parnassus in the Elizabethan age whose initials were E. G. was Edward Guilpin, the author of the *Skialetheia*. He was an eastern counties' man, and he had been identified with Donne in that series of sudden experiments in satire which we have already examined. I have little doubt, then, that this obscure and trivial, but very characteristic, piece was addressed to Guilpin. The reference to closed theatres and abandoned streets suggests the plague months from the autumn of 1592 to the close of 1593. If so, this epistle denotes an easy friendship, and would probably accompany a transcript of those "slimy rhymes," the first three Satires, sent to Guilpin at the time of their composition, as an incitement to push on with his own "Shadow of Truth in Certain Epigrams and Satires."

With one great poet Donne was certainly in considerable communication during his youth. He was an isolated figure, unlike the men around him, but so was Ben Jonson, in whom Donne evidently inspired both curiosity and respect. In Jonson's Conversations with Drummond of Hawthornden, jotted down after the English poet's tramp on foot to Scotland in 1618-19, the references to Donne are numerous and of extreme value, in spite of their acid and meagre quality. Ben Jonson told Drummond " that Donne, for not keeping of accent, deserved hanging"; that he had introduced him, under the pseudonym of Criticus, into his Preface to the "Art of Poesy" (but here Drummond seems to have committed some blunder); that "he esteemeth John Donne the first poet in the world in some things; his verses of 'The Lost Chain' (Elegy xii.) he hath by heart; and that passage of 'The Calm'

'In one place lay
Feathers and dust, to-day and yesterday;'"

that "Donne himself, for not being understood, would perish." Several other curious critical *dicta* of Ben Jonson on Donne will more properly occupy us when we reach the works to which they refer. It is possible that the introduction of Criticus, which it would be exceedingly interesting to regain, was made in some excursus to the "Art of Poesy" as we now possess it. Probably it perished among those notes regarding

" All the old Venusine, in poetry,
And lighted by the Stagyrite, could spy,"

the loss of which, in the fire of 1623, Ben Jonson deplores in his "Execration upon Vulcan." His interest in Donne was genuine, and he expressed it on occasions more responsible than his chats in the library at Hawthornden. We shall speak later on of the epistle which Donne addressed to him on the 9th of November 1603. From Ben Jonson's "Epigrams" may here be quoted one in which there is no grudging note of praise—

" DONNE, the delight of Phœbus and each Muse,
Who, to thy one, all other brains refuse,
Whose every work, of thy most early wit,
Came forth example, and remains so yet:
Longer a knowing than most wits do live,
And which no affection praise enough can give!
To it, thy language, letters, arts, best life,
Which might with half mankind maintain a strife;
All which I meant to praise, and yet I would,
But leave, because I cannot as I should."

It was to Donne, too, that in later years Ben Jonson sent his *Epigrams* to be revised and read, as to the best living critic of poetry, and the one whose censures were most above suspicion. Oddly enough, too, one of Donne's poems, the Sixteenth Elegy, was reprinted in the 1641 edition of Ben Jonson's *Underwoods*, and has been challenged as the work of that poet, to which its versification has an unusual resemblance. Possibly it was touched up by Jonson, and was found in his handwriting among his posthumous papers. These are the slight and tantalising evidences of a lifelong acquaintance and esteem existing between these two great writers. It would be exaggeration, on the documents before us, confidently to assume that their relations amounted to intimate friendship.

MARRIAGE

1597–1604

CHAPTER IV

MARRIAGE

1597–1604

FOUR days before Donne had been entered at Lincoln's Inn, the particular glory and shining star of that society had been appointed by Queen Elizabeth her Attorney-General. This was Thomas Egerton, one of the most brilliant and successful lawyers of the day, whose career had from early youth been a series of rapid and steady advances. According to Dugdale and Wood, he was the natural son of Sir Richard Egerton of Ridley, in Cheshire, head of one of the most ancient families in the kingdom. Born about 1540, he was educated at Brasenose College, Oxford, and in 1559 removed to Lincoln's Inn, where he devoted his distinguished talents to the study and practice of law. In 1581 he was made Solicitor-General; on the 2nd of June 1592, as we have seen, he was advanced to be Attorney-General, a post then, according to Bacon, "honestly worth £6000 a year." He was presently knighted, and on the 10th of April 1594 Sir Thomas Egerton was appointed Master of the Rolls.

Through all this shower of honours, however, Sir Thomas Egerton remained faithful to Lincoln's Inn, where, since 1582, he had held the office of Lent-Reader. It was not until the duties of Master of the Rolls pressed too heavily upon him that he withdrew from being one of the Governors of the Society. It is not possible but that Donne must have been aware of the existence of the most influential member and patron of Lincoln's Inn; it is more than probable that Egerton's attention was drawn to the erratic and gifted Catholic student. Meanwhile,

Sir Thomas Egerton was becoming a person of importance second to few in the realm, and when Sir John Puckering died in 1596, Egerton, on the 6th of May, received from the Queen at Greenwich the Great Seal of England, with the title of Lord Keeper; at the same time he was sworn of the Privy Council, and by a special grace was permitted to continue to enjoy the lucrative office of Master of the Rolls. Sir Thomas Egerton, in thus becoming the Lord Keeper of England, was welcomed by the learned lawyers and the public *magna expectatione et integritatis opinione*—as Camden tells us—"with high anticipations and a settled reputation for honesty." No judicial appointment of the reign awakened more universal applause.

The Lord Keeper was but lately married for the second time, his first wife, Elizabeth Ravenscroft, who had borne him two sons, having deceased some years before. In his second nuptials he had taken another Elizabeth, the widow of Sir John Wooley of Pyrford. She was the sister and under the guardianship of another knight of the same county of Surrey, Sir George More of Loseley. With all these people the fate of Donne was to be very closely identified, and we may therefore pause for a moment to consider of what persons their families consisted. Sir Thomas Egerton, who was to beget no children by this second, or by an ultimate third, wife, had been left two sons by the first; these were Thomas and John. Lady Wooley had a young son, Francis, born in 1582, whom she brought with her when she married Sir Thomas Egerton. Sir George More, who had been a widower since 1590, possessed several children; his third daughter, Anne, was born in 1584. It has been suggested that from the first an alliance was projected between Francis Wooley and Anne More, but this does not seem to me to be borne out by the evidence. In the first place, marriage between persons so near of kin were held in abhorrence in Elizabethan times, although by no means unknown; in the second, the relations of Anne and Francis, throughout the subsequent events, were of an eminently fraternal nature.

Donne's connection with this group of people probably

began when he joined the Islands expedition in 1597. The Lord Keeper was a personal friend of Essex, and his own son and stepson were attached to that adventurous enterprise. Young Thomas Egerton may have been with the English fleet at Cadiz in 1596, Francis Wooley scarcely, since he was but in his fourteenth year. Next autumn, however, unquestionably both lads were in the Azores expedition. Both would surely be personally attached to the Earl of Essex, like Donne, who "waited upon his lordship." It is open to us to conjecture, either, that the Lord Keeper, in pursuance of that zealous interest in Lincoln's Inn which he continued to cultivate, introduced to Essex a young student already received at court and well considered among the learned; or that, on board Essex's ship in the Azores, Donne continued to make himself serviceable to the two boys, and to win their grateful friendship. All that we know positively is that, soon after the return of the expedition to England in October 1597, Donne attracted the notice of the Lord Keeper, who, having made inquiry into "his learning, languages, and other abilities, and much affecting his person and behaviour, took him to be his chief secretary." From Donne's own words, four years later, we find that the appointment took place in the winter of 1597.

The home of the Lord Keeper was York House, in the Strand. The family consisted, as we have seen, of Sir Thomas and Lady Egerton, of their sons Thomas and John, of Francis Wooley, and as it would seem, at frequent intervals and for increasing lengths of time, of the new Lady Egerton's favourite niece, Anne More. Sir George More, that young lady's father, who was Chancellor of the Garter and Lieutenant of the Tower, lived at the paternal mansion of Loseley, and seems to have used York House whenever his business brought him up to Westminster. Into this intelligent, polite, and distinguished circle Donne was now introduced on terms which were almost those of an equal. A secretary in such a household would be apt to hang painfully in air between the master and his family on one hand, and the higher domestics on the other. This was obviated by the graceful tact of the Lord Keeper, who did not, from the beginning of Donne's attendance upon him, " account him to be so much his servant, as to forget he was his friend; and to testify it, did always use him with much courtesy, appointing him a place at his own table, to which he esteemed his company and discourse to be a great ornament."

It is likely that employer and secretary were very constantly thrown together in such retirement as fell to the lot of the Lord Keeper. Of the sons of Sir Thomas Egerton one was a soldier, the other a schoolboy. Francis Wooley went back from the wars to Oxford, where he took his degree in 1599. Young Thomas Egerton, who had been knighted for gallantry in 1597, was killed in August 1599 while attempting, under the command of the ill-starred Essex, to subdue the Irish rebellion. Meanwhile the Lord Keeper obtained great credit for his conduct on the Committee for treating with the Dutch in 1598, and it is more than probable that Donne was at this time sent over on secretarial work to the Low Countries, allusions to which abound in his poetry of this epoch. The passage of a new treaty with the ambassadors of the States was of vast pecuniary and political advantage to the Queen, and Egerton shared with Lord Buckhurst the credit of this brilliant piece of financial diplomacy. In 1600 the same authorities conducted a similar, though rather less magnificent, set of affairs with the court of Denmark. We may conjecture, if we will, and with some probability, that Donne was sent on this occasion to Copenhagen. It is quite certain, however, that Donne, who was throughout this time the confidential amanuensis and chief private secretary, was a witness of most of the more striking events with which his illustrious employer was intimately connected.

An Oxford friend of Donne's, who now reappears for a moment, is Sir William Cornwallis, who was knighted in Dublin in this year, 1599, by the Earl of Essex. He was the eldest son of Sir Charles Cornwallis of Beeston-in-Sprouston, Norfolk, who survived him. (He must not be confounded with the contemporary Sir William Cornwallis of Brome, who had married Jane, daughter of Hercules Meautys; she afterwards became the wife of Sir Nathaniel Bacon, and moved in the circle of Donne's Twickenham friends.) A MS. poem, preserved in the Bodleian, celebrates this friendship [1]—

> "As in times past the rustic shepherds sent
>   Their tidiest lambs or kids for sacrifice
> Unto their gods, sincere being their intent,
>   Though base their gift, if that should moralise
> Their loves, yet no direct discerning eye
> Will judge their act, but full of piety.
>
> So offer I my best affection,
>   Apparallèd in these harsh tatter'd rhymes;
> Think not they want love, though perfection;
>   Or that my love's no truer than my lines;
> Smooth is my love, tho' rugged be my verse,
> Yet well they mean, tho' well they ill rehearse.
>
> What time thou mean'st to offer Idleness,
>   Come to my den, for here she always stays:
> If then for change of hours you seem careless,
>   Agree with me to lose them at the plays.
> Farewell, dear friend, my love, not lines respect,
> So shall you show my friendship you affect.
>   Yours,
>   WILLIAM CORNWALLYS.

"To my ever to be respected friend, Mr. JOHN DONE, Secretary to my Lord Keeper, give these."

If Donne and Cornwallis went to "lose their hours" at the new plays brought out in 1599, they may have witnessed the first performances of *Much Ado about Nothing* and *As you like It.* If so, in all probability the verse of Shakespeare left the exotic Donne now, as always, perfectly indifferent

In the year 1599 a strange visitor was transferred to the guardianship of Sir Thomas Egerton. That sage and loyal man had suffered much from the eccentricities of his brilliant young friend, the second Devereux, Earl of Essex,

---
[1] Tanner MSS., 306, fol. 237.

and had expostulated with him on his riotous behaviour in letters remarkable equally for their firmness and for their tact. All was in vain, and when, after his return from Ireland, the turbulence of Essex became intolerable, he was placed, in a sort of semi-durance, under the personal charge of the Lord Keeper. From October 1, 1599, to July 5, 1600, Essex was obliged to reside at York House, and it was there that in June 1600 his trial was held.

Very odd must have been the scenes in which Donne took a keenly observant part. In particular, we may with confidence identify him with one of the spectators who, on the 8th of February 1601, took part in the dramatic seizure of Essex in his own house, when the Lord Keeper, accompanied by the Earl Worcester, Sir William Knollys, and the Lord Chief Justice Popham, with their respective servants, were sent to invite the rebellious favourite to return to his duty. It was but a very short excursion from York House, and Essex had but just left the custody of the Lord Keeper. The gates of the house were shut upon the dignified envoys, but, after some stay, as Camden tells us, they were let in by the wicket, although all their servants were kept out. It was an exciting crisis, and Donne, shut outside, would, as his master entered, see for a moment the whole courtyard full and buzzing like a wasp's nest with malcontents, while Essex himself, half demented, was shouting and gesticulating in the midst of his creatures. Further into the adventure, one of the most picturesque in our social history, we must not proceed, since whoever was present when the Queen's envoys were guarded with cocked muskets in Essex's inner apartments, Donne certainly was not. But to him who had waited upon Essex, and experienced in the easy life of travel the fascination of his character, all these events must have been among the most poignant which he had to encounter; and their culmination on the scaffold, when Essex was executed on the 25th of February, an epoch in the life of Donne.

The cordiality and courtesy of Sir Thomas Egerton towards his secretary were shown in many ways, and the

MARRIAGE

position of the young poet became, as we shall see, only too perilously secure at York House. The Lord Keeper declared that Donne was "fitter to serve a king than a subject," and entrusted to his charge all his most important secretarial business. How great Donne's influence must have been at this time, and how wide the sphere of his patronage, we may easily divine; while a solitary letter, preserved from those busy years when he spoke mainly in the voice of his master, gives us an idea of his discretion. This was written to a person of honour, who, unfortunately languishing for a while, like so many other people of quality towards the end of Elizabeth's reign, in one of Her Majesty's gaols, was very eager indeed to emerge from it. How often G. H. had already importuned the young secretary, appears in the faintly sarcastic humour of "I owe you a continual tribute of letters":—

"*To my good friend* G. H.[1]

"SIR,—The little business which you left in my hands is now despatched; if it has hung longer than you thought, it might serve for just excuse that these small things make as many steps to their end, and need as many motions for the warrant, as much writing of the clerks, as long expectation of a seal, as greater. It comes now to you sealed, and with it as strong and assured seals of my service and love to you, if it be good enough for you.

"I owe you a continual tribute of letters. But, sir, even in princes and parents, and all states that have in them a natural sovereignty, there is a sort of reciprocation, and as decent to do some offices due to them that serve them: which makes me look for letters from you, because I have another as valuable a pawn therefore as your friendship, which is your promise; lest by the gaoler's fault this letter stick long, I must tell you, that I wrote and sent it 12th December 1600.—Your friend and servant and lover,
                              "J. DONNE.

"12*th December* 1600."

---

[1] The *Letters* of 1651.

These four years of constant commerce, in public and private life, with one of the most remarkable men of the age, put their stamp on the character of the poet. Egerton was a man who impressed every one with his gravity and stately charm. Bacon, who, though he owed much to Egerton, did not like him, and afterwards grossly desired his office of High Chancellor, confessed that Egerton's sagacity distinguished him as "a true sage, or *salvia*," in the garden of the State. His temper was solemn; he loved wit and the play of fancy, but was seldom seen to smile. Such a companion was exactly suited to appreciate and to determine Donne's aptitude toward a sardonic and casuistical species of humour. Egerton was famous for the rapid movement of his thought and for his readiness and elegance of speech. In these he took a reasonable pride, and in the extremity of his age it was his special subject of despair that his mind seemed to him to be becoming "dull and heavy" and his utterance "faltering." Donne was his companion from the Lord Keeper's fifty-seventh to his sixty-second years, during the period when Egerton was at the height of his prestige as a lawyer and as a statesman. He was much tried and often bereaved; he was conscious of jealousy in younger men; by degrees these things oppressed him, and he became subject to fits of deep dejection. At these times his figure, always dignified and early venerable, was clothed about with such a majestic melancholy that no one dared to address him. But while Donne was being thrown daily into his company, the Lord Keeper was at the zenith of his powers, and the effect of such a companionship upon a young man like Donne, of tastes so eclectic, of intellect so subtle, of observation so caustic, cannot but have been extreme. I do not question that the most important influence to which Donne was ever subjected was that of Egerton, and that to the great sobriety of this lawyer we owe the radical change in the poet's outlook upon life and men.

The household life was complicated during the year 1600 by more troubles than the enforced presence of the Earl of Essex and his suite. In January of that year the

MARRIAGE

second Lady Egerton died, and by this event the tie with Loseley and with the More family would naturally have been broken. But it was not convenient for Sir George More that the death of his sister should close York House to him. He was in a somewhat awkward position at Loseley, where his father, although now extremely old, retained his position as head of the household. Sir George More, already in his forty-seventh year, was a man of great activity of mind and body, and more than considerable capacity. He had the political instinct strongly developed, and from 1584 to 1611 he was in every Parliament, now as the representative of Guildford, now of the county of Surrey. He had been knighted in 1597, and his father and he entertained on a large scale at their mansion of Loseley. Sir George More was an impulsive, emotional man, of insatiable energy. Something in his bearing and conversation made him a very great favourite with the Queen, who visited Loseley four times. Sir George More, whose wife Anne died in 1590, had nine children, of whom the third daughter, Anne, born in 1584, seems to have been partly adopted by the second Lady Egerton.

When that lady died, Anne More appears to have stayed on at York House to conduct the Lord Chancellor's establishment in the interim. She was barely sixteen, but doubtless, with the methods of education then in use, she was as mature as most young ladies of twenty years of age to-day. It is not to be doubted that she had already attracted the notice of the romantic and not too scrupulous secretary. Moreover, the death of Lady Egerton removed a very serious obstacle in the way of his attentions. It is to be noted as a curious chance that in the three families of Egertons, Mores, and Wooleys, who now united at York House, there was not one woman of mature years. It has been suggested that the Fourth Elegy must be taken as "a recital of facts" in the chain of relations between John Donne and Anne More. It is agreeable to be able to point out that the young lady's mother, who plays so very unpleasant a part in that powerful and disagreeable poem, had died when Anne was six years old. This alone makes it impossible that the Fourth Elegy should be the narrative of Donne's courtship of his wife. That it is "a recital of facts" I do not for a moment doubt, but the seduction so cynically described—and, so far as I can discover, alluded to in no other of his poetical writings—must date from 1598 at latest; and I conjecture, in fact, that the incident belongs to the first year after the unregenerate poet's return from the Islands Voyage. An item of internal evidence is the versification of this elegy, which links it with earlier and distinguishes it from later compositions.

The complexion which Donne, looking back from the sanctity of old age to this period of his youth, desired to be thrown on the compromising episode of his clandestine courtship, is no doubt reflected by Izaak Walton. The letters of Donne from prison in 1602 confirm in the main his later recollections. It would seem that the opportunities for unguarded conversation which the young couple met with after Lady Egerton's death insensibly led them through the year 1600 into closer and closer sentimental relations. Donne "fell into such a liking as, with her approbation, increased into a love for this young gentlewoman." The courting took place at York House, where the juvenile Anne seems to have enjoyed complete immunity from the protecting wing of any chaperon. What brought their easy friendship to a crisis was the announcement that the Lord Keeper was about to marry for the third time, an intention which he carried out on the 20th of October 1600. About the same time Sir William More died, and the mansion and estates of Loseley fell into the custody of Sir George. No longer needed at York House, and called to aid her father at Loseley, a double cord of duty drew Anne More away from the perilous and fascinating purlieus of York House.

But it was too late. In the agony of parting "some faithful promises were so interchangeably passed as never to be violated by either party." To Loseley the distressed maiden withdrew, unquestionably in tears, while Donne no less certainly relieved his feelings in bad sonnets to his faithful confidants, Christopher and Samuel Brooke. It is to be remarked that at this moment of his life his poetical talent seems to have almost entirely quitted him. It was to return in the course of a few years, and with not a little of its early splendour. But most of such few poems as we can plausibly attribute to the period of his courtship and early marriage display all the faults of his style and hardly a trace of its felicities. It was doubtless under the inspiration of Donne himself that Walton stated that Sir George More had, thus early, "some intimation" of the liaison between Donne and his daughter. Walton says that Sir George, "knowing prevention to be a great part of wisdom, did therefore remove her [about Christmas 1600] from [York House] to his own house at Loseley, in the county of Surrey; but too late." No doubt this is how the circumstances were recalled to Donne's memory; but we find that Anne More was in town several times after the meeting of Parliament in 1601, and that Donne saw her in private on these occasions. Moreover, the letters he wrote from prison, though they suggest that surely Sir George must have noticed that something unusual was going on, preclude the idea that any "intimation" was given to the lady's father.

Certain friends, however, became aware in the course of 1601 that events between the lovers were approaching a climax. Among these young Francis Wooley was one, and John Egerton perhaps another. That extremely odd and impish person, the Earl of Northumberland, presently takes a part in the intrigue scarcely compatible with ignorance of its earlier stages. No one, however, seems to have guessed how far things had gone, nor what mutual pledges had been made. "The friends of both parties," Walton says, "used much diligence and many arguments to kill or cool their affections for each other, but in vain; for love is a flattering mischief, that hath denied aged and wise men a foresight of those evils that too often prove to be the children of that blind father; a passion that carries us to commit errors with as much ease as whirlwinds remove feathers, and begets in us an unwearied industry to the attainment of what we desire. And such an industry did, notwithstanding much watchfulness against it, bring them secretly together (I forbear to tell the manner how), and at last to a marriage too, without the allowance of those friends, whose approbation always was, and ever will be, necessary to make even a virtuous love become lawful." Walton's parenthesis—"I forbear to tell the manner how"—seems to be a circumstantial suggestion that a member of the triple family circle helped the lovers, and for my own part I feel little doubt that this was Francis Wooley. So, and so only, can we explain his future treatment of the married lovers.

Three weeks before Christmas 1601 John Donne and Anne More were married. Only five persons were present. Christopher Brooke gave away the bride, a gift which he was certainly in no way competent to bestow, and his young brother Samuel, who must have only just taken orders, performed the ceremony. Who the fifth individual was we do not know; probably a servant. Donne was very particular afterwards to assure Sir George More that none but strangers to the families at York House were involved, and that even those who regarded the courtship with some favour were not informed of the wedding. It is difficult to grasp the reason for Donne's complacency, but he certainly writes as one desiring credit on this point, not merely for prudence, but for straightforwardness. If the secret wedding took place about the 5th, it was doubtless hurried on by the impending dissolution of Parliament, which took place on the 19th inst. Anne's visit to York House would then close, and the marriage of the Lord Keeper had probably made her position there so difficult that she was doubtful of returning. It was now or never with the plighted lovers, and they rushed into an adventure, the danger of which they had evidently not taken into consideration.

The furtive ceremony completed, Anne Donne returned to York House, and in due course to Loseley. What the lovers expected the next step to be, it is impossible to say. But they had chosen the date for their escapade unluckily.

Sir George More was distended with pride and ambition; the Queen's favours made any exaltation seem natural to his hopes. The Lord Keeper, on the other hand, had just received the first check which had ruffled the unparalleled smoothness of his professional advance. In November he had come into collision with the Speaker of the House of Commons, and in spite of his learning and his prestige, he had met with an undeniable rebuff. His father-in-law excited with a sort of *manie des grandeurs*, his employer as sullen as a bear with a sore foot—it must be admitted that Donne had not chosen a happy moment for kidnapping the daughter of the one from the hearth-stone of the other. Yet he seems to have had no idea of the seriousness of his position, and when he was asked why he did not openly declare his suit, he replied that to have announced it would have been to spoil all.

But the act so gaily performed was one of the gravest indecorum. As Dr. Jessopp says, "A double offence had been committed by the parties concerned. First, an offence against the Canon Law in marrying a girl without the consent of her father; and secondly, the civil offence against the Common Law. It was a very serious business. It became plain that a disclosure must be made; the only question was, Who should act as mediator between the bridegroom and his father-in-law?" The plan was adopted of gradually dropping hints and half-intimations into the ear of Sir George More, who, reflecting that he now had his daughter safe at Loseley, and never dreaming of the enormity of a marriage, was made extremely angry by these innuendoes, but came no nearer to a knowledge of the real state of affairs. To vow that Anne should visit York House no more was, in her father's belief, to cut off the poisoned stream at its source.

It became obvious to those in the secret that somebody must sooner or later bell the cat. For this purpose that extraordinary person, the "Wizard Earl," was chosen. Henry Percy, ninth Earl of Northumberland, now in his thirty-eighth year, was one of the most curious men of the age. He was a bundle of paradoxes. Not an avowed

Catholic, and with very little feeling of any kind for religion, he was looked upon as a secret partisan of the Catholic cause, mainly, it would appear, because of his want of sympathy with Anglican theology. His greatest friend had been Essex and was to be Raleigh. He enjoyed the exotic, the lawless, the untrammelled for their own sake. He had no social prejudices, but cultivated with eagerness the prohibited sciences, dreaming out the falls of princes in the crystal globe, or sharing in the pseudo-scientific experiments of disreputable astrologers. He had the appearance of a necromancer himself, and was looked at askance as one who, like Master Foresight, could "judge of motions direct and retrograde, of sextiles, quadrates, trines and oppositions, fiery trigons and aquatical trigons." His curiosity was insatiable, and his love for acting as a go-between in delicate affairs amounted to a dangerous passion. Northumberland was a learned and eager person, filled with strange scholastic knowledge, whose sceptical and audacious intellectual temperament was sure to be highly attractive to Donne, and the poet seems to have been at this time on terms of some intimacy with the Earl. To Northumberland, at all events, Donne turned to get him out of disgrace.

On the 2nd of February 1602, then, the Earl of Northumberland proceeded to Loseley on a mission of peace, and broke to the astonished Sir George the fact that his daughter was the wife of Sir Thomas Egerton's secretary. He was armed with this curious letter from the culprit:—

"*To* Sir GEORGE MORE.[1]

"SIR,—If a very respective fear of your displeasure, and a doubt that my lord (whom I know, out of your worthiness, to love you much) would be so compassionate with you as to add his anger to yours, did not so much increase my sickness as that I cannot stir, I had taken the boldness to have done the office of this letter by waiting upon you myself to have given you truth and clearness of

[1] From the Loseley MSS.

this matter between your daughter and me, and to show you plainly the limits of our fault, by which I know your wisdom will proportion the punishment.

"So long since as her being at York House this had foundation, and so much then of promise and contract built upon it as, without violence to conscience, might not be shaken.

"At her lying in town this Parliament I found means to see her twice or thrice. We both knew the obligations that lay upon us, and we adventured equally; and about three weeks before Christmas we married. And as at the doing there were not used above five persons, of which I protest to you by my salvation there was not one that had any dependence or relation to you, so in all the passage of it did I forbear to use any such person, who by furtherance of it might violate any trust or duty towards you.

"The reasons why I did not fore-acquaint you with it (to deal with the same plainness I have used) were these:— I knew my present estate less than fit for her. I knew (yet I knew not why) that I stood not right in your opinion. I knew that to have given any intimation of it had been to impossibilitate the whole matter. And then, having these honest purposes in our hearts and these fetters in our consciences, methinks we should be pardoned if our fault be but this, that we did not, by fore-revealing of it, consent to our hindrance and torment.

"Sir, I acknowledge my fault to be so great, as I dare scarce offer any other prayer to you in mine own behalf than this, to believe this truth,—that I neither had dishonest end nor means. But for her, whom I tender much more than my fortunes or life (else I would, I might neither joy in this life nor enjoy the next), I humbly beg of you that she may not, to her danger, feel the terror of your sudden anger.

"I know this letter shall find you full of passion; but I know no passion can alter your reason and wisdom, to which I adventure to commend these particulars;—that it is irremediably done; that if you incense my lord, you destroy her and me; that it is easy to give us happiness, and that my endeavours and industry, if it please you to prosper them, may soon make me somewhat worthier of her.

"If any take the advantage of your displeasure against me, and fill you with ill thoughts of me, my comfort is that you know that faith and thanks are due to them only that speak when their informations might do good, which now it cannot work towards any party. For my excuse I can say nothing, except I knew what were said to you.

"Sir, I have truly told you this matter, and I humbly beseech you so to deal in it as the persuasions of Nature, Reason, Wisdom, and Christianity shall inform you; and to accept the vows of one whom you may now raise or scatter—which are, that as my love is directed unchangeably upon her, so all my labours shall concur to her contentment, and to show my humble obedience to yourself.

"Yours in all duty and humbleness,
"J. DONNE.

"From my lodging by the Savoy,
 2nd February 1601[2].
"To the Right Worshipful Sir GEORGE MORE, Kt."

In spite, however, of these moving casuistries, of all the Earl's tact, and of the favourable light in which he must have placed the prospects and the talents of the young bridegroom, the news was to Sir George More "so immeasurely unwelcome and so transported him, that his passion of anger and inconsideration exceeded theirs of love and error." He lost his head altogether, and, as angry people often do, thought to console his pride for having been outwitted by cruelly punishing those who had annoyed him. Walton here makes two of those little errors which are extremely venial and natural, but which ought to put us on our guard against accepting his narrative in detail without careful examination. He tells us that Sir George More "presently engaged his sister, the Lady Ellesmere, to join with him to procure her Lord to discharge Mr. Donne of the place he held under his Lordship." In the first place, it was not until after the accession of James I., and when he was made Lord High Chancellor of England in July 1603, that Sir Thomas Egerton was created Baron Ellesmere of Ellesmere; and in the second (and much more important) place, Sir George More cannot have asked his sister to interfere in the matter, because she had been dead for more than a year. The existing, and third, Lady Egerton was not related to the Loseley family.

By whatever means, however, Sir George approached his brother-in-law, he pushed his suit with vindictive violence. Sir Thomas Egerton was not inclined, at first, to take a very serious view of the escapade. He was attached to Donne, and, though doubtless conscious of his faults, appreciated his gifts and his fidelity highly. He reminded More that " errors might be overpunished, and desired him therefore to forbear till second considerations might clear some scruples." Agitation and disappointment had meanwhile reduced Donne to a wretched state. He had already left York House, and withdrawn to a lodging in the Savoy, where he presently fell ill. Sir George More meanwhile redoubled his complaints, and the Lord Keeper, bowing before his brother-in-law's vociferations, dismissed Donne from his service. The poet was overwhelmed with despair. He knew not where to turn, for his estate was now greatly diminished, and he foresaw a tedious interval of labour at the bar before he could earn enough to support a wife. He wrote to Mrs. Donne to acquaint her with the fact of his dismissal. This letter appears to be lost, but Walton tells us that after signing it he wrote this, the briefest of his lyrical effusions—

" John Donne—Ann Donne—Undone." [1]

But worse was at hand. Sir George More, who seems to have had no idea of bowing to the inevitable, used his influence with such effect that, about the 10th of February, Donne and the two Brookes were thrown into separate prisons, charged with a conspiracy to break the Common

---

[1] It is desirable to note that the name *Donne* was pronounced exactly as though it rhymed to *gun*.

and the Canon Law. Donne addressed to his father-in-law next day the following letter :—

"*To* the right wor. Sir Geo. More, kt.[1]

"Sir,—The inward accusations in my conscience, that I have offended you beyond any ability of redeeming it by me, and the feeling of my Lord's heavy displeasure following it, forceth me to write, though I know my fault make my letters very ungracious to you.

"Almighty God, whom I call to witness that all my grief is that I have in this manner offended you and Him, direct you to believe that which out of an humble and afflicted heart I now write to you. And since we have no means to move God, when He will not hear our prayers, to hear them, but by praying, I humbly beseech you to allow by His gracious example my penitence so good entertainment, as it may have a belief and a pity.

"Of nothing in this one fault that I hear said to me can I disculp myself, but of the contemptuous and despiteful purpose towards you, which I hear is surmised against me. But for my dutiful regard to my late Lady, for my religion, and for my life, I refer myself to them that may have observed them. I humbly beseech you to take off these weights, and to put my fault into the balance alone, as it was done without the addition of these ill reports, and though then it will be too heavy for me, yet then it will less grieve you to pardon it.

"How little and how short the comfort and pleasure of destroying is, I know your wisdom and religion informs you. And though perchance you intend not utter destruction, yet the way through which I fall towards it is so headlong, that, being thus pushed, I shall soon be at bottom, for it pleaseth God, from whom I acknowledge the punishment to be just, to accompany my other ills with so much sickness as I have no refuge but that of mercy, which I beg of Him, my Lord, and you, which I hope you will not repent to have afforded me, since all my

[1] From the Loseley MSS.

endeavours and the whole course of my life shall be bent to make myself worthy of your favour and her love, whose peace of conscience and quiet I know must be much wounded and violenced if your displeasure sever us.

"I can present nothing to your thoughts which you knew not before, but my submission, my repentance, and my hearty desire to do anything satisfactory to your just displeasure. Of which I beseech you to make a charitable use and construction. From the Fleet, 11th Feb. 1601[2].—Yours in all faithful duty and obedience,

"J. Donne."

More, on receipt of this, refused all communication with his son-in-law, and referred him to the Lord Keeper. Accordingly, a few hours later the following very humble letter was addressed from the Fleet Prison to Sir Thomas Egerton:[1]—

"To excuse my offence, or so much to resist the just punishment for it, as to move your Lordship to withdraw it, I thought till now were to aggravate my fault. But since it hath pleased God to join with you in punishing thereof with increasing my sickness, and that He gives me now audience by prayer, it emboldeneth me also to address my humble request to your Lordship, that you would admit into your favourable consideration how far my intentions were from doing dishonour to your Lordship's house, and how unable I am to escape utter and present destruction, if your Lordship judge only the effect and deed.

"My services never had so much worth in them as to deserve the favours wherewith they were paid; but they had always so much honesty as that only this hath stained them. Your justice hath been merciful in making me know my offence, and it hath much profited me that I am dejected. Since then I am so entirely yours, that even your disfavours have wrought good upon me. I humbly beseech you that all my good may proceed from your

[1] From the Loseley MSS.

Lordship, and that since Sir George More, whom I leave no humble way unsought to regain, refers all to your Lordship, you would be pleased to lessen that correction which your just wisdom hath destined for me, and so to pity my sickness and other misery as shall best agree with your honourable disposition.

"Almighty God accompany all your Lordship's purposes, and bless you and yours with many good days. Fleet, 12 Febr. 1601[2].—Your Lordship's most dejected and poor servant.   JOHN DONNE.

"To the Right Honourable my very good
   L. and Master Sr. THOMAS EGERTON,
   Knight, L. Keeper of the Great Seal
   of England."

The result of these appeals was permission to leave the Fleet Prison and be confined in his chamber in the Strand. Probably his state of health procured him this indulgence, for Christopher Brooke was kept on in the Marshalsea for at least another fortnight. No sooner had Donne arrived in his lodgings than he poured forth another, and this time a very curious, epistle to Sir George More:[1]—

"SIR,—From you, to whom next to God I shall owe my health, by enjoying by your mediation this mild change of imprisonment, I desire to derive all my good fortune and content in this world; and therefore, with my most unfeigned thanks, present to you my humble petition that you would be pleased to hope that, as that fault which was laid to me of having deceived some gentlewomen before, and that of loving a corrupt religion, are vanished and smoked away (as I assure myself, out of their weakness they are), and that as the devil in the article of our death takes the advantage of our weakness and fear, to aggravate our sins to our conscience, so some uncharitable malice hath presented my debts double at least.

"How many of the imputations laid upon me would fall off, if I might shake and purge myself in your presence!

[1] From the Loseley MSS.

But if that were done, of this offence committed to you I cannot acquit myself, of which yet I hope that God (to whom for that I heartily direct many prayers) will inform you to make that use, that as of evil manners good laws grow, so out of disobedience and boldness you will take occasion to show mercy and tenderness. And when it shall please God to soften your heart so much towards us as to pardon us, I beseech you also to undertake that charitable office of being my mediator to my Lord, whom as upon your just complaint you found full of justice, I doubt not but you shall also find full of mercy, for so is the Almighty pattern of Justice and Mercy equally full of both.

"My conscience, and such affection as in my conscience becomes an honest man, emboldeneth me to make one request more, which is, that by some kind and comfortable message you would be pleased to give some ease of the afflictions which I know your daughter in her mind suffers, and that (if it be not against your other purposes) I may with your leave write to her, for without your leave I will never attempt anything concerning her. God so have mercy upon me, as I am unchangeably resolved to bend all my courses to make me fit for her, which if God and my Lord and you be pleased to strengthen, I hope neither my debts, which I can easily order, nor anything else shall interrupt. Almighty God keep you in His favour, and restore me to His and yours.

"From my chamber, whither by your favour I am come, 13th Feb. 1601[2]. J. DONNE.

'To the Right Worshipful
  Sir GEORGE MORE, Knight."

Donne was a very active correspondent this week, and the Lord Keeper received the following incoherent note:—

"*To* Sir THOMAS EGERTON.[1]

"Only in that coin, wherein they that delight to do benefits and good turns for the work's sake love to be

[1] From the Loseley MSS.

paid, am I rich, which is thankfulness, which I humbly and abundantly present to your Lordship, beseeching you to give such way and entertainment to this virtue of mercy, which is always in you, and always awake, that it may so soften you, that as it hath wrought for me the best of blessings, which is this way to health, so it may give my mind her chief comfort, which is your pardon for my bold and presumptuous offence.

"Almighty God be always so with you in this world, as you may be sure to be with Him in the next. 13th Feb. 1601[2].

"Your Lordship's poor and repentant servant,

"J. DONNE.

"To the Right Honourable my very good Lord and Master, Sir THOMAS EGERTON, Knight, Lord Keeper of the Great Seal of England."

His energies were called forth by the straits into which his rashness had thrown him. His private means, in spite of the relief which four years of salaried life at York House ought to have given them, were greatly reduced; he was heavily in debt. Walton attributes the undermining of his estate to "youth, and travel, and needless bounty," but the entire Donne family were suffering from a diminution of their income. In 1617 the poet reminded his mother that "all the wealth which [my father] left, God hath suffered to be gone from us all," which indicates that the property was badly placed, and gradually dwindled away. That Donne had been wasteful and reckless between 1592 and 1600 is obvious also, and between careless expenditure and a diminishing income it was only his salary as a private secretary which kept him from feeling pinched. His dismissal alarmed him, and the following note[1] shows that he had turned for employment to the famous political antiquary, Mr. (afterwards Sir) Robert Cotton. This eminent man was only three years the senior of Donne, but he was already "courted, admired, and esteemed by the greatest men in the nation." Cotton was actively

[1] Cotton MS., Julius C., iii. f. 153.

Sr

I ame gone to Royston, and I make account that hys m:tie may receive the bookf they Eve minyte: So that if I may at yor first lyī=sure deliuer thys bookf to my L: to who I be=seech yow to recommend me must humble seruice

J.W Euer to E, Sr
commander

J. Donne

24 Jan:

FACSIMILE OF LETTER FROM DONNE TO SIR ROBERT COTTON

From the Original, now in the British Museum

employed on jurisprudential and constitutional inquiries, in which, no doubt, Donne was astute enough to hope that he also might be made helpful. We have no reason to suppose that anything ultimately came of his appeal to Robert Cotton.

"*To* Robert Cotton.

"Sir,—I send you back by this bearer the letters which I borrowed of you. If you will now to ease my imprisonment spare me some of the French negotiations, you shall have them as faithfully kept, and as orderly returned, as these, and when I am worth your commanding, I am wholly yours. From my prison in my chamber 20th February 1601[2].[1]—Your honest assured friend,
"J. Donne.
"To my very honest and very assured friend
Robert Cotton, Esq., at his house in Blackfriars."

Three days later Donne is no longer in prison, but writing in very high spirits, as follows, to Sir Henry Goodyer, from lodgings in the Savoy:[2]—

"Sir,—Of myself (who, if honesty were precious, were worth the talking of) let me say a little. The Commissioners by imprisoning the witnesses and excommunicating all us, have implicitly justified our marriage. Sir George will, as I hear, keep her till I send for her: and let her remain there yet, his good nature and her sorrow will work something. I have liberty to ride abroad, and feel not much of an imprisonment. For my return to my Lord, and Sir George's pacification, you know my means, and therefore my hopes.

"Of Ostend it is said there hath been a new blow given. Losses of men somewhat equal, but the enemy hath recovered a trench which Sir Francis had held out of the town. The States have honoured him by publishing an edict with sharp punishment to any that spoke dishonourably of his

---

[1] From the original in the British Museum.
[2] MS. in possession of J. H. Anderdon, Esq.

parley with the Archduke. If the Emperor were dead before you went, perchance he is buried by this time.

"I hope somebody else hath had the ill luck to tell you first, that the young Bedford[1] is dead. The King of Spain intends to spend this summer in Italy: and there I think by that time will be our Lords of Pembroke, Willoughby, and Worcester.[2] The Lord-Deputy hath cut off some of Tyrrells now lately, but no great number. I send this letter to ask the way to Polesworth: if I hear it, find it, I shall cost you half-an-hour a week to read the rest. I hear nothing of your warrant from Mr. Andrew Lee. Take my love and honesty into the good opinion, and commend my poor unworthy thanks and service to your good lady. 23rd February 1601[2] from my chamber at Mr. Haines' house by the Savoy (for this language your subscriptions use).

"Your true certain friend,
"Jo. Donne.

Meanwhile poor Christopher Brooke, more severely punished than the bridegroom himself, was still confined in the Marshalsea Prison. On the 25th of February he wrote a long letter to the Lord Keeper begging to be released. He was a lawyer, and he was due on the York Circuit, where he ought to have made his appearance on the 21st inst. He offered sureties for the very large sum of £1100, and he referred the Lord Keeper to the fortune of his mother, a wealthy woman. It was particularly annoying for Brooke to be imprisoned at this moment, for he now had more professional business on hand than he had ever had in his life before. Yet, in his exasperation, he is absolutely loyal to his friend; with really admirable courage he says: "Pardon me a word for Mr. Donne, my Lord. Were it not now best that every one whom he any way concerns should become his favourer or his friend, who wants, my

---

[1] The only son of Donne's future patroness, Lucy, Countess of Bedford.
[2] This was Edward, the second Somerset Earl of Worcester (1553-1628). Donne had met him at York House in the Essex days. Lady Worcester was the aunt of Donne's friend, Lord Huntingdon. In 1682 the Worcester earldom was merged in the Duchy of Beaufort.

good Lord, but fortune's hands and tongue to rear him up, and set him out?"

Sir George More, meanwhile, abating as yet nothing of his vindictive anger, gave such information to the legal authorities as led to the appointment of special commissioners to report upon the validity of the marriage, hoping to profit by the fact that his niece had hitherto been prevented from all cohabitation with Donne, to secure an adjudication of nullity of the marriage. The scandal having now become public, the Lord Keeper could no longer hesitate, and he indicated his displeasure to his former secretary in the sternest terms. Now, and only now, Donne woke up to the extreme peril of his situation. He found himself face to face with ruin, domestic and professional. He adopted a tone of humility, and having persuaded Sir George More to pay him a visit, he managed so to impress him by tact and submission, that he extorted from him a promise that, although he was still inexorable in his opposition to the marriage, he would endeavour to persuade Sir Thomas Egerton to take Donne back into his service. Friends exerted themselves to act in a mollifying degree upon Sir George More, who now began to regret that he had adopted so extremely choleric a tone.

It would seem that among these friends were some recent additions to the household at York House, of whom it is now time to speak in some detail. The manners of Donne, which erred in the direction of vivacity and a sort of brilliant impertinence when he felt himself secure, could, at will, and under the stimulus of a desire to please, become extremely insinuating. He had with women especially a mode of roguish and fantastic respectfulness, a familiar and yet not obtrusive gaiety, which were absolutely irresistible. He had not failed to exercise these arts upon Alice Spencer, the third wife of Sir Thomas Egerton, and upon her children. This lady, when she married for a second time in October 1600, was the widow of Ferdinand Stanley, fifth Earl of Derby, who had died in 1594; she was a great heiress, daughter of Sir John Spencer of Althorpe. The Countess of Derby had three young daughters, all of whom married, and married well, soon after the re-marriage of their mother. Anne, the eldest, became Lady Chandos of Sudeley; Frances, the second, took John Egerton, and immediately after the death of the Lord Keeper became Countess of Bridgewater;[1] the third, whose name will frequently recur in this narrative, was married at Christmas 1601 to Henry Hastings, fifth Earl of Huntingdon.

It might be supposed that this bevy of great ladies, whose introduction to York House raised the family of the Lord Keeper to a higher, indeed to the highest, stratum of aristocratic society, would be profoundly indifferent to the fate of the indiscreet and even indelicate secretary who had vexed the new head of their house by a tiresome mésalliance. But Donne had not wasted the few months in which he had enjoyed the advantage of their society. They all took a romantic and sympathetic interest in his fate; they all favoured his fortunes, and became, and remained, among the staunchest of his friends. It is certain that Sir George More desired to retain that easy admission to York House which had been so advantageous to him, and which he might well expect the death of his sister and the escapade of his daughter to bring abruptly to a close. We cannot question that the attitude of the Countess of Derby had not a little to do with the change of Sir George's attitude to Donne. His feelings would be further conciliated by the fact that, on their first superficial examination of the circumstances, the Commissioners gave him little hope that they would be able to pronounce the marriage invalid. We may not unsafely conjecture that it was by the advice of Lady Derby herself, who was throughout a true friend to Donne, that he was induced to write the following sensible and manly letters:—

"*To* Sir George More.[2]

"Sir,—If I could fear that in so much worthiness as is in you there were no mercy, or if these weights oppressed

[1] Lord Ellesmere was designated Earl of Bridgewater on the very day of his death, March 15, 1617, and his son was confirmed in the title on the subsequent May 27.
[2] From the Loseley MSS.

only my shoulders and my fortunes and not my conscience and hers whose good is dearer to me by much than my life, I should not thus trouble you with my letters; but when I see that this storm hath shaked me at root in my Lord's favour, where I was well planted and have just reason to fear that those ill-reports which malice hath raised of me may have troubled hers, I can leave no honest way untried to remedy these miseries, nor find any way more honest than this, out of an humble and repentant heart, for the fault done to you, to beg both your pardon and assistance in my suit to my Lord.

"I should wrong you as much again as I did if I should think you sought to destroy me; but though I be not headlongly destroyed, I languish and rust dangerously. From seeking preferments abroad, my love and conscience restrains me; from hoping for them here, my Lord's disgracings cut me off. My imprisonments, and theirs whose love to me brought them to it, hath already cost me £40. And the love of my friends, though it be not utterly grounded upon my fortunes, yet I know suffers somewhat in these long and uncertain disgraces of mine.

"I therefore humbly beseech you to have so charitable a pity of what I have, and do, and must suffer, as to take to yourself the comfort of having saved from such destruction as your just anger might have laid upon him, a sorrowful and honest man. I was bold in my last letter to beg leave of you that I might write to your daughter. Though I understand thereupon, that after the Thursday you were not displeased that I should, yet I have not, nor will not without your knowledge, do it. But now I beseech you that I may, since I protest before God it is the greatest of my afflictions not to do it. In all the world is not more true sorrow than in my heart, nor more understanding of true repentance than in yours. And therefore God, whose pardon in such cases is never denied, gives me leave to hope that you will favourably consider my necessities.

"To His merciful guiding and protection I commend you and cease to trouble you. March 1601[2].
"Yours in all humbleness and dutiful obedience,
"J. DONNE.
"To the Right Worshipful
 Sir GEORGE MORE, Knight."

"*To* Sir THOMAS EGERTON.[1]

"That offence, which was to God in this matter, His mercy hath assured my conscience is pardoned.

"The Commissioners who minister His anger and mercy incline also to remit it.

"Sir George More, of whose learning and wisdom I have good knowledge, and therefore good hope of his moderation, hath said before his last going that he was so far from being any cause or mover of my punishment or disgrace, that if it fitted his reputation he would be a suitor to your Lordship for my restoring. All these irons are knocked off, yet I perish in as heavy fetters as ever whilst I languish under your Lordship's anger.

"How soon my history is despatched! I was carefully and honestly bred; enjoyed an indifferent fortune; I had (and I had understanding enough to value it) the sweetness and security of a freedom and independency, without marking out to my hopes any place of profit. I had a desire to be your Lordship's servant, by the favour which your good son's love to me obtained. I was four years your Lordship's secretary, not dishonest nor greedy. The sickness of which I died is that I began in your Lordship's house this love. Where I shall be buried I know not. It is late now for me (but yet necessity, as it hath continually an autumn and a withering, so it hath ever a spring, and must put forth) to begin that course which some years past I purposed to travel, though I could now do it, not much disadvantageously. But I have some bridle upon me now more than then by my marriage of this gentlewoman, in providing for whom I

---

[1] From the Loseley MSS.

can and will show myself very honest, though not so fortunate.

"To seek preferment here with any but your Lordship were a madness. Every great man to whom I shall address any such suit will silently dispute the case, and say, 'Would my Lord Keeper so disgraciously have imprisoned him and flung him away if he had not done some other great fault of which we hear not?' So that to the burden of my true weaknesses I shall have this addition of a very prejudicial suspicion that I am worse than I hope your Lordship doth think me, or would that the world should think. I have therefore no way before me, but must turn back to your Lordship, who knows that redemption was no less work than creation.

"I know my fault so well, and so well acknowledge it, that I protest I have not so much as inwardly grudged or startled at the punishment. I know your Lordship's disposition so well, as though in course of justice it be of proof against clamours of offenders, yet it is not strong enough to resist itself, and I know itself naturally inclines it to pity. I know mine own necessity, out of which I humbly beg that your Lordship will so much intender your heart towards me, as to give me leave to come into your presence. Affliction, misery, and destruction are not there; and everywhere else where I am they are. 1 *Martii* 1601[2].—Your Lordship's most poor and most penitent servant,

"J. DONNE.

"To the Right Honourable my very good Lord and Master, Sir THOMAS EGERTON, Knight, Lord Keeper of the Great Seal of England."

This request was presently endorsed by Sir George More himself, who found himself placed in the very foolish position of begging his brother-in-law to undo the act which had been forced upon him by Sir George's own importunity. Donne was set at liberty, no doubt on the recommendation of the Commissioners, and every one supposed that all would be forgiven and forgotten. Society, taking its cue from the distinguished ladies of the Derby family, "approved his daughter's choice," and was disposed to congratulate Sir George More on having unwittingly secured for his daughter—who, however, was still separated from Donne—so brilliant and so promising a husband. More was one of those men who admire what others assure them to be admirable; he had always liked Donne, and now he thought to gratify everybody by gradually forgiving him. And if he was to be his son-in-law in fact, what could be more convenient than that Donne should return to his lucrative employment at York House?

But More reckoned without the Lord Keeper. He, as we have seen, had been very unwilling to take the clandestine wedding too seriously. He had urged moderation upon Sir George More, had expressed his satisfaction with Donne's previous conduct, and had professed himself willing to overlook his secretary's indiscretion. But More had insisted, and Donne had been dismissed. The widest publicity had been given to the adventure, and the law had been forced to take cognisance of it. Whatever might be Sir Thomas Egerton's private esteem for the young man, he could not revoke a sentence so publicly given. His position in the State and before the Queen was too prominent and too delicate for him to reinstate in a highly confidential post a secretary whose error had brought about such an open scandal. To Sir George More's importunity, which must have seemed to him painfully ridiculous, the Lord Keeper replied, "That though he was unfeignedly sorry for what he had done, it was yet inconsistent with his place and credit to discharge and re-admit servants at the request of passionate petitioners."

While all this was being mooted, however, Donne found himself liberated, while those friends whose generous indulgence on his behalf had led to such painful results were still in durance. There was no reason why they should be imprisoned if Donne himself were released, and little difficulty seems to have been made in allowing Christopher Brooke to leave the Marshalsea, and young Samuel Brooke, whose offence was graver, since he actually officiated at the wedding, to quit the unnamed prison in which he was confined. The proceedings of the Commissioners were not long delayed, and on the 27th of April the Court of the Archbishop of Canterbury removed the last obstacles, and finally confirmed the marriage of John and Anne Donne.[1] It appears from Walton's account that even now difficulties were made for a while in allowing the young couple to live together. "His days," says Donne's earliest biographer, "were still cloudy; and, being past these troubles, others did still multiply upon him; for his wife was, to her extreme sorrow, detained from him; and though with Jacob he endured not a hard service for her, yet he lost a good one, and was forced to make good his title, and to get possession of her by a long and restless suit in law; which proved troublesome and sadly chargeable to him."

It was about this time that Donne wrote his noble poem, "The Canonization," which affords us an index to the feelings of indignant and irritated impatience with which he regarded the obstacles set in the way of his happiness. It is marked by some of the most characteristic features of his genius, and shows that he had regained to the full the lyric fire which had for some years been dormant—

> "For God's sake hold your tongue, and let me love!
>   Or chide my palsy, or my gout;
>   My five gray hairs, or ruin'd fortune flout;
> With wealth your state, your mind with arts improve;
>   Take you a course, get you a place,
>   Observe his Honour or his Grace,
> Or the king's real, or his stamp'd face
>   Contemplate; what you will, approve,
>   So you will let me love.
>
> Alas! alas! who's injured by my love?
>   What merchant's ships have my sighs drown'd?
>   Who says my tears have overflow'd his ground?
> When did my colds a forward spring remove?
>   When did the heats which my veins fill
>   Add one more to the plaguey bill?[2]
> Soldiers find wars, and lawyers find out still
>   Litigious men, which quarrels move,
>   Tho' she and I do love."

---

[1] There is an official and attested copy of this decree, dated 27th April 1602, among the Loseley MSS.

[2] That is to say, to the official weekly bill of deaths caused by the Plague.

He dwells on the mysterious unity which removes his wife and himself from the general category of individuality, and makes them a conjoint and mystic body, a modern Phœnix. And then he closes thus—

> "We can die by it, if not live by love,
>   And if unfit for tomb or hearse
>   Our legend be, it will be fit for verse;
> And if no piece of chronicle we prove,
>   We'll build in sonnets pretty rooms;
>   As well a well-wrought urn becomes
> The greatest ashes, as half-acre tombs,
>   And by these hymns all shall approve
>   Us canonized for love.
>
> And thus invoke us 'You, whom reverend love
>   Made one another's hermitage;
>   You, to whom love was peace, that now is rage;
> Who did the whole world's soul contract, and drove
>   Into the glasses of your eyes;
>   So made such mirrors, and such spies,
> That they did all to you epitomise—
>   Countries, towns, courts beg from above
>   A pattern of your love.'"

His transcendental fancy, however, might thus see in the conjointure of Anne and himself a microcosm of the eternal; in the eyes of the world they cut a meagre and impoverished figure. For the young maiden-bride, kept in unkind durance at her choleric father's house, we may feel much more sympathy than for Donne. Her mind had been cruelly ruffled by a needless and probably an exaggerated report of his wild life in days before he knew her, and his character was blackened to her in various ways. She remained quite faithful to him, in spite of the inexperience and weakness of her seventeen years. It must be admitted that Anne Donne is, and remains, rather shadowy to us. A gentle, enduring creature, yielding to the relief of silent tears, not (it would seem) intellectual or particularly companionable, she clung with absolute fidelity to the husband to whom she had given herself in a tumult of girlish confidence. He, on his part, although his caprices sometimes wandered, remained at heart true to her, gradually learning that the fantastic metaphor of his youth, the pair of compasses of which one limb sweeps the circle while the other remains still at home, though both are all the while but one, can be true to the letter of a contented and fortunate married couple. Love, not the fiery passion that he had played with in younger days, but the sweet and lambent influence which sanctifies life, grew with the years, and though the poem probably belongs to a slightly later period, and to the peaceful days at Mitcham, we may here quote some earnest lines from "Love's Growth"—

> "I scarce believe my love to be so pure
>   As I had thought it was,
>   Because it doth endure
> Vicissitude, and season, as the grass;
> Methinks I lied all winter, when I swore
> My love was infinite, if spring make it more."

He has discovered that love is not such an abstract quality as he used to say it was in those wild days when he owned no mistress but his Muse. He has learned to value the positive and mundane love which is "not too wise or good for human nature's daily food." And then he rises into heights of mystical psychology where the timid Anne Donne could have had no ambition to follow him, and traces in marvellously concentrated imagery the apotheosis of this gentle, wedded love which he enjoys—

> "And yet no greater, but more eminent,
>   Love by the spring is grown;
>   As in the firmament
> Stars by the sun are not enlarged, but shown,
> Gentle love-deeds, as blossom on a bough,
> From love's awakened root do bud out now.
>   If, as in water stirr'd more circles be
>   Produced by one, love such additions take,
>   Those like so many spheres but one heav'n make,
> For they are all concentric unto thee;
> And tho' each spring do add to love new heat,
>   As princes do in times of action get
>   New taxes, and remit them not in peace,
> No winter shall abate this spring's increase."

Sir George now relaxed his guard over his daughter, whom, indeed, he had no longer any legal pretext for confining. He even gave the young couple his paternal blessing, but that was all that he gave them. He was living at Loseley in a style of ostentation which left him very little margin, and we may suppose, without any impropriety, that he considered that Donne, now in his thirtieth year, with talents so versatile and brilliant, was capable of supporting a wife. But Donne's "estate was the greatest part spent in many and changeable travels, books, and dear-bought experience: he out of all employment that might yield a support for himself and wife, who had been curiously and plentifully educated: both their natures generous, and accustomed to confer, and not to receive courtesies: these and other considerations, but chiefly that his wife was to bear a part in his sufferings, surrounded him with many sad thoughts, and some apparent apprehensions of want."

At this juncture a friend stepped in in the person of Mrs. Donne's cousin, Sir Francis Wooley. By the death of his father, Sir John Wooley, the Queen's private secretary, this young man, who had been Donne's companion by sea and land, inherited the very handsome estate of Pyrford, or Pirford, in Surrey, seven miles north-east of Guildford, with a magnificent dwelling-house on the Wey, where Queen Elizabeth had herself twice been a visitor, and a large deer-park. In the course of 1602 Wooley came of age, and he immediately invited the Donnes to make Pyrford their temporary home. As a matter of fact, they appear to have resided there until the close of 1604. But those years of calm and retired existence are absolutely blank to us. We know not what were Donne's occupations in them, nor what his friendships. All but a few of the letters from these thirty months or so are lost.

It would be amusing to believe that Donne was serving the Queen abroad in the autumn of 1602. This would follow if we could be convinced that the letter from John Allsop[1] to John Donne at Bremen, in which the latter is styled "the Honourable Her Majesty's Ambassador," could possibly be addressed to the youthful poet. The letter is

[1] MSS. Tanner in the Bodleian Library.

all about diplomatic relations with Denmark and Sweden, and is dated September 26, 1602. It is difficult to know what John Donne (or Dunne) was at that time at all likely to be engaged on such business, but I cannot persuade myself that it was the subject of this biography.

One of the very few indications of Donne's mode of life in these years is found in a dignified epistle addressed to Ben Jonson on the 9th of November 1603. In this he represents himself as threatened by an impending law-suit and in much trouble about his affairs, yet confident in his own integrity, and determined that the attacks of fate shall only force him "to a stricter goodness." Donne writes as though Ben Jonson were thoroughly acquainted with the circumstances, and had frankly assured the writer of his sympathy. Ben Jonson had in this year presented his masque of *The Satyr* at Althorpe, and it is not unlikely that it was through the Spencers that the old friendship of the two poets was sustained.

In 1603, moreover, Donne writes an epistle in verse to Thomas Roe, to be in the following year knighted, and to begin his glorious and rather romantic career as an ambassador. Roe, with whom Donne kept up a lifelong friendship, was several years his junior. The epistle refers to some amatory episode, now hopelessly obscured, and is interesting mainly for the familiarity of its address to "Dear Tom," showing that already an intimacy existed between them. The active part of Roe's life had not yet begun, but he had successfully served the Queen, at the close of her life, as Esquire of the Body. The Queen, by the way, died while Donne was at Pyrford, on the 24th of March 1603, and the world of England was presently electrified by the advent and progress of James I. In all this Donne had no part: he neither prepared an entertainment nor rhymed an encomium. His days of standing before royalty were not yet come.

An undated letter survives to show Donne's attitude towards his father-in-law, Sir George More, who was now his close country-neighbour, and with whom the young people were once again on terms of familiarity. This letter, which throws an interesting light on the writer's mental occupations, probably belongs to 1603 or 1604:—

"*To* Sir G. M[ORE].[1]

"If you were here, you would not think me importune if I bid you good-morrow every day; and such a patience will excuse my often letters. No other kind of conveyance is better for knowledge, or love. What treasures of moral knowledge are in Seneca's letters to only one Lucilius? and what of natural in Pliny's? how much of the story of the time is in Cicero's letters? And how all of these times, in the Jesuit's eastern and western epistles? where can we find so perfect a character of Phalaris as in his own letters, which are almost so many writs of execution? Or of Brutus, as in his privy seals for money? The Evangels and Acts teach us what to believe, but the Epistles of the Apostles what to do. And those who have endeavoured to dignify Seneca above his worth, have no way fitter than to imagine letters between him and St. Paul. As they think also that they have expressed an excellent person, in that letter which they obtrude, from our Blessed Saviour to King Agabarus.

"The Italians, which are most discursive, and think the world owes them all wisdom, abound so much in this kind of expressing, that Michel Montaigne says, he hath seen (as I remember) 400 volumes of Italian letters. But it is the other capacity which must make mine acceptable, that they are also the best conveyers of love. But, though all knowledge be in those authors already, yet, as some poisons, and some medicines, hurt not, nor profit, except the creature in which they reside contribute their lively activity and vigour; so, much of the knowledge buried in books perisheth, and becomes ineffectual, if it be not applied, and refreshed by a companion or friend. Much of their goodness hath the same period which some physicians of Italy have observed to be in the biting of their tarantula, that it affects no longer than the fly lives.

[1] From the *Letters* of 1651.

"For with how much desire we read the papers of any living now (especially friends) which we would scarce allow a box in our cabinet, or shelf in our library, if they were dead? And we do justly in it, for the writings and words of men present we may examine, control, and expostulate, and receive satisfaction from the authors; but the other we must believe, or discredit; they present no mean. Since, then, at this time I am upon the stage, you may be content to hear me.

"And now that perchance I have brought you to it (as Thomas Badger did the King), now I have nothing to say. And it is well, for the letter is already long enough, else let this problem supply, which was occasioned by you, of women wearing stones; which, it seems, you were afraid women should read, because you avert them at the beginning with a protestation of cleanliness. Martial found no way fitter to draw the Roman matrons to read one of his books, which he thinks most moral and cleanly, than to counsel them by the first epigram to skip the book, because it was obscene. But either you write not at all for women, or for those of sincerer palates. Though their unworthiness and your own ease be advocates for me with you, yet I must add my entreaty that you let go no copy of my problems till I review them. If it be too late, at least be able to tell me who hath them.

"Yours,
"J. Donne."

"*To* Robert Cotton.[1]

"Sir,—I have read Valdesius, which you sent me, with much delight, as well because the question is important, as perplexed. He is extremely full of authorities and citations, as almost every Spaniard is, and every lawyer. But all his arguments are from the merits of their Church, which must be allowed by all to be the competentest judge of this. That the Spaniards are forenamed in your Acts of councils, and in authors reciting them, is wild proof. For every-

[1] British Museum MSS.

where you shall find those relations to have been done expressly and promiscuously because the matter was not controverted at the time. In the first quarrel at Constance France was not a party. Nor by the connivancy of the council which would not pronounce for us, nor the fury of the Basil, at least of the Castilian legate there, where we were dejected, after long pretences (saith Valdesius) is France wounded at all. She and Spain jostled first at Trent. And there because the Imperial legate was never asked by the French whether he were also legate for Spain, nor protested against, if he sat in that right, though it appeared there was no other Spaniard legate there, therefore this seems a position of the place, as Spaniard, not only as Imperial. And after the Emperor's death, when it was questioned, after exagitation of that privilege, he spake first by order; and that done, left not the place to the French, but to all the world, and sat with the clerk. And in the end this council, as the others also did, safeguarded by decree the rights of all princes from any prejudice by any Act done or omitted there.

"So no council witnessing any precedency in the French before, nor any forfeiture bearing on the Spanish part here, and the Spanish having done here the last acts of precedency, sitting first and speaking first as long as he stayed, the matter seems at least as integral on the Spanish side, though you shall scarce light upon any Frenchman but considers this as *rem confectam.* Not upon these councils, but upon the decision of Pius IV. for Charles IX. against Philip II. But to it Valdesius says it was not done juridically. An appeal was put in. The case nor parties are not now the same, Spain being increased by Portugal. And the Spanish legate at Rome then was by the King's express commandment remiss in it because France had solemnly made his protestations there of departing from the Roman Church, except it were pronounced for him. But before or after these Valdesius meddles with no exposition; I think because he respects no other judge. Therefore he remembers not the decree of the Venetian State 1558, nor that at Vienna since, where his party was so strong, and yet the Emperor did no more but forbid intermeetings. Nor that in Poland Monluc had it after.

"Almost all the French offer this for the issue, that before '58 at Venice it was never asked, and Valdesius makes the quarrel, I know not how old, for his words are, *mille sæculis*. But before '58 I have observed our time of differing, at Calais 1521, when the point was whether it then belonged to the Spanish, Charles being then elect Emperor and King of your Rome, for without that essential circumstance it seems no offer had been there made on your part. And though Valdesius profess liberality, to give more than their authors ask (as indeed he is often more submiss than his nation useth to be, in arms or argument, where they have reasonable appearance of conquest), yet it is easy to remember him of many such circumstances for the French as he swells up for the Spanish. As that Clement gave a hundred days' indulgence to any who prayed for the French King and Innocent IV. added ten which is in Tho: Aquin: and many times your French King hath gone *lateraliter* with the Emperor. But there are such heaps of these on both sides, as it will, I think, ever remain perplexed, for since in Henry II. of France his time, the Pope would not judge for him, since Philip II. could never procure it, in all Henry III. his bravery against Rome, nor in Henry IV. his grovelling to creep into the Church, nor in such a succession of cousin Emperors, I know not where he should hope for it.

"Sir, I have both held your book longer than I meant, and held you longer by this letter, now I send it back. But you that are a real and foredoer of benefit, I presume are also an easy pardoner of unmalicious faults.

"Your affectionate friend and servant,
"J. Donne.

"Pyrford [1603?]."

By Valdesius here is not meant the Spanish mystic Juan de Valdés, who died in 1541, but a later and less illustrious Don Diego de Valdés (Jacobus Valdesius). He was the author of a volume entitled *De dignitate regum regnorumque*

Hispaniæ, et honoratiori loco eis, seu eorum legatis, a conciliis ac Romana sede jure debito. Written at Madrid in 1600, this treatise was published in 1602; and it is evidently this work which Cotton lent to Donne. The letter refers to a dispute which took place between Queen Elizabeth's ambassador, Henry Neville, and the Spanish ambassador, at Calais, in 1599, on precedence. The subject may have cropped up again, for Cotton appears to have desired Donne's opinion on the Spanish case as stated by Valdesius. The book still exists in the Cottonian collection.

It is possible that Donne was first presented to the new monarch on the 12th of August 1603, when the King and Queen were entertained at Loseley[1] with profuse hospitality by Sir George More.

Among the Tobie Mathew collections there are certain letters, without signature or address, internal evidence in which points unmistakably to their having been written to Donne while he was at Pyrford. The writer speaks of events which can be dated in 1603 and 1604; he refers to his own repeated entertainment by Sir Francis Wooley when he has come down to Pyrford to visit Donne. It has occurred to me that the author of these lively letters may have been Christopher Brooke. In one of these he reproaches Donne with remaining so constantly at Pyrford:—

"Your friends [in London] are sorry that you make yourself so great a stranger, but you best know your own occasions. Howbeit, if you have any design towards the Court, it was good you did prevent the loss of any more time. . . . The King's hand is neither so full nor so open as it hath been. You have not a poor friend that would be gladder [than I] of your good fortunes. . . . Sir Henry Goodyer is well, but no better than when you saw him. When I was at Pyrford, I left behind me Mr. Bacon's Discourse of matters ecclesiastical; I pray you return it by this bearer. . . . It cannot be but we shall see you shortly."

Another and much longer letter evidently belongs to May 1604. The writer complains "it is long since you

---
[1] See Nichols' *Progresses*, 251.

were in London and long since I was in Pyrford"; and he upbraids Donne for giving way to an indolent depression of spirits:—

"I trust it shall be no offence to interrupt your melancholy, in which soever of the fair walks it shall possess you, with this remembrance of my good wishes. . . . I know not what intelligence you have here, or what spies you are in fee withall"—that is to say, in what degree you know the current news.

"I could be content to wait till I were weary, and it would be long first. . . . Rather than kill you, I would punish your absence with silence—silence after a sort, for somewhat I will say, for my part. And if Sir Goodyer shall discharge himself upon any promise of mine, he wrongs me and he deceives you."

Then comes a flood of little gossip of the moment, especially about Parliament:—

"And surely, saving that Sir George More is your father (in law and not in conscience), he speaks as ill as ever he did, saving that he speaks not so much. . . . Sir William Cornwallis hath taken upon him to answer the objections against the Union, but so lamely as (if he were not a kind friend of yours) I would express that wonder which I have in my heart, how he keeps himself from the coat with the long sleeves. It is incredible to think, if it were not true, that such simplicity of conceit could be joined in him with so impudent utterance."

Cornwallis' pamphlet on the Union was published in 1604; and thus the anonymous friend rattles on, supplying us not with much real news of Donne, but with a sort of dust of information. "If your wife had been delivered a little later," is evidently a reference to the birth of John Donne, junior, to be his father's not too reputable editor some thirty years later.

When Mrs. Donne died in 1617 her husband stated, in the inscription which he placed in the old church of St. Clement Danes, that she had borne him twelve children, of whom seven then survived. Of these, two are believed to have been born at Pyrford—Constance in 1603, and John in 1604. The latter lived to publish his father's posthumous writings, and to do more than any one else to preserve his reputation and prestige.

A brief note, condoling with Sir Henry Goodyer on the death of his wife, concludes our scanty record of the life at Pyrford :—

"*To* Sir H[enry] G[oodyer].[1]

"Sir,—I live so far removed that even the ill news of your great loss (which is ever swiftest and loudest) found me not till now. Your letter speaks it not plain enough; but I am so accustomed to the worst, that I am sure it is so in this. I am almost glad that I knew her so little, for I would have no more additions to sorrow. If I should comfort you, it were an alms acceptable in no other title than when poor give to poor, for I am more needy of it than you. And I know you well provided of Christian and learned and brave defences against all human accidents. I will make my best haste after your messenger; and if myself and the place had not been ill-provided of horses, I had been the messenger, for you have taught me by granting more to deny no request.—Your honest unprofitable friend,   J. Donne.

"Pyrford, 3 o'clock,
    Just as yours came."

---

[1] From the *Letters* of 1651.

THE PROGRESS OF THE SOUL

CHAPTER V

THE PROGRESS OF THE SOUL

DURING the latter part of his residence in the house of Sir Thomas Egerton, Donne proposed to himself to compose a metaphysical narrative in verse in a manner which should remind his readers of no previous work. He made considerable advance with this, and when he abandoned it, it had already run to more than five hundred lines; the existing fragment, therefore, is by far the most extended of his poetical productions. It is very satisfactory to the biographer of the mind of Donne that this poem, which he began by naming "Metempsychosis," and which is now known as *The Progress of the Soul*, happens to be exactly dated, since it is a highly characteristic example of his style, and displays it at its climacteric. As we now possess it, the brief prose preface is headed with the words "Infinitati Sacrum, 16 Augusti 1601."

The preface is a curious tirade, not lacking in a certain unexpected lucidity and modernness of style, but of the most fantastic and even giddy import. Donne announces that he is going to paint his own picture at the head of his poem, " if any colours can deliver a mind so plain and flat and throughlight [translucent] as mine." Here sarcasm stalks unabashed, for Queen Elizabeth possessed no subject whose mind was less translucent, flat or plain, than that of Donne. He presents himself as still above all things a satirist, but he is tired of damning others, especially authors. He has therefore determined to contribute to contemporary literature, as we should say, an independent work of his own, thus to give other men a chance of censuring him. But he will borrow nothing, either from the classics or from the poets of his own day; the only person to whom he will be indebted shall be an unnamed scholar, who from some obscure Rabbinical or Spanish source has digged out the treasure of the odd subject he chooses. That is to say, some one has pointed out to Donne that if he wants to write a startling poem, illustrative of his peculiarities of soul and style, here is a theme made to his hand.

The theme is an adaptation of the Pythagorean theory of metempsychosis, which has been too narrowly bound down to a circulation through men and animals; the vegetable world is no less open to its incursions; a soul may fly from a whale to a cauliflower, and from a bean to a mammoth. What resided in an emperor yesterday, may animate a post-horse to-day, and flit into a "macaroon" (or fop) to-morrow. And Donne flings himself forth upon the glittering and elastic strands of his fancy. The soul may forget that it once lived in a melon, yet dimly recall the lascivious banquet at which it was served. It may remember not the time when it was a spider, yet recollect the vivid moment when a secret hand dropped it as poison into a cup of wine. The poet, therefore, will recount the adventures of the memory of a soul from Paradise until the present year of grace, sparing us all but its spasms of passion, its moments of intensest experience.

The scheme of this poem offers not a little attraction, and might have been treated with brilliant success in prose by some such follower of Rabelais as Bonaventure des Périers, who would have brought to the task of its composition a bitter scepticism and a pedantic erudition, wrapping up caustic and detestable insinuations in a cloak of wilful obscurity. It seems as though, for a moment, Donne had intended to adopt this line, and we cannot doubt that Ben Jonson, with whom he took counsel, commended this conception of the task. *The Progress of the Soul*, as it now stands, is not an easy poem to read, and our critics have found it simple to accept, as appropriate to its text, the words of Ben Jonson to Drummond of Hawthornden: "The conceit of Donne's Transformation, or Μετεμψύχωσις, was, that he sought the soul of that apple which Eve pulled, and thereafter made it the soul of a bitch,

THE PROGRESS OF THE SOUL

then of a she-wolf, and so of a woman: his general purpose was to have brought in all the bodies of the Heretics from the soul of Cain, and at last left it in the body of Calvin. Of this he never wrote but one sheet, and now, since he was made Doctor, repenteth highly, and seeketh to destroy all his poems."

This is an invaluable piece of information, but it does not absolve us from a study of the poem itself. The poet begins, in the approved epic manner, by announcing to us his subject—

> " I sing the progress of a deathless soul,
> Whom Fate,—which God made, but does not control,—
> Placed in most shapes."

He will make the adventures of this hunted soul his theme,

> " And the great world to's agèd evening
> From infant morn, through manly noon, I draw:
> What the gold Chaldee, or silver Persian saw,
> Greek brass, or Roman iron, is in this one."

He then addresses the sun, as he did long afterwards in his great sonnet to Lord Doncaster, celebrating the fecundity of its "hot masculine flame," its "male force," which first drew out the island spices in the far, dim chambers of the East. He bids the wheeling luminary concede that the fragile Soul of whom the poet sings has seen as many realms as he in his loose-reined career, and shall long survive his frail flight. Noah, under the name of "holy Janus," is then introduced, with a humorous description of the varieties of life provisionally cooped up together, and we are reminded that this Soul has moved and informed more different shapes than inhabited the Ark. After an appeal, suddenly serious, to the Destiny of God to guide the poet in his task of chronicling the strange divagations of the Soul, these stanzas occur. As the text at present exists, copied in all probability by careless hands from one rude draft, it is evident that they are corrupt in themselves, and are embedded without proper fusion in the general mass of the poem. But they possess great autobiographical value, and the body of their obscurity flashes with embedded jewels of poetry—

> "To my six lusters[1] almost now outwore
> Except thy book owe me so many more,
> Except my legend be free from the lets
> Of steep ambition, sleepy poverty,
> Spirit-quenching sickness, dull captivity,
> Distracting business, and from beauty's nets,
> And all that calls from this, and to others whets,
> O let me not launch out, but let me save
> Th' expense of brain and spirit, that my grave
> His right and due, a whole unwasted man, may have."

The meaning of this seems to me, that, being nearly thirty years of age, Donne is not inclined, unless the book of destiny promises him at least thirty more, with a fair prospect of health and wealth and bodily comfort, to adventure in arduous, intellectual enterprise. If he is going to continue the distracting life he has endured hitherto, without respite from illness and business, the ennuis of love and the frets of ambition, the game is positively not worth the candle; he will retire from the intolerable struggle, and will go down quietly to his grave, when his time comes, "a whole, unwasted man." This is what he fancies he would prefer—a quiet life, without events, where there should be no "expense of brain or spirit," and rest should come early to him—

> "But if my days be long, and good enough,
> In vain this sea shall énlarge or enrough
> Itself, *for I will through the wave and foam;*
> *And shall in sad lone ways, a lively sprite,*
> *Make my dark heavy poem light,* and light.
> For, though through many straits and lands I roam,
> *I launch at Paradise, and I sail towards home;*
> The course I there began shall here be stay'd,
> Sails hoisted there, struck here, and anchors laid
> In Thames, which were at Tigris and Euphrates weigh'd."

It will be remembered that Ben Jonson reported that the Soul was at last to be left in the body of Calvin. This

---

[1] That is to say, Donne was advanced in his twenty-ninth year.

seems to be either a misunderstanding on Jonson's part or else to indicate a change of Donne's intention, for it now becomes certain that the Soul was to be represented as finding its final habitation in Queen Elizabeth—

> "For the great Soul which here amongst us now
> Doth dwell, and moves that hand, and tongue, and brow,
> Which, as the Moon the sea, moves us,"

can be none other than she of whom Shakespeare a few months later was to say—

> "The mortal Moon hath her eclipse endured,"

and, if so, Donne's language is explicit. The story of the Queen, perhaps as the great tyrannical persecutor of the Catholics, was to wind up his satire—

> "For 'tis the crown and last strain of my song—
> This Soul, to whom Luther and Mahomet were
> Prisons of flesh; this Soul, which oft did tear
> And mend the wracks of th' Empire and late Rome,
> And lived when every great change did come,
> Had first in Paradise a low, but fatal room."

We are then informed what room that was. It hung in Paradise, at the flushed end of one of the boughs of that "forbidden learnèd tree" whence came all our woe. It was born in the flesh of the fruit of the knowledge of good and evil—

> "Prince of the orchard, fair as dawning morn,
> Fenced with the law, and ripe as soon as born,
> That apple grew, which this Soul did enlive."

When the Serpent offered it to Eve, the Soul went with the apple, and

> "Man all at once was there by Woman slain,"

yet it was not delivered for a moment into Eve's custody, for—

> "Just in that instant when the Serpent's grip
> Broke the slight veins and tender conduit-pipe,
> Thro' which this Soul from the tree's root did draw
> Life and growth to this apple, fled away
> This loose Soul,"

and, fluttering to the ground, sank through a boggy piece of ground into the roots of a Mandrake. Donne had a great partiality for mandrakes, in the half-human roots of which the superstition of the age saw aphrodisiac and lethal powers. They grew naturally beneath the gallows; they shrieked when torn out of the earth, so that, as we learn in *Romeo and Juliet*, "living mortals, hearing them, ran mad"; dried, they spoke oracularly; and worn in an amulet, they had the potency of cantharides. In one of the best known of his lyrics Donne had suggested, as an adventure of extraordinary romance, to "get with child a mandrake-root." Here the Soul in her progress now resides, and a most vivid and grotesque picture is given of the malign human vegetable. But Eve disturbs the Soul in this "lone, unhaunted place," for, sin having come into the world, her child is vexed with fever, and she seeks in waste places for a herb to restore it to health. In her search she is led to the mandrake and the poppy,

"And tore up both, and so cool'd her child's blood."

Donne reflects that these plants were the first to die because of their virtues; had they been base weeds they might have lived long.

"Thinner than burnt air flies this soul,"

and, seeking for a fresh habitation, insinuates herself

"Into a small blue shell, the which a poor
Warm bird o'erspread, and sat still evermore,
Till her enclos'd child kick'd, and peck'd itself a door."

The Soul occupies as its new inn a grim little freshly-hatched sparrow, which is thus described, in Donne's most vigorously realistic manner—

"Out crept a sparrow . . .
On whose raw arms stiff feathers now begin,
As children's teeth thro' gums, to break with pain;
His flesh is jelly yet, and his bones threads;
All a new downy mantle overspreads;
A mouth he opes, which would as much contain
As his late house, and the first hour speaks plain,

THE PROGRESS OF THE SOUL

> And chirps aloud for meat.   Meat fit for men
> His father steals for him, and so feeds then
> One that, within a month, will beat him from his hen."

The little cock-sparrow has a brilliant existence, but might have sheltered the Soul longer if it had garnered its forces better; it is a spendthrift of its vital energy, and dies of exhaustion.   The Soul flits down into a brook, and hides in one ovum of a fish's roe.   It is next swallowed by a swan, and the Soul has two prisons,

> " Till, melted by the Swan's digestive fire,
> She left her house, the Fish, and vapour'd forth."

She enters another fish, is pursued by a pike, and swallowed by an oyster-catcher.   Her vicissitudes lead the future friend of Izaak Walton to make the following reflections with regard to the finny race in general—

> " Is any kind subject to rape like fish ?
> Ill unto man they neither do nor wish ;
>   Fishers they kill not, nor with noise awake ;
> They do not hunt, nor strive to make a prey
> Of beasts, nor their young sons to bear away ;
>   Fowls they pursue not, nor do undertake
> To spoil the nests industrious birds do make ;
> Yet them all these unkind kinds feed upon ;
>   To kill them is an occupation,
> And laws make fasts and Lents for their destruction."

A sudden stiff land-wind drives the oyster-catcher out to sea, and the Soul enters the embryo of a whale.   Donne outdoes himself in the preposterous description of this monster, which seems to be copied from a print in some fabulous book of voyages.   As an example of style mis-applied, a portion of this may be quoted—

> " At every stroke his brazen fins do take,
> More circles in the broken sea they make
>   Than cannons' voices, when the air they tear.
> His ribs are pillars, and his high-arch'd roof
> Of bark, that blunts best steel, is thunder-proof.
>   Swim in him swallow'd dolphins without fear,
>   And feel no sides, as if his vast womb were
> Some inland sea ; and ever as he went
> He spouted rivers up, as if he meant
> To join our seas with seas above the firmament."

This whale is long the tyrant of the ocean, but at length two little fishes, a thresher and a swordfish, combine to attack and slay him. The Soul, indignant that even so enormous a mansion can be battered down about her ears, flies to shore again, and for her next home

"Got the strait cloister of a wretched mouse."

The mouse climbs up the proboscis of an elephant, and gnaws its brain, but is killed by the death-fall of the huge beast; the Soul flies forth and takes refuge in a wolf, and then in a whelp, and then in an ape, which intrudes itself on Siphatecia, Adam's fifth daughter, sister and wife to Cain. Here, at last, the Soul finds a human habitation; but we have not yet advanced out of sight of the Garden of Eden, and at this rate of progress it would have taken millions of verses to bring us safely down to Queen Elizabeth. The poet evidently felt the inherent weakness of his scheme, and here abandoned it, drawing the threads loosely together in a final stanza when he says that his "sullen" poem is written to please himself and not other people, and declares that there is no such thing as positive good or positive evil, but all is a question of relative values, and to be judged by the average of public opinion.

The Progress of the Soul may help us to understand why, with gifts of intellectual appreciation and keen refinement perhaps unsurpassed even in that consummate age, Donne never contrived to reach the first rank among men of letters. The puerility of the central idea is extraordinary; the Soul flits from body to body, without growth, without change, as a parasite leaps from one harbouring object to another. In this notion of the undeveloping restlessness of the Soul, if there is any thought at all, it is the bare satiric one, too cheap to be so magnificently extended and embroidered. It is probable that Donne's intention was to irradiate the dark places of ignorance and brutality as his narrative descended the ages, but, as we have seen, he could not induce the hare to start. He had little dramatic and positively no epic talent; and this is implicitly admitted even by De Quincey, who

THE PROGRESS OF THE SOUL

is the solitary uncompromising admirer of *The Progress of the Soul* whom three centuries have produced.

But when all this is conceded, the poem remains one of the most extraordinary in a majestic age. De Quincey, to quote him at the height of his argument, declares that "massy diamonds compose the very substance of this poem on the Metempsychosis, thoughts and descriptions which have the fervent and gloomy sublimity of Ezechiel or Æschylus." If a sober criticism may hesitate to admit the "massy diamonds," there is yet no question that diamond dust is sprinkled broadcast over the stanzas of this grotesque poem. The effort after a complete novelty of style is apparent, and the result of this is occasionally, although not invariably, happy. What we notice in it first is resistance to the accepted Spenserian glow and amenity. The author is absolutely in revolt against the tendency and mode of Spenser. He is not less opposed to a dry and even manner of writing intellectual poetry, which was a revival, in measure, of what Spenser had cast forth, and which had been exemplified in the graceful and highly popular miscellanies of Samuel Daniel, first collected in this very year 1601; in the *Nosce Teipsum* of Sir John Davys, in 1599; and in the historical verse of Drayton (1597 and onwards). My own conviction is that it was the even flow of versification of these academic writers which, more than anything else, goaded Donne to the cultivation of that violently varied tonality in verse of which *The Progress of the Soul* gives innumerable examples. We have an exact parallel in the exacerbation of Wagner's genius through his impatience with the smoothness of Donizetti.

If we look around for any contemporary poetry which shall in measure remind us of Donne, we are confined to one or two works of pure eccentricity, such as Chapman's *Amorous Zodiac*, published in 1595, and Cyril Tourneur's *Transform'd Metamorphosis* of 1600. In the former unseemly and ingenious rhapsody there is a certain resemblance to *The Progress of the Soul* in its superficial aspect, while the verse of Tourneur may be said to suit Donne's ear better than that of any other contemporary. But Donne affects neither the turbidity of Chapman nor the Alexandrian allusiveness of Cyril Tourneur, while his language, although frequently hard and abrupt, is genuine and lucid English, and not darkened by a thick flight of detestable and useless neologisms. Our quotations will suffice to show with what brilliant intrepidity he will dart in a moment into the very central shrine of imaginative expression. Here, as in his lyrics, the general aspect of the work is, as he said himself, "sullen," with the leaden colours of the thunderstorm, but ever and again the lightning plays amongst it in lambent and intolerable radiance.

From the biographical standpoint, *The Progress of the Soul* offers us a few details of importance. The entire tone and character of it are un-Christian; it is penetrated by the mocking, sensuous scepticism of the Renaissance. The author is akin to Marlowe's Faustus, without veneration, without fear, pursued by an absolutely unflinching curiosity into unfamiliar fields of physical inquiry. No one can read this poem of August 1601 and believe that Donne's memory was not, in later years, amiably deceived when he told Izaak Walton that he continued through these years to "proceed with humility and diffidence in disquisition and search" after religious truth. It is quite certain, from all the evidence we possess—if we regard it honestly—that Donne's conscience was not yet touched. He had lost his traditional faith as a Catholic, and no light had come to him at present from the other Church. In a feverish crisis of intellectual pride he wrote this extraordinary poem—one of the least pietistic and least "diffident" essay in psychological imagination ever presented to the public. No wonder that in his holier years he desired wholly to destroy such an evidence of his arrogant worldliness.

The text of *The Progress of the Soul*, although, or perhaps because, the poem is so elaborate and difficult, is comparatively clear. The earliest version which I have met with is a manuscript, apparently of the first quarter of the seventeenth century, which belonged to a certain Bradon,

THE PROGRESS OF THE SOUL

and passed into the Phillipps collection. It is now in my own library. This is a copy, not very intelligently made, either from the poet's handwriting or from an early transcript of the same. It presents some fifty or sixty slight variants, many of them obvious misreadings, but several which are distinct improvements upon the printed text, and one or two which actually clear up difficulties in the latter. It is headed "Dr. Donne's Μετεμψύχωσις." In the first quarto (1633) *The Progress of the Soul* opens the volume; in subsequent editions, with slight alterations of text, it takes a less prominent place. The date of composition (16 Augusti 1601), given in 1633, does not occur upon the Phillipps MS. In all the seventeenth century texts the punctuation is so wild that we are forced to suppose that the editors were unable to follow the poet's meaning.

LIFE AT MITCHAM

1605–1608

CHAPTER VI

LIFE AT MITCHAM

1605-1608

It was Walton's belief, in which no doubt he had followed a lapse of memory in Donne himself, that the poet and his family continued to live with Sir Francis Wooley until the death of the latter. The two families, indeed, remained on terms of affectionate intimacy until the lamented and premature decease of Sir Francis Wooley in 1610; but Donne had been obliged to quit Pyrford, on account of its distance from town, five years earlier. He was called to London by professional work, the nature of which we shall presently examine; it was absolutely needful that he should live within easy reach of the City. In the spring of 1605 the Donnes were residing, or at least lodging, at Camberwell, where Mrs. Donne's sister Jane, Lady Grymes, had a house. It is probable that they were the guests of Sir Thomas Grymes while looking about for a dwelling of their own. The Grymes continued to be Donne's intimate and lifelong friends. At all events, here George Donne was born on the 9th of May 1605. Finally, the Donnes settled not far off, at Mitcham, in a small manorial house, which remained in existence until about half a century ago, when it was pulled down. Mr. Richard Simpson, the author of the *Life of Edmund Campion*, played in the garden of it when he was a child, and was told that certain of the trees there had been planted by Donne. Simpson made a slight but intelligible and valuable drawing of the house before its destruction; this was reproduced by Dr. Jessopp in 1897. The letters of Donne do not conceal the discomforts of this little dwelling. He particularly complains of the thinness of the walls—no trifling drawback, when we consider the rude and imperfect methods of warming houses which were alone familiar to the early seventeenth century. His health was seriously undermined during the years he spent at Mitcham, but whether from privation or neglect of himself or constitutional tendency, it is now difficult to decide. His symptoms in later life point to his having had an attack of typhoid fever in his youth.

While he left his wife and the steadily growing army of babies at Mitcham, he himself had a "lodging" or apartment in the Strand. This also was a cheerless place, built over a vault, and pervious to cold and damp. He seems, however, to have made one room of it comfortable with an increasing library of books. As far as we can make out, he divided his time pretty equally—with that remarkable restlessness of the Jacobean age—between the Strand and Mitcham, riding, as it would seem, several times a week from one residence to the other, and sleeping perhaps half his nights in one and half in the other. There is no evidence that Donne took any exercise, except on horseback, and as years advanced he became more and more a bookworm. At Mitcham he was among his relations and friends. His brother-in-law, Sir Nicholas Throckmorton Carew, was lord of the manor of Mitcham; and Donne either found or immediately made a fast friend in the generous and splendid Sir Julius Cæsar, a lawyer of Italian extraction, born in 1558, of great wealth, who possessed at Mitcham a mansion of such magnificence that Queen Elizabeth had paid him a visit, spending the night of September 12, 1598, in his house. Cæsar had been knighted on the 20th of May 1603, and, soon after Donne's arrival at Mitcham, became Chancellor of the Exchequer (April 7, 1606). Sir Julius Cæsar, a man of exquisite manners and courtly hospitality, was a lover of literature, and continued to be a friend of Donne until the death of the latter; he died in 1636. Among Donne's friends has been included, but on somewhat slight evidence, Sir Richard Martin, the Master of the Mint, who was Sir Julius Cæsar's father-in-law. He was seventy-two years of age when Donne came to Mitcham, and his own house was at Tottenham, on the other side of London. We can say no more than that Sir Richard Martin probably visited Sir Julius Cæsar, and that on some such occasion Donne may possibly have been presented to him.

We now come to the nature of the professional work which called Donne from Pyrford up to town in 1605. While he lived with Sir Francis Wooley he had made a serious study of the Civil and Canon Laws, "in which he acquired such a perfection as was judged to hold proportion with many who had made that study the employment of their whole life." With these labours he had combined an immense amount of miscellaneous reading of the scholastic sort, and in particular of the foreign casuists of the sixteenth century. The fame of this peculiar combination of somewhat eccentric lines of learning reached the ears of a man to whom, more than to any one else at that time, such attainments might prove serviceable. Thomas Morton, born in 1564, was by nine years Donne's senior. He had taken a brilliant degree at Cambridge, but at the age of thirty-four had found no preferment, when he was advanced to the rectory of Long Marston, in Yorkshire. Here his talents attracted the notice of Henry Hastings, Earl of Huntingdon, Lord President of the Council of the North, who made him his chaplain. This Lord Huntingdon it was whose nephew, the fifth earl, married Elizabeth, third daughter of the Countess of Derby, who, after his death, became Countess of Worcester. Morton thus became known to that circle of great ladies into which Donne had already begun to be admitted.

The recrudescence of Catholicism in England in the first year of his reign was a subject of alarm and of bewilderment to James I. Bancroft, still Bishop of London, but soon to be Archbishop of Canterbury, had expended his energies mainly against the Puritan nonconformists, whom his celebrated canons of ecclesiastical law, drawn up in the Convocation of March 20, 1604, filled with consternation. But James shrewdly perceived that in concentrating attack upon the Dissenters the Catholics had been given an opportunity to reassert themselves. He did not wish to persecute anybody, yet he was determined to insist upon uniformity in the national religion. On the 17th of May 1604 he consulted Parliament as to the propriety of passing new laws "to hem in" the Papists. Three weeks later a bill for the due execution of the statutes against Jesuits, seminary priests, and recusants was introduced into the House of Lords. This bill, the severity of which was intensified by the Commons, passed in July; but James repented of his harshness, and refused to take advantage of it. In a decree, issued from his manor of Oatlands on the 16th of July 1604, the King desired a moderation in treating recusants, that "that uniformity which we desire may be wrought by clemency and by weight of reason, and not by rigour of law."

Then resulted an immense output of theological and argumentative literature. Everybody wrote a "letter" or an "appeal," and the censorship of the press was greatly relaxed. As Egeon Askew, of Queen's College, Oxford, put it—in a remarkably mixed metaphor—"pamphleteers ran to the printer as horses rush into battle, where they were wounded with their own quills." William Covell timidly expressed, in the autumn of 1604, the general tendency towards conciliation. All promised to resolve itself into a mere war of ink and paper. The impudent demand of Spain that Prince Charles should be educated as a Catholic produced another change in James I.'s attitude towards the Papists. Incensed by the Spanish proposals, and alarmed at the increase in the numbers of the recusants at home, the King determined on more strenuous measures for the banishment of the priests and the conversion of the laity.

With the former, and with its melodramatic consequences, we have nothing here to do. As the principal engine of the latter was selected the supple and active intellect of Morton. He had already attracted notice "for his dexterity and acuteness in disputing with the Romish Recusants."[1] His disputes with the Jesuits had

---
[1] See Dr. Barwick's Τερονίκης, 1660, pp. 67, 68.

been carried on with urbanity on both sides, and Serarius, Rector of the College at Mainz, in his work against Scaliger, specially acknowledges the civility of Morton as an opponent.

The Earls of Huntingdon, succeeding one another with great rapidity, offer a danger to the hasty biographer. The death of the third Hastings earl in 1595 seems to have given a momentary check to the fortunes of Morton, who took the opportunity to go to Frankfurt, where he made the recusant arguments his peculiar study. His talents, however, were not long obscured, and Queen Elizabeth, in her last years, had frequently distinguished him. He attended her ambassador to Denmark, and presently became chaplain to the Earl of Rutland at Belvoir, an appointment which he expressly appreciated, because it brought him nearer to London. He had already become prominent for a persuasive adroitness in disputing with Roman Catholics. Now in his fortieth year, encouraged by the particular favour of James I., he undertook to contend with the new opponents of uniformity in the even lists of purely theological controversy. Morton had hitherto confined himself to oral discourse and debate. Perhaps the practice of writing found him at first ill-prepared; perhaps he needed somebody to make his cross-references for him and to correct his proof-sheets. He was wealthy, busy, much called away from London by his multiplying duties.

The fourth Earl of Huntingdon, dying on the last day of 1604, left as his heir to the title a cousin, Henry, the husband of Donne's friend, and Morton seems to have returned to influence in the Hastings family. It would seem that Donne was suggested to him, very possibly by the young Countess of Huntingdon, as possessing exactly the qualities which he required, and as eager to increase in this way his very scanty income. I believe that from 1605 to the summer of 1607 Donne was mainly employed in revising, collecting, and even perhaps composing, for Morton.

What was desired was, to distinguish between the various species of recusants and deal with them discreetly. It is difficult for us to comprehend a situation, in which political feeling ran so high that no distinction was made between a Presbyterian and a Roman Catholic. But such a pamphlet as the *Puritanopapismus* of Oliver Ormerod of Emmanuel found many supporters to respond to its suggestion that Papists, Anabaptists, and Brownists were all much the same, and equally detestable to the pure loyal Protestant. The King was little pleased by such fanatical confusions as these, and one of his chaplains, Dr. William Wilkes, was set to explain the King's meaning more at full in a treatise of *Obedience, or Ecclesiastic Union*. Meanwhile the casuistical or intellectual aspect of the discussion was left in the hands of Morton. In the middle of his labours he was startled, but not distracted, by the amazing revelations of Gunpowder Plot.

Evidence of Donne's activity in working for Morton still exists in the shape of various controversial pamphlets on which are found his signature or slight observations in his handwriting. Among those which have passed through my hands are the tract of Ormerod, printed in 1605, and containing a discussion of the relative merits of Anabaptists and Papists; Sutcliffe's *Subversion of Robert Parsons' confused and worthless Work*, 1606; and William Perkins' *Second Part of the Reformation of a Catholic*, 1607. Donne possessed, moreover, Hill's *Defence of Christ's Descent into Hell* and Covell's defence of Hooker, to which reference will be made later on. These pamphlets bear indications of careful reading and reference on their possessor's part, and are interesting as bearing out, in an unexpected way, the accuracy of Walton's account of Donne's relations with Morton.

The publications in which Donne assisted Morton are somewhat numerous, and are printed in Latin and English. The first is the *Apologia Catholica* of 1605. In the course of the same year Morton produced a quarto volume on Gunpowder Plot, entitled *Conspiracy and Rebellion*. Meanwhile a continuation of his original controversy was on the stocks, and appeared in 1606 as *Apologiæ Catholicæ secunda pars*. This publication excited a storm of anger, and led to a rainfall of pamphlets. Morton, exhilarated by the glow of battle, responded with *A full Satisfaction concerning a double Romish Iniquity: Heinous Rebellion and more than Heathenish Æquivocation,* in three parts, 1606. This was a rather full examination of Romish positions and practices, with a justification of the Protestant standpoint, all tending to an encouragement of the Government in taking a very strenuous line with the Catholics. The sensation caused by this attack was extreme, and the Jesuits were alarmed. Partly concealed by the initials P. R., the famous Robert Parsons was directed to reply to it, under the title of *A treatise tending to Mitigation towards Catholic subjects in England,* 1607. With this the first period of Morton's literary activity closes, and throughout this we are to believe that the assistance and co-operation of Donne were incessant.

There is reason, however, to believe that during a part of this time Donne was on the Continent. On the 16th of February 1606[1] licence was granted to Sir James Bourchier, Sir Alexander Morrison, Sir William Chute, and John Donne to travel for three years. Whether they were to travel separately or in a party does not appear. I suppose the licence did not imply that the absence was bound to extend to three years, but that that must be the limit. It was doubtless on this occasion that Mrs. Donne jestingly proposed to accompany her husband in the dress of a page. Matron as she was, she was only twenty-one, and of a delicate figure; she might have played the part with a sufficiently graceful petulance. But what concerns us is that the whimsical idea inspired her husband with a poem which, if stained by certain rather egregious faults of taste, is one of the cleverest and most original that he ever composed—

"By our first strange and fatal interview,
By all desires which thereof did ensue,
By our long starving hopes, by that remorse
Which my words' masculine persuasive force
Begot in thee, and by the memory
Of hurts, which spies and rivals threaten'd me,

---

[1] Domestic State Papers—Feb. 16, 160$\frac{5}{6}$.

> I calmly beg. But by thy father's wrath,
> By all pains, which want and divorcement hath,
> I conjure thee, and all the oaths which I
> And thou have sworn to seal joint constancy,
> Here I unswear, and overswear them thus;
> Thou shalt not love by ways so dangerous.
> Temper, O fair love, love's impetuous rage;
> Be my true mistress still, not my feign'd page.
> I'll go, and, by thy kind leave, leave behind
> Thee, only worthy to nurse in my mind
> Thirst to come back; O! if thou die before,
> My soul from other lands to thee shall soar.
> Thy else-almighty beauty cannot move
> Rage from the seas, nor thy love teach them love."

It appears that his intended destinations were Italy and Germany, the land of the "spongy hydroptic Dutch." The poem closes with a really exquisite and tender, although playful, injunction to Mrs. Donne, who is treated as if she were still a child, to refrain from any such romantic adventure as she threatens—

> "O stay here, for, for thee
> England alone's a worthy gallery,
> To walk in expectation, till from thence
> Our greatest King call thee to His presence.
> When I am gone, dream me some happiness,
> Nor let thy looks our long-hid love confess,
> Nor praise, nor dispraise me, nor bless nor curse
> Openly Love's force, nor in bed fright thy nurse
> With midnight startings, crying out, 'O! O!
> Nurse, O! my love is slain! I saw him go
> O'er the white Alps alone; I saw him, I,
> Assail'd, fight, taken, stabb'd, bleed, fall and die.'"

If Donne really went to Italy in 1606, as he certainly planned to do, this was doubtless one of the "many and chargeable travels" which reduced him to such a lamentable state of poverty and to melancholy years of "dear-bought experience." It is, on the other hand, conceivable that he went on a secret mission to obtain information for Morton.

We should know little of the mind of Donne in these critical years if it were not for the fragments which have come down to us, in a tormented condition, without arrangement, very often without indication of date, of his correspondence with a friend who has been already mentioned, Sir Henry Goodyer. This gentleman, not in himself a man of any commanding ability, belonged to the sympathetic and appreciative class to which genius, in every age, owes its main support. Throughout his life, Donne, who called friendship his "second religion," possessed many tender and loyal friends. Of those who were pre-eminent for their bright fidelity, Sir Henry Goodyer took a leading place. Wotton, especially about this time, distracted with business and the duties of diplomacy, could not, as Donne complained, give much time to correspondence. Goodyer's leisure, on the other hand, seems to have been infinite, and he devoted a large section of it to the entertainment of the friend whom he admired and warmly loved, not perhaps without some admixture of apprehension.

Henry Goodyer is to be so often mentioned in the course of this narrative, and demands so much gratitude from all lovers of Donne, that we must pause here to reconstruct, as well as we may, his somewhat shadowy figure. After the monasteries were suppressed in 1538, the abbey of St. Edith of Polesworth, of black or Benedictine nuns, was sold to a London merchant, Francis Goodyer, Gent., with the whole lordship of Polesworth, in Warwickshire, in 1544. The eldest son of this man died without male issue, but there was a younger son, who must have shown some ambition or energy, since he was knighted. This Sir William Goodyer, of Monk's Kirby, married Mary Brook, and had a son, Henry, who was baptized on the 21st of August 1571, being thus two years older than his eminent friend. Sir William died in 1578, and Henry in due time married his cousin Frances, succeeding at the death of her father to the estates at Polesworth.

During the reign of Elizabeth, Henry Goodyer does not seem to have been heard of, but in the Parliament of 1603 he was M.P. for Porthpean and West Looe, in Cornwall, and he contrived to attract the attention of James I., who appointed him "one of the Gentlemen of his Majesty's Privy Chamber." On the 19th of July 1603 he was knighted at Lamer, Sir John Gerard's seat in Hertfordshire. Goodyer was an extravagant man, and we shall have occasion to notice the painful straits to which he was ultimately put to support his family and himself. He died in almost abject poverty. But in these first years we are to conceive him as a tolerably wealthy and certainly very open-handed country gentleman, recently admitted to Court, and still a little dazzled by the splendours of London. For a long time Donne wrote to Goodyer a weekly letter; it is much to be feared that those portions of this correspondence which we would now be most glad to possess, the picturesque and trivial parts, are precisely those which were not preserved. Among these letters the following, which seems to refer to the birth of Francis Donne, baptized at Mitcham on the 8th of January 1607, appears to be the earliest :—

"*To the Honourable Knight* Sir H[ENRY] GOODYER.[1]

"SIR,—Though you escape my lifting up of your latch by removing, you cannot my letters; yet of this letter I do not much accuse myself, for I serve your commandment in it, for it is only to convey to you this paper opposed to those, with which you trusted me. It is (I cannot say the weightiest, but truly) the saddest lucubration and night's passage that ever I had. For it exercised those hours, which, with extreme danger of her, whom I should hardly have abstained from recompensing for her company in this world, with accompanying her out of it, increased my poor family with a son. Though her anguish, and my fears and hopes, seem divers and wild distractions from this small business of your papers, yet because they all narrowed themselves, and met in *Via regia*, which is the consideration of ourselves and God, I thought it time not unfit for this dispatch. Thus much more than needed I have told you, whilst my fire was lighting at Tricombs [at] ten o'clock.—Yours ever entirely, J. DONNE."

[*January* 1607 ?]

---

[1] From the *Letters* of 1651.

Francis Donne was one of the children who died in infancy, probably at Mitcham.

When Ben Jonson published *The Fox* in 1607, with a preface dated February 11, there was prefixed to it a copy of commendatory Latin verses "Amicissimo et Meritissimo Ben Jonson, in *Volponem*." The continued esteem and friendship which existed between these two men is the more noticeable in that Donne extended a like indulgence to no other poet of his own or of the preceding generation. He was obviously in far closer intellectual and artistic sympathy with Jonson than with any other professional writer.

In 1607, after the preparation for the press of *A Full Satisfaction*, Donne's position once more became critical. Thomas Morton had more than served his apprenticeship; he had attracted the favourable notice of all the Anglican authorities. James I. had made him his chaplain-in-ordinary; he had been received under the protection of Bancroft, Archbishop of Canterbury. The time was now come for Morton to take a higher position in the Church of England, and, before the close of 1606, he was informed that the King intended to reward his services against the Catholics by the next piece of preferment. Donne's occupation, therefore, was likely at any moment to slip from him, and he was made painfully conscious of his own unsatisfactory position. He was still a kind of Goethe, but without a Weimar. One of the most learned of living Englishmen in the law, he was not a lawyer; a profound theologian, he was not in orders; with a throng of exalted relations and friends, he possessed no post at Court. He began, at the age of thirty-four, to look out once again for some means of gaining a livelihood. The following letter lifts, for a moment, the veil from Donne's life at this time, and shows him to us endeavouring to obtain a post in the house of Queen Anne, through the good offices of William Fowler, her secretary. This letter has, I think, been misunderstood as implying that Donne desired to take Fowler's place. If the language, which was purposely obscured, be carefully examined, it will be seen, I believe, that Donne has been vaguely promised some employment by Fowler, and, being alarmed by a rumour that Fowler is retiring, desires his suit to be pressed while there is yet time for Donne to enjoy the Secretary's patronage. At the same time, the expression about Fowler's taking "steps therein" seems to bear the contrary significance:—

"*To the Honourable Knight* Sir H. GOODYER, *one of the Gentlemen of his Majesty's Privy Chamber.*

"SIR,—You may remember that long since you delivered Mr. Fowler possession of me, but the wide distance in which I have lived from court, makes me reasonably fear, that now he knows not his right and power in me, though he must of necessity have all, to whom you and I join in a gift of me, as we did to him, so that perchance he hath a servant of me, which might be passed in a book of concealment.

"If your leisure suffer it, I pray find whether I be in him still, and conserve me in his love; and so perfect your own work, or do it over again, and restore me to the place, which by your favour I had in him. For Mr. Powell who serves her Majesty as clerk of her council, hath told me that Mr. Fowler hath some purpose to retire himself; and therefore I would fain, for all my love, have so much of his, as to find him willing when I shall seek him at court, to let me understand his purpose therein; for if my means may make me acceptable to the Queen and him, I should be very sorry, he should make so far steps therein with any other, that I should fail in it, only for not having spoke to him soon enough. It were an injury to the forwardness of your love to add more; here therefore I kiss your hands, and commend to you the truth of my love.

"Your very affectionate servant and lover,
"JO. DONNE.
"From my lodging in the Strand, whither
    I shall return on Monday, 13 June, 1607."

These and other propositions came to nothing, but the admirable Morton was otherwise ambitious for the friend whose splendid penetration of intellect and inherent force of virtue he had enjoyed so full occasion of appreciating. He had himself by this time been assured of the vacant Deanery of Gloucester, and he was anxious to make his own promotion the opportunity for securing the talents and graces of Donne for the English Church. On the 22nd of June 1607 Thomas Morton was presented to the Deanery of Gloucester. What he immediately attempted to do for Donne was preserved to us, through the most fortunate chance of the great prolongation of Morton's life, by Izaak Walton. The following account was received by Walton from "that most laborious and learned Bishop of Durham"—for so Morton became in 1632—"one whom God hath blessed with perfect intellectuals and a cheerful heart at the age of ninety-four years, and is yet living." As the Bishop of Durham only survived a few months longer, dying in his ninety-fifth year, on the 22nd of September 1659, it is impossible to be too thankful that Walton was just in time to secure this most important document, "the following relation, which I received from this good man, my friend," and printed no doubt mainly in the Bishop's own words:—

"He sent to Mr. Donne, and entreated to borrow an hour of his time for a conference the next day. After their meeting, there was not many minutes passed before he spake to Mr. Donne to this purpose: 'Mr. Donne, the occasion of sending for you is to propose to you what I have often revolved in my own thought since I last saw you; which, nevertheless, I will not declare but upon this condition, that you shall not return me a present answer, but forbear three days, and bestow some part of that time in fasting and prayer; and after a serious consideration of what I shall propose, then return to me with your answer. Deny me not, Mr. Donne; for it is the effect of a true love, which I would gladly pay as a debt due for yours to me.'"

This request being granted, the Doctor expressed himself thus:—

"'Mr. Donne, I know your education and abilities; I

know your expectation of a state-employment; and I know your fitness for it; and I know, too, the many delays and contingencies that attend court promises; and let me tell you, that my love, begot by our long friendship and your merits, hath prompted me to such an inquisition after your present temporal estate, as makes me no stranger to your necessities; which I know to be such as your generous spirit could not bear, if it were not supported with a pious patience. You know I have formerly persuaded you to waive your court hopes, and enter into holy orders; which I now again persuade you to embrace, with this reason added to my former request: the King hath yesterday made me Dean of Gloucester, and I am also possessed of a benefice, the profits of which are equal to those of my Deanery. I will think my Deanery enough for my maintenance (who am and resolve to die a single man), and will quit my benefice, and estate you in it (which the Patron is willing I shall do), if God shall incline your heart to embrace this motion. Remember, Mr. Donne, no man's education or parts make him too good for this employment, which is to be an ambassador for the God of glory, that God who by a vile death opened the gates of life to mankind. Make me no present answer; but remember your promise, and return to me the third day with your resolution.'

"At the hearing of this, Mr. Donne's faint breath and perplexed countenance gave a visible testimony of an inward conflict; but he performed his promise, and departed without returning an answer till the third day, and then his answer was to this effect:—

"'My most worthy and most dear friend, since I saw you I have been faithful to my promise, and have also meditated much of your great kindness, which hath been such as would exceed even my gratitude; but that it cannot do; and more I cannot return you; and I do that with a heart full of humility and thanks, though I may not accept of your offer: but, sir, my refusal is not for that I think myself too good for that calling, for which kings, if they think so, are not good enough; nor for that my education and learning, though not eminent, may not, being assisted with God's grace and humility, render me in some measure fit for it: but I dare make so dear a friend as you are my confessor: some irregularities of my life have been so visible to some men, that though I have, I thank God, made my peace with Him by penitential resolutions against them, and, by the assistance of His grace, banished them my affections: yet this, which God knows to be so, is not so visible to men, as to free me from their censures, and, it may be, that sacred calling from a dishonour. And besides, whereas it is determined by the best of casuists, that God's glory should be the first end, and a maintenance the second motive to embrace that calling; and though each man may propose to himself both together; yet the first may not be put last without a violation of conscience, which He that searches the heart will judge. And truly my present condition is such, that if I ask my own conscience, whether it be reconcilable to that rule, it is at this time so perplexed about it, that I can neither give myself nor you an answer. You know, sir, who says, Happy is that man whose conscience doth not accuse him for that thing which he does. To these, I might add other reasons that dissuade me; but I crave your favour that I may forbear to express them, and thankfully decline your offer.'"

It would be very interesting to us to know whether this most important document is to be taken as representing the *ipsissima verba* of Morton and Donne, or as the recollection of an old man half a century after the event. If the former, were Donne's words preserved in a written letter to the Dean, or are they a report of what he said? If the latter, did the Dean take down notes of the conversation at the time? On the whole, I incline to the last of these suppositions. The account is far too circumstantial not to be in the main exact, and the high character of Morton precludes the idea of fiction. On the other hand, the actual verbiage is scarcely that of Donne, to which by usage the ear becomes highly sensitive. Nor can it be supposed to be that of Walton, but is probably entirely the composition of Morton, who may have founded it, not merely on notes in a diary, but on letters from Donne of which he made this précis.

It seems to me the more certain that we have not here the precise words of Donne, because I think that Morton has, very innocently and naturally, modified the real objections made by the poet to his proposition. We must remember that, before this thrilling narrative was written down, Donne had risen to perhaps the foremost place in the English church, in fame though not in rank. He had passed away in the very glory of holiness, leaving all England bereaved of its noblest preacher and most sanctified divine. But, meanwhile, the secular poetry of Donne had been published, and the animalism of his natural temper had been almost unduly dwelt upon. People had discovered that their majestic Dean of St. Paul's had, in his youth, been as other wild young men. They had not been scandalised, as we should be, since that was not the seventeenth-century fashion; but they had become accustomed to the idea that this great and holy man had been loose and fiery in his youth. It went to the further glorification of God's infinite judgment and mercy that He should have saved so noble a being from the nets of the flesh.

By this conception I think that, looking back fifty years, Morton was slightly led astray; for Donne's objection to taking orders at thirty-five could hardly have rested upon the consciousness that up to his thirtieth year he had lived for pleasure. There is no evidence, internal or external, that since his marriage he had been guilty of any infidelity to his poor, patient wife. On the contrary, his conduct to her and in the face of the world had clearly been exemplary. But the real difficulty which so suddenly checked him, which led him with so much anguish to refuse Morton's offer in 1607, as the King's repeated wishes later on, must have been theological. Penitence and a genuine sorrow for faults of instinct, which were wholly matters of the past, might be insufficient to give confidence to a weaker man, but it is absurd to think that they kept such a stalwart will as that of Donne hovering on the brink of holy orders.

He may, it is more than probable, have confessed to the Dean his errors of past life, but it is inconceivable to any one who has studied the characteristics of his temperament, that remorse—that torture of the morally bewildered—could unhinge such a perspicuous conscience as his.

In the career of Donne all the crises are intellectual ones. When he halts, when he plunges forward, it is the brain that steers him. We look, therefore, at this tremendous moment of his career, when his whole future hung in the balance, for an intellectual difficulty, not for a moral scruple. To the aged Bishop of Durham, doubtless, the wild controversies and theological passions of his own youth seemed dim and remote. He had forgotten, perhaps, what had brought Donne into relations with him, and what their work together had been. All this time, we must reflect, Donne, although he had long since abandoned the ceremonial of the Roman Church, had not ceased to be a Roman Catholic so far as to enter any other communion. He had preserved, as the *Pseudo-Martyr* shows us, a lively curiosity in Catholic dogma, and it was his late peculiar position, as a Roman Catholic without fervour and yet with great erudition, which had commended him to Morton. My own impression is that Donne was actually detached at this time from either church, although I am not unaware that such detachment, common enough in France and Italy, was very rare in England. It is inconceivable that Morton should have employed Donne if he were still a Roman Catholic, yet he was hardly at this time an Anglican. In his secretarial and editorial work for that excellent man Donne's condition of soul must often have revealed itself. Morton, we must recollect, was specially distinguished at this time for his minglement of the serpent and the dove in dealing with Roman Catholics. His public conference with the Romish Recusants at York in 1601, and his subsequent courtesy to his opponents, had made his talents in this direction universally acknowledged, and for the next ten years Morton was pre-eminently the persuader and proselytiser of weak-kneed Catholics.

When a man achieves such a reputation as this, to

justify and to maintain it becomes a passion. Queen Elizabeth had given express commands that the Papists in Yorkshire should be enticed into the national fold by the gentlest means; *nolo mortem peccatoris*, she had said to Lord Sheffield. For this purpose Morton was the chosen instrument, and we can easily believe that he would peculiarly rejoice in gently securing for the Anglican communion so powerful, brilliant, and unusual a young man as Donne. In their long talks together, of which the *Pseudo-Martyr* gives us an idea, he had found no irresistible prejudice in Donne's mind, but rather an indifferency, a lack of conviction, a total want of compelling zeal. But doubtless, with his generous perspicacity, Morton looked ahead, and saw a Donne more advanced and settled than Donne could find in his own bosom. At all events, the step into Anglican orders was one which Donne could not honestly take at present. But he had now been brought to the door of the Church of England; he needed but conviction and a call to open it. These were somewhat slow to come, but they were now upon their journey. Nor can we to-day explain more reasonably Donne's strange reluctance to respond to the heavenly voices calling—

"Dunque che è? perchè, perchè ristai?"

It would appear that in the summer of 1607 Donne received encouragement, or even a command, to correspond with Mrs. Herbert. He entered with alacrity into the engagement, and promised, as will be seen, letters by hundreds and fifties. These which we now print were preserved by Izaak Walton, who published them as an appendix to his *Life of George Herbert*. (Another, although dated by Walton July 11, 1607, probably belongs to a different month, and will be given later on.) Walton had more of the correspondence, but did not print it, and the originals doubtless perished among Lady Cook's collection of MSS. when Higham House was burned by the Roundheads. Mrs. Herbert was Magdalen, the widow of Richard Herbert, of Montgomery Castle, himself the son of Sir Edward Herbert, who died in 1593. Richard survived his father but three years, leaving in their early infancy ten children, two at least of whom were afterwards to attain high and varied celebrity. Their mother was a woman eminent alike for her piety and her beauty. Mrs. Herbert, who had been the daughter and heiress of Sir Richard Newport, devoted herself to the education of her children, of whom the eldest was Edward, the future Lord Herbert of Cherbury, born in 1583, while the fifth son was George, the poet of *The Temple*. The circumstances of the connection of this lady with Donne have been told by Izaak Walton in his *Life of Mr. George Herbert*, in terms which may be here repeated :—

"In this time of her widowhood, she being desirous to give Edward, her eldest son, such advantages of learning and other education as might suit his birth and fortune, and thereby make him the more fit for the service of his country, did, at his being of a fit age, remove from Montgomery Castle with him, and some of her younger sons, to Oxford; and having entered Edward into Queen's College, and provided him a fit tutor, she commended him to his care; yet she continued there with him, and still kept him in a moderate awe of herself, and so much under her own eye, as to see and converse with him daily; but she managed this power over him without any such rigid sourness as might make her company a torment to her child; but with such a sweetness and compliance with the recreations and pleasures of youth as did incline him willingly to spend much of his time in the company of his dear and careful mother; which was to her great content: for she would often say, 'That as our bodies take a nourishment suitable to the meat on which we feed, so our souls as insensibly take in vice by the example or conversation with wicked company': and would therefore as often say, 'That ignorance of vice was the best preservation of virtue; and that the very knowledge of wickedness was as tinder to inflame and kindle sin, and to keep it burning.' For these reasons she endeared him to her own company, and continued with him in Oxford four years, in which time her great and harmless wit, her cheerful gravity, and her obliging behaviour gained her an acquaintance and friendship with most of any eminent worth or learning that were at that time in or near that University, and particularly with Mr. John Donne, who then came accidentally to that place, in this time of her being there."

Walton is hopelessly confusing as to his dates in this passage, and he presently tells us that the "amity" between Donne and Magdalen Herbert began "in a happy time for him, he being then near to the fortieth year of his age," a statement which brings us to 1612, and is absolutely unintelligible.

The remainder of Walton's evidence on this subject, however, is interesting and important, and we must quote from him again:—

"There might be more demonstrations of the friendship and the many sacred endearments betwixt these two excellent persons (for I have many of their letters in my hand), and much more might be said of her great prudence and piety."

The letters now following were selected by Walton to illustrate his *Life of George Herbert*. We shall have frequent occasion to dwell on Donne's intimacy with this illustrious family. It is enough to point out here that, although he may, as Walton thought, have met Mrs. Herbert at Oxford some years earlier, this correspondence seems to mark the commencement of their real intimacy.

"*To the Worthiest Lady* Mistress MAGDALEN HERBERT.

"MADAM,—Every excuse hath in it somewhat of accusation; and since I am innocent, and yet must excuse, how shall I do for that part of accusing? By my troth, as desperate and perplexed men grow from thence bold, so must I take the boldness of accusing you, who would draw so dark a curtain betwixt me and your purposes, as that I had no glimmering, neither of your goings, nor the way which my letters might haunt. Yet have I given this licence to travel, but I know not whither, nor it. It is therefore rather a pinnace to discover; and the entire

colony of letters, of hundreds and fifties, must follow; whose employment is more honourable than that which our State meditates to Virginia, because you are worthier than all of that country, of which that is a wretched inch; for you have better treasure, and a harmlessness. If this sound like a flattery, tear it out. I am to my letters as rigid as a Puritan, as Cæsar was to his wife. I can as ill endure a suspicion and misinterpretable word as a fault. But remember that nothing is flattery which the speaker believes; and of the grossest flattery there is this good use, that they tell us what we should be. But, madam, you are beyond instruction, and therefore there can belong to you only praises; of which, though you be no good hearer, yet allow all my letters leave to have in them one part of it, which is thankfulness towards you.—Your unworthiest servant, except your accepting have mended him,
JOHN DONNE.
"Micham, *July* 11, 1607."

"*To the Worthiest Lady* Mrs. MAGDALEN HERBERT.

"MADAM,—This is my second letter, in which, though I cannot tell you what is good, yet this is the worst, that I must be a great part of it; yet to me, that is recompensed, because you must be mingled. After I knew you were gone (for I must little less than accusingly tell you, I knew not you would go), I sent my first letter, like a Bevis of Hampton, to seek adventures. This day I came to town, and to the best part of it, your house; for your memory is a state-cloth and presence, which I reverence, though you be away; though I need not seek that there, which I have about and within me. There, though I found my accusation, yet anything to which your hand is, is a pardon: yet I would not burn my first letter; because as in great destiny no small passage can be omitted or frustrated, so, in my resolution of writing almost daily to you I would have no link of the chain broken by me, both because my letters interpret one another, and because only their number can give them weight. If I had your commission and instructions to do you the service of a lieger ambassador here, I could say something of the Countess of Devon, of the States, and such things. But since to you, who are not only a world alone, but the monarchy of the world yourself, nothing can be added, especially by me, I will sustain myself with the honour of being, your servant extraordinary, and without place, JOHN DONNE.

"London, *July* 23, 1607."

"*To the Worthiest Lady* Mrs. MAGDALEN HERBERT.

"MADAM,—As we must die before we can have full glory and happiness, so before I can have this degree of it, as to see you by a letter, I must also die, that is, come to London, to plaguy London—a place full of danger and vanity and vice, though the Court be gone; and such it will be till your return redeem it. Not that the greatest virtue in the world, which is you, can be such a marshal as to defeat or disperse all the vice of this place; but as higher bodies remove, or contract themselves, when better come, so at your return we shall have one door open to innocence. Yet, madam, you are not such an Ireland as produceth neither ill nor good; no spiders nor nightingales, which is a rare degree of perfection. But you have found and practised that experiment that even Nature, out of her detesting of emptiness, if we will make that our work to remove bad, will fill us with good things. To abstain from it was therefore but the childhood and minority of your soul, which had been long exercised since, in your manlier active part of doing good. Of which since I have been a witness and subject, not to tell you sometimes, that by your influence and example I have attained to such a step of goodness, as to be thankful, were loth to accuse your power and judgment of impotency and infirmity.— Your Ladyship's in all services, JOHN DONNE.

"*August* 2, 1607."

The following letter to Mrs. Magdalen Herbert is dated by Walton "July 11, 1607"; this, however, is an impossible date, as the correspondence with that lady already printed proves. Whatever may be its exact date, this graceful epistle suits very well with the year 1607, and I therefore give it in this place, though with no assurance of correctness.

"*To* Mrs. MAGDALEN HERBERT.

"MADAM,—Your favours to me are everywhere; I use them and have them. I enjoy them at London, and leave them there, and yet find them at Mitcham. Such riddles as these become things inexpressible; and such is your goodness. I was almost sorry to find your servant here this day, because I was loth to have any witness of my not coming home last night, and indeed of my coming this morning. But my not coming was excusable, because earnest business detained me; and my coming this day is by the example of your St. Mary Magdalen, who rose early upon Sunday to seek that which she loved most; and so did I. And, from her and myself, I return such thanks as are due to one to whom we owe all the good opinion that they whom we need most have of us. By this messenger, and on this good day, I commit the enclosed holy hymns and sonnets (which for the matter, not the workmanship, have yet escaped the fire) to your judgment, and to your protection too, if you think them worthy of it; and I have appointed this enclosed sonnet to usher them to your happy hand.—Your unworthiest servant, unless your accepting him to be so have mended him, Jo. DONNE."

To the Lady MAGDALEN HERBERT.
Of St. Mary Magdalen.

HER of your name, whose fair inheritance
  Bethina was, and jointure Magdalo,
An active faith so highly did advance,
  That she once knew more than the Church did know,
The resurrection; so much good there is
  Deliver'd of her, that some fathers be
Loth to believe one woman could do this;
  But think these Magdalens were two or three.

> Increase their number, Lady, and their fame :
>   To their devotion add your innocence :
> Take so much of th' example, as of the name ;
>   The latter half ; and in some recompense
> That they did harbour Christ Himself a guest,
> Harbour these hymns, to His dear name addrest.
>
> J. D.

Meanwhile, with little expectation of further employment from Morton, who would retire to his Deanery, and with his applications for court posts invariably postponed or rejected, Donne fell into grievous depression and poverty. This condition reached an almost intolerable climax in 1608, but before dwelling upon it, we have to print certain letters, mainly addressed to Sir Henry Goodyer, which show something of the mind of Donne and its lack of preparation for the clerical discipline. Of these, the first is a kind of essay on epistolary friendship, and seems to mark the opening of that regular weekly correspondence with Sir Henry Goodyer to which we owe so much enlightenment.

"*To* Sir H[ENRY] G[OODYER].[1]

"SIR,—In the history or style of friendship, which is best written both in deeds and words, a letter which is of a mixed nature, and hath something of both, is a mixed parenthesis ; it may be left out, yet it contributes, though not to the being, yet to the verdure and freshness thereof. Letters have truly the same office as oaths. As these amongst light and empty men are but fillings and pauses and interjections ; but with weightier they are sad attestations. So are letters to some complement, and obligation to others.

"For mine, as I never authorised my servant to lie in my behalf (for if it were officious in him, it might be worse in me), so I allow my letters much less that civil dishonesty, both because they go from me more considerately and because they are permanent ; for in them I may speak to you in your chamber a year hence before I know not whom and not hear my self. They shall therefore ever keep the

---

[1] From the *Letters* of 1651.

sincerity and intemperateness of the fountain, whence they are derived. And as wheresoever these leaves fall, the root is in my heart, so shall they, as that sucks good affections towards you there, have ever true impressions thereof.

"Thus much information is in very leaves, that they can tell what the tree is, and these can tell you I am a friend and an honest man. Of what general use the fruit should speak, and I have none; and of what particular profit to you, your application and experimenting should tell you, and you can make none of such a nothing; yet even of barren sycamores, such as I, there were use, if either any light flashings, or scorching vehemencies, or sudden showers, made you need so shadowy an example or remembrancer. But (Sir) your fortune and mind do you this happy injury, that they make all kind of fruits useless unto you. Therefore I have placed my love wisely where I need communicate nothing. All this, though perchance you read it not till Michaelmas, was told you at Mitcham, 15th August, 1607."

In this next letter, which is neither signed nor dated, but which I incline to attribute to the summer of 1607, we find Donne for the first time definitely distinguishing himself from the Roman Catholics, and speaking of the English Church as "ours." This, at least, Morton's generous and impulsive action had accomplished; it had tired Donne of hanging in a no-man's land between the rival religious bodies, and had brought him definitely into that which was for the future to be his home. The entertainment of the French Prince no doubt refers to the visit to England of the Prince de Joinville, brother of the Duc de Guise, who was here for four or five weeks in May and June 1607.

"*To* Sir H[ENRY] G[OODYER].[1]

"This Tuesday morning, which hath brought me to London, presents me with all your letters. Methought it was a rent day, I mean such as yours, and not as mine; and

[1] From the *Letters* of 1651.

yet such too, when I considered how much I owed you for them, how good a mother, how fertile and abundant the understanding is, if she have a good father; and how well friendship performs that office. For that which is denied in other generations is done in this of yours: for here is superfetation, child upon child, and that which is more strange, twins at a latter conception.

"If in my second religion, friendship, I had a conscience, either *errantem* to mistake good and bad and indifferent, or *opinantem* to be ravished by other's opinions or examples, or *dubiam* to adhere to neither part, or *scrupulosam* to incline to one, but upon reasons light in themselves, or undiscussed in me (which are almost all the diseases of conscience), I might mistake your often, long, and busy letters, and fear you did but entreat me to have mercy upon you and spare you; for you know our Court took the resolution, that it was the best way to despatch the French Prince back again quickly, to receive him solemnly, ceremoniously, and expensively, when he hoped a domestic and durable entertainment.

"I never meant to excel you in weight nor price, but in number and bulk I thought I might, because he may cast up a greater sum who hath but forty small monies, than he with twenty Portugueses. The memory of friends (I mean only for letters) neither enters ordinarily into busied men, because they are ever employed within, nor into men of pleasure, because they are never at home. For these wishes therefore which you won out of your pleasure and recreation, you were as excusable to me if you write seldom, as Sir H. Wotton is, under the oppression of business, or the necessity of seeming so; or more than he, because I hope you have both pleasure and business: only to me, who have neither, this omission were sin; for though writing be not of the precepts of friendship, but of the counsels, yet, as in some cases to some men counsels become precepts, and though not immediately from God, yet very roundly and quickly from His Church (as selling and dividing goods in the first time, continence in the Roman Church, and order and decency in ours), so to me who can do nothing else, it seems to bind my conscience to write; and it is sin to do against the conscience, though that err.

"Yet no man's letters might be better wanted than mine, since my whole letter is nothing else but a confession that I should and would write. I owed you a letter in verse before by mine own promise, and now that you think that you have hedged in that debt by a greater by your letter in verse, I think it now most seasonable and fashionable for me to break. At least, to write presently, were to accuse myself of not having read yours so often as such a letter deserves from you to me.

"To make my debt greater (for such is the desire of all, who cannot or mean not to pay) I pray read these two problems: for such light flashes as these have been my hawkings in my Surrey[1] journeys. I accompany them with another rag of verses, worthy of that name for the smallness, and age, for it hath long lain among my other papers, and laughs at them that have adventured to you: for I think till now you saw it not, and neither you nor it should repent it. Sir, if I were anything, my love to you might multiply it, and dignify it: but infinite nothings are but one such; yet since even chimeras have some name and titles, I am also   Yours."

[*July* ? 1607.]

The copy of verses exists, an epistle in the four-line stanza of Sir John Davys' *Nosce Teipsum*. From its dignified appeal to the higher life some passages may here be given, in illustration of the relations existing between the two friends. Donne, who saw Goodyer open-handed, genial, and intelligent, but lacking in sobriety, spares not his affectionate exhortations—

> "Who makes the last a pattern for next year
> Turns no new leaf, but still the same thing reads;
> Seen things he sees again, heard things doth hear,
> And makes his life but like a pair of beads.
> . . . .

---

[1] Misprinted "sorry" in the printed copy.

> So had your body her morning, hath her noon,
>   And shall not better; her next change is night;
> But her fair, larger guest, to whom sun and moon
>   Are sparks and short-liv'd, claims another right.
>
> The noble soul by age grows lustier;
>   Her appetite and her digestion mend.
> We must not starve, nor hope to pamper her
>   With women's milk, and pap, until the end.
>
> Provide you manlier diet. You have seen
>   All libraries, which are schools, camps and courts;
> But ask your garners if you have not been
>   In harvest too indulgent to your sports."

He advises Goodyer to go abroad to recover the exhaustion of his fortunes, but the recommendation came too late. From this time forth the knight's difficulties seem to have grown upon him steadily. Donne has not much hope that his friend's easy, graceful faults will ever mend; but he has too much tact to scold him—

> "However, keep the lively taste you hold
>   Of God; love Him as now, but fear Him more;
> And in your afternoons think what you told
>   And promised Him, at morning prayer before."

And the epistle closes, very pleasantly, with one of those directly personal touches which make the whole relation suddenly a living one to us—

> "But thus I make you keep your promise, sir;
>   Riding I had you, tho' you still stay'd there;
> And in these thoughts, altho' you never stir,
>   You came with me to Mitcham, and are here."

We may notice, as a fresh anxiety to Donne, that the loss of means which is plainly spoken of in this poem came to Sir Henry Goodyer at the very time when his friend was beginning most to need the help he could no longer supply.

The friend addressed in the following highly elaborate specimen of Jacobean letter-writing was Sir Thomas Lucy of Charlcote, a young man at this time not much more than twenty-one years of age. He was the grandson of Shakespeare's man, and the son of another Sir Thomas, who had died in 1605. This latter gentleman had cultivated intellectual tastes, and had collected a large library of French and Italian books, which it was his son's pride to tend and augment. The mother of Sir Thomas Lucy was Constantia Kingsmill, whose family was connected in friendship with Donne. It is possible that Donne had been employed to read with Sir Thomas Lucy, who was intimate with the Herberts, as we shall see later on. Lucy presently married Alice, granddaughter of Sir John Spencer of Althorpe, niece of Lady Derby and cousin of her daughters. In 1608 Lucy travelled with Edward Herbert in France for a year, and was involved with him in many romantic adventures; he does not seem to have been in London again until 1610.

"*To my honoured friend* Sir T. LUCY.

"SIR,—I make account that the writing of letters, when it is with any seriousness, is a kind of ecstasy, and a departure and secession and suspension of the soul, which doth then communicate itself to two bodies: and as I would every day provide for my soul's last convoy, though I know not when I shall die, and perchance I shall never die; so for these ecstasies in letters, I oftentimes deliver myself over in writing when I know not when those letters shall be sent to you, and many times they never are, for I have a little satisfaction in seeing a letter written to you upon my table, though I meet no opportunity of sending it.

"Especially this summer, when either by my early retiring home, or your irresolutions of your own purposes, or some other possessions of yours you did less reveal to me your progresses and stations, and where I might cross you by letters, than heretofore: I make shift to lay little fault upon you, because my pardon might be easier, if I transgress into a longer and busier letter than your country sports admit; but you may read it in winter.

"And by that time I may more clearly express myself

for those things which have entered into me, concerning your soul: for as the greatest advantage which man's soul is thought to have beyond others, is that which they call *Actum reflexum*, and *iteratum* (for beasts do the same things as we do, but they do not consider nor remember the circumstances and inducements; and by what power and faculty it is that they do them), so of those which they call *Actum reflexum* the noblest is that which reflects upon the soul itself, and considers and meditates it, into which consideration when I walk after my slow and unperfect pace, I begin to think that as litigious men tired with suits admit any arbitrament, and princes travailed with long and wasteful war descend to such conditions of peace as they are soon after ashamed to have embraced; so philosophers, and so all sects of Christians, after long disputations and controversies, have allowed many things for positive and dogmatical truths which are not worthy of that dignity; and so many doctrines have grown to be the ordinary diet and food of our spirits, and have place in the pap of catechisms, which were admitted but as physic in that present distemper, or accepted in a lazy weariness, when men so they might have something to rely upon, and to excuse themselves from more painful inquisition, never examined what that was. To which indisposition of ours the casuists are so indulgent, as that they allow a conscience to adhere to any probable opinion against a more probable, and do never bind him to seek out which is the more probable, but give him leave to dissemble it and to depart from it, if by mischance he come to know it.

"This, as it appears in all sciences, so most manifestly in physic, which for a long time considering nothing but plain curing, and that but by example and precedent, the world at last longed for some certain canons and rules, how these cures might be accomplished; and when men are inflamed with this desire, and that such a fire breaks out that rages and consumes infinitely by heat of argument, except some of authority interpose.

"This produced Hippocrates his Aphorisms; and the world slumbered or took breath in his resolution divers hundreds of years: and then in Galen's time, which was not satisfied with the effect of curing, nor with the knowledge how to cure, broke out another desire of finding out the causes why those simples wrought those effects. Then Galen, rather to stay their stomachs than that he gave them enough, taught them the qualities of the four elements, and arrested them upon this, that all differences of qualities proceeded from them.

"And after (not much before our time), men perceiving that all effects in physic could not be derived from these beggarly and impotent properties of the elements, and that therefore they were driven often to that miserable refuge of specific form, and of antipathy and sympathy, we see the world hath turned upon new principles which are attributed to Paracelsus, but (indeed) too much to his honour.

"Certainly it is also so in the physic of our soul, divinity, for in the Primitive Church, when amongst the Fathers there were so divers opinions of the state of the soul, presently after this life, they easily inclined to be content to do as much for them dead as when they were alive, and so concurred in a charitable disposition to pray for them; which manner of prayer then in use no Christian Church at this day, having received better light, will allow of.

"So also when in the beginning of S. Augustine's time, grace had been so much advanced that man's nature was scarce admitted to be so much as any means or instrument (not only no kind of cause) of his own good works: and soon after in S. Augustine's time also man's free-will (by fierce opposition and arguing against the former error) was too much over-valued, and admitted into too near degrees of fellowship with grace: those times admitted a doctrine and form of reconciliation which, though for reverence to the time, both the Dominicans and Jesuits at this day in their great quarrel about grace and free-will would yet seem to maintain; yet indifferent and dispassioned men of that Church see there is no possibility in it, and therefore accuse it of absurdity and almost of heresy.

"I think it falls out thus also in the matter of the soul; for Christian religion presuming a soul, and intending principally her happiness in the life to come, hath been content to accept any way which hath been obtruded, how this soul is begun in us. Hence it is that whole Christian Churches arrest themselves upon propagation from parents; and other whole Christian Churches allow only infusion from God. In both which opinions there appear such infirmities as it is time to look for a better; for whosoever will adhere to the way of propagation, can never evict necessarily and certainly a natural immortality in the soul, if the soul result out of matter, nor shall he ever prove that all mankind hath any more than one soul: as certainly of all beasts, if they receive such souls as they have from their parents, every species can have but one soul. And they which follow the opinion of infusion from God, and of a new creation (which is now the more common opinion), as they can very hardly defend the doctrine of original sin (the soul is forced to take this infection, and comes not into the body of her own disposition), so shall they never be able to prove that all those whom we see in the shape of men have an immortal and reasonable soul, because our parents are as able as any other species is to give us a soul of growth and of sense, and to perform all vital and animal functions.

"And so without infusion of such a soul may produce a creature as wise and well disposed as any horse or elephant, of which degree many whom we see come far short; nor hath God bound or declared Himself that He will always create a soul for every embryon, there is yet therefore no opinion in philosophy nor divinity so well established as constrains us to believe both that the soul is immortal, and that every particular man hath such a soul, which, since out of the great mercy of our God we do constantly believe, I am ashamed that we do not also know it by searching further.

"But as sometimes we had rather believe a traveller's lie than go to disprove him, so men rather cleave to these ways than seek new: yet because I have meditated therein, I will shortly acquaint you with what I think, for I would not be in danger of that law of Moses, That if a man dig a pit and cover it not, he must recompense those which are damnified by it, which is often interpreted of such as shake old opinions, and do not establish new as certain, but leave consciences in a worse danger than they found them in. I believe that law of Moses hath in it some mystery and appliableness, for by that law men are only then bound to that indemnity and compensation if an ox or an ass (that is, such as are of a strong constitution and accustomed to labour) fall therein, but it is not said so if a sheep or a goat fall; no more are we, if men in a silliness or wantonness will stumble or take a scandal, bound to rectify them at all times. And therefore because I justly presume you strong and watchful enough, I make account that I am not obnoxious to that law, since my meditations are neither too wide nor too deep for you, except only that my way of expressing them may be extended beyond your patience and pardon, which I will therefore tempt no longer at this time.

"Your very affectionate friend and servant and lover,
"J. DONNE.
"From Mitcham, my close prison ever since I saw you, 9th *October* [1607]."

Dr. Jessopp kindly points out to me that any one who feels curiosity regarding the transcendental question discussed in the central part of this letter, or who desires information upon the history of the controversy alluded to, will find a very full and most learned discussion and summary of it in Pererius' *Commentary on Genesis*, ii. 7.

"*To* Sir H[ENRY] G[OODYER].[1]

"SIR,—Nature hath made all bodies alike, by mingling and kneading up the same elements in every one. And amongst men, the other nature, custom, hath made every mind like some other; we are patterns or copies, we inform or imitate. But as he hath not presently attained to write a good hand which hath equalled one excellent Master in his *A*, another in his *B*, much less he which

[1] *Letters* of 1651.

hath sought all the excellent Masters, and employed all his time to exceed in one letter, because not so much an excellency of any, nor every one, as an evenness and proportion, and respect to one another gives the perfection; so is no man virtuous by particular example.

"Not he that doth all actions to the pattern of the most valiant, or liberal, which histories afford; nor he which chooses from every one their best actions, and thereupon doth something like those. Perchance such may be *in via perficiendorum*, which divines allow to monastical life, but not *perfectorum*, which by them is only due to prelacy. For virtue is even, and continual, and the same, and can therefore break nowhere, nor admit ends nor beginnings; it is not only not broken, but not tied together.

"He is not virtuous, out of whose actions you can pick an excellent one. Vice and her fruits may be seen, because they are thick bodies, but not virtue, which is all light; and vices have swellings and fits, and noise, because being extremes, they dwell far asunder, and they maintain both a foreign war against virtue, and a civil against one another, and affect sovereignty, as virtue doth society. The later physicians say, that when our natural inborn preservative is corrupted or wasted, and must be restored by a like extracted from other bodies; the chief care is that the mummy have in it no excelling quality, but an equally digested temper.

"And such is true virtue. But men who have preferred money before all, think they deal honourably with virtue if they compare her with money: and think that as money is not called base till the alloy exceed the pure; so they are virtuous enough if they have enough to make their actions current, which is, if either they get praise, or (in a lower abasing) if they incur not infamy or penalty. But you know who said, *Angusta innocentia est ad legem bonum esse:* which rule being given for positive laws, severe mistakers apply even to God's law, and (perchance against His commandment) bind themselves to His counsels, beyond His laws. But they are worse that think that because some men, formerly wasteful, live better with half their rents than they did with all, being now advantaged with discretion and experience, therefore our times need less moral virtue than the first, because we have Christianity, which is the use and application of all virtue: as though our religion were but an art of thrift, to make a little virtue go far. For as plentiful springs are fittest, and best become large aqueducts, so doth much virtue such a steward and officer as a Christian.

"But I must not give you a homily for a letter. I said a great while since, that custom made men like; we who have been accustomed to one another are like in this, that we love not business: this therefore shall not be to you nor me a busy letter. I end with a problem, whose errand is, to ask for his fellows. I pray before you engulf yourself in the progress, leave them for me, and such other of my papers as you will lend me till you return. And besides this allegorical lending, lend me truly your counsels, and love God and me, whilst I love Him and you."

"*To the best Knight* Sir H. Wotton.[1]

"Sir,—When I saw your good Countess last, she let me think that her message by her footman would hasten you up. And it furthered that opinion in me, when I knew how near M. Mathews' day of departing this kingdom was. To counterpoise both these, I have a little letter from you brought to me to Mitcham yesterday, but left at my lodging two days sooner, and because that speaks nothing of your return, I am content to be perplexed in it; and as in all other, so in this perplexity to do that which is safest.

"To me it is safest to write, because it performs a duty and leaves my conscience well: and though it seem not safest for the letter, which may perish, yet I remember that in the Crociate [Crusade] for the wars in the Holy Land, and so in all pilgrimages enterprised in devotion, he which dies in the way enjoys all the benefit and indulgences which the end did afford. Howsoever, all that can increase the danger of your letter increase my merit, for, as where they immolate

[1] *Letters* of 1651.

men, it is a scanter devotion to sacrifice one of many slaves, or of many children, or an only child, than to beget and bring up one purposely to sacrifice it, so if I ordain this letter purposely for destruction, it is the largest expressing of that kind of piety, and I am easy to believe (because I wish it) your haste hither.

"Not that I can fear any slackness in that business which drew you down, because your fortune and honour are a pair of good spurs to it; but here also you have both true business and many *quasi negotia*, which go two and two to a business; which are visitations, and such, as though they be not full businesses, yet are so near them that they serve as for excuses in omissions of the other. As when abjurations was in use in this land, the State and law were satisfied if the abjuror came to the seaside and waded into the sea when winds and tides resisted; so we think ourselves justly excusable to our friends and ourselves if, when we should do business, we come to the place of business, as Courts and the houses of great princes and officers.

"I do not so much intimate your infirmity in this as frankly confess mine own. The master of Latin language says, *Oculi et aures aliorum te speculantur et custodiunt*. So those two words are synonymous, and only the observation of others upon me is my preservation from extreme idleness, else I profess that I hate business so much, as I am sometimes glad to remember, that the Roman Church reads that verse *A negotio perambulante in tenebris*, which we read 'from the pestilence walking by night,' so equal to me do the plague and business deserve avoiding, but you will neither believe that I abhor business if I enlarge this letter, nor that I would afford you that ease which I affect: therefore return to your pleasures.

"Your unprofitablest friend,
"Jo. Donne.

"*March* 14, 1607[8]."

"It is my third letter, which I tell you, because I found not Mr. Rogers, but left the letter which I sent last with a stranger at Clifford's Inn."

In the foregoing letter Tobie Matthew is mentioned; we shall presently recur to his name.

"*To a Person of Honour.*[1]

"Sir,—Though my friendship be good for nothing else, it may give you the profit of a tentation, or of an affliction; it may excuse your patience; and though it cannot allure, it shall importune you. Though I know you have many worthy friends of all ranks, yet I add something, since I which am of none, would fain be your friend too. There is some of the honour and some of the degrees of a Creation to make a friendship of nothing.

"Yet, not to annihilate myself utterly (for though it seem humbleness, yet it is a work of as much almightiness to bring a thing to nothing as from nothing), though I be not of the best stuff for friendship, which men of warm and durable fortunes only are, I cannot say that I am not of the best fashion, if truth and honesty be that, which I must ever exercise towards you, because I learned it of you; for the conversation with worthy men, and of good example, though it sow not virtue in us, yet produceth and ripeneth it.

"Your man's haste and mine to Mitcham cuts off this letter here; yet, as in little patterns torn from a whole piece, this may tell you what all I am. Though by taking me before my day, which I accounted Tuesday, I make short payment of this duty of letters, yet I have a little comfort in this, that you see me hereby willing to pay those debts which I can before my time.

"Your affectionate friend,
"J. Donne.

"First Saturday in
  March 1607[8]."

"You forget to send me the 'Apology'; and many times I think it an injury to remember one of a promise, lest it confess a distrust. But of the book, by occasion of

[1] *Letters* of 1651.

reading the Dean's answer to it, I have sometimes some want."

The Dean, of course, is Thomas Morton, now Dean of Gloucester. The "Apology" was Robert Parsons' *Treatise tending towards Mitigation.* The general tenor of the postscript gives us the impression that Donne's work for Morton was even yet not absolutely concluded. He was probably helping the Dean to prepare his final shot at the Jesuits, *A Preamble unto an Encounter with P. R.*, which appeared in 1608, and closed this particular section of the Dean of Gloucester's controversial writings.

We now reach a little group of letters which belong to the early months of the next year. The "last of 1607" was what we should call March 24, 1608. The person addressed is Sir Thomas Roe. "The Mask" must have been Ben Jonson's *The Hue and Cry after Cupid*, prepared at Court for Lord Haddington's marriage with Lady Elizabeth Radcliffe on Shrove Tuesday.

"*To* Sir T[HOMAS] R[OE].

"SIR,—I have bespoke you a New Year's gift, that is, a good New Year, for I have offered your name with my soul heartily to God in my morning's best sacrifice. If for custom you will do a particular office in recompense, deliver this letter to your Lady now, or when the rage of 'The Mask' is past. If you make any haste into the country, I pray let me know it. I would kiss your hands before you go, which I do now, and continue your affectionate servant and lover, J. DONNE.

"Mitcham, the last of 1607,
  as I remember."

"*To* Sir H[ENRY] G[OODYER].[1]

"SIR,—I cannot obey you if you go to-morrow to Parson's Green; your company, that place, and my promise

[1] *Letters* of 1651.

are strong inducements; but an ague flouts them all, of which I have had two such threatenings, that I provide against it by a little physic. This is one fetter; but I have a pair; for I attend Sir George More's answer in a little business, of which I can have no account till his return, so I am fastened here till after Sunday. As you are sure that I love you thoroughly, so think this a good expressing of that, that I promise now that I will certainly go with you on Monday, in despite of these interruptions, and serve you with my company to the Bath, which journey it is time to hasten. But I pray think this promise so much worth, that it may deserve your coming this way on Monday, for I make it with that reservation. God send you hawks and fortunes of a high pitch.—Your honest affectionate   J. DONNE."

The next letter, which I attribute conjecturally to the spring of 1608, was headed by John Donne the younger "To Sir H. G." There is, however, one great difficulty in the way of accepting this address, namely, that the letter speaks of the health of the recipient's father. But Sir William Goodyer had died in 1578, and Sir Henry's wife's father was also dead. The letter, to whomever it may have been addressed, is of particular value on account of the revelation it gives of Donne's temperament, his liveliness in company, his violent freakish high spirits, followed in solitude by equally violent depressions, by what Gray long afterwards called a mechanical dejection. No better phrase could be found to describe the animation of a sociable, highly nervous man in congenial society than this, "I kindle squibs about me, and fly into sportfulness and company." But the letter [1] is also important as foreshadowing the state of nervous disease or at least acute discomfort into which he was presently to fall:—

"SIR,—I hope you are now welcome to London, and well, and well comforted in your father's health and love, and well contented that we ask you how you do, and tell

[1] From the *Letters* of 1651.

you how we are, which yet I cannot of myself. If I knew that I were ill, I were well; for we consist of three parts, a soul, and body, and mind: which I call those thoughts and affections, and passions, which neither soul nor body hath alone, but have been begotten by their communication, as music results out of our breath and a cornet.

"And of all these the diseases are cures, if they be known. Of our soul's sicknesses, which are sins, the knowledge is to acknowledge, and that is her physic, in which we are not dieted by drams and scruples, for we cannot take too much. Of our body's infirmities, though our knowledge be partly *ab extrinseco*, from the opinion of the physician, and that the subject and matter be flexible and various, yet their rules are certain, and if the matter be rightly applied to the rule, our knowledge thereof is also certain.

"But, of the diseases of the mind there is no criterion, no canon, no rule, for our own taste and apprehension and interpretation should be the judge, and that is the disease itself. Therefore sometimes when I find myself transported with jollity and love of company, I hang leads at my heels, and reduce to my thoughts my fortunes, my years, the duties of a man, of a friend, of a husband, of a father, and all the incumbencies of a family; when sadness dejects me, either I countermine it with another sadness, or I kindle squibs about me again, and fly into sportfulness and company: and I find ever after all, that I am like an exorcist, which had long laboured about one, which at last appears to have the mother, that I still mistake my disease.

"And I still vex myself with this, because if I know it not, nobody can know it. And I comfort myself because I see dispassioned men are subject to the like ignorances. For divers minds out of the same thing often draw contrary conclusions, as Augustine thought devout Anthony to be therefore full of the Holy Ghost, because not being able to read, he could say the whole Bible, and interpret it; and Thyreus the Jesuit, for the same reason, doth think all the Anabaptists to be possessed. And as often out of contrary things men draw one conclusion.

"As to the Roman Church, magnificence and splendour hath ever been an argument of God's favour, and poverty and affliction to the Greek. Out of this variety of minds it proceeds, that though our souls would go to one end, heaven, and all our bodies must go to one end, the earth; yet our third part, the mind, which is our natural guide here, chooses to every man a several way: scarce any man likes what another doth, nor advisedly, that which himself.

"But, sir, I am beyond my purpose; I mean to write a letter, and I am fallen into a discourse, and I do not only take you from some business, but I make you a new business by drawing you into these meditations. In which let my openness be an argument of such love as I would fain express in some worthier fashion."

"*To* Sir H[ENRY] G[OODYER].[1]

"SIR,—Because I am in a place and season where I see everything bud forth, I must do so too, and vent some of my meditations to you; the rather because all other buds being yet without taste or virtue, my letters may be like them. The pleasantness of the season displeases me. Everything refreshes, and I wither, and I grow older and not better, my strength diminishes, and my load grows, and being to pass more and more storms, I find that I have not only cast out all my ballast which nature and time gives, reason and discretion, and so am as empty and light as vanity can make me; but I have over-fraught myself with vice, and so am riddingly subject to two contrary racks, sinking and oversetting, and under the iniquity of such a disease as inforces the patient when he is almost starved, not only to fast, but to purge. For I have much to take in, and much to cast out; sometimes I think it easier to discharge myself of vice than of vanity, as one may sooner carry the fire out of a room than the smoke; and then I see it was a new

[1] *Letters* of 1651.

vanity to think so. And when I think sometimes that vanity, because it is thin and airy, may be expelled with virtue or business, or substantial vice; I find that I give entrance thereby to new vices.

"Certainly as the earth and water, one sad, the other fluid, make but one body; so to air and vanity, there is but one *centrum morbi*. And that which later physicians say of our bodies, is fitter for our minds; for that which they call destruction, which is a corruption and want of those fundamental parts whereof we consist, is vice; and that *collectio stercorum*, which is but the excrement of that corruption, is our vanity and indiscretion; both these have but one root in me, and must be pulled out at once or never. But I am so far from digging to it, that I know not where it is, for it is not in mine eyes only, but in every sense, nor in my concupiscence only, but in every power and affection.

"Sir, I was willing to let you see how impotent a man you love, not to dishearten you from doing so still (for my vices are not infectious, nor wandering, they came not yesterday, nor mean to go away to-day; they inn not, but dwell in me, and see themselves so welcome, and find in me so good bad company of one another, that they will not change, especially to one not apprehensive, nor easily accessible); but I do it, that your counsel might cure me, and if you deny that, your example shall, for I will as much strive to be like you as I will wish you to continue good."

The next letter, evidently from Mitcham in the spring of 1608, shows that the melancholy fit was gaining ground. He was becoming more and more cast down by the hopelessness of his fortunes. That his wife was well connected, and that her father, brothers, and sisters were wealthy, was no comfort to the Donnes; they starved in the midst of plenty. According to Walton, they had friends near them at Mitcham who "were bountiful" to them, but the bounty of neighbours is a sore weight upon the pride of a man of thirty-five years, conscious of vast intellectual and moral resources, and yet unable to use them. The work for Morton was over: I suspect that a year or two later the lodging in the Strand was given up for reasons of economy. Donne was miserable in the little thin-walled house at Mitcham, which he calls his "prison" and his "hospital." In one letter he says: "I write from the fireside in my parlour, and in the noise of three gamesome children, and by the side of her whom, because I have transplanted into such a wretched fortune, I must labour to disguise that from her by all such honest devices, as giving her my company and discourse." It is extraordinary that Sir George More, who had shown considerable complaisance in forgiving his daughter, should have been so obstinate in refusing to contribute to her support. Possibly he thought to force his brilliant, eccentric son-in-law to adopt some profession by cutting off supplies, but Donne was not to be affected by such considerations.

It may have been about this time that his "very learned friend," Dr. Lancelot Andrews, lent Donne a printed book, which fell into the hands of the children in the Mitcham house, and was by them torn to pieces. It was a copy of "Mœnus," whatever that might be, and it had already passed to Paris, and on to Frankfort, with Andrews on his travels. I would venture to suggest that by "Mœnus" may be meant Molinus or Molinæus—Pierre du Moulin (1568–1658), with whom Andrews entered into controversy. Donne was obliged to have the whole volume copied, and returned to Andrews in manuscript, accompanied by a set of agreeable apologetic verses. This must have been before Lancelot Andrews was consecrated Bishop of Ely on the 22nd of September 1609, and while he was still Bishop of Chichester. He was by eight years Donne's senior, but is spoken of as one of Donne's particular friends; of this, however, there is little evidence, save what is contained in these whimsical verses.

Perhaps, because of Sir Henry Goodyer's misfortunes, certainly because of the cessation of work for Morton, and the persistent illness in Donne's family, doubtless from other causes now obscure to us, the summer and autumn of 1608 formed a period of unmitigated distress at Mitcham.

This was the nadir of Donne's life, his point of deepest moral and physical wretchedness. But first comes a letter addressed to Sir John Harington, the poet and translator:—

"*To* Sir I. H.[1]

"SIR,—I would not omit this, not commodity, but advantage of writing to you. This emptiness in London dignifies any letter from hence, as in the seasons, earliness and lateness makes the sourness, and after the sweetness of fruits acceptable and gracious. We often excuse and advance mean authors by the age in which they lived, so will your love do this letter; and you will tell yourself that if he which writ it knew wherein he might express his affection, or anything which might have made his letter welcomer, he would have done it.

"As it is, you may accept it so, as we do many china manufactures, of which when we know no use, yet we satisfy our curiosity in considering them, because we knew not how, nor of what matter they were made.

"Near great woods and quarries it is no wonder to see fair houses, but in Holland which wants both, it is. So were it for me who am as far removed from Court and knowledge of foreign passages as this city is now from the face and furniture of a city, to build up a long letter and to write of myself, were but to enclose a poor handful of straw for a token in a letter: yet I will tell you that I am at London only to provide for Monday, when I shall use that favour which my Lady Bedford hath afforded me of giving her name to my daughter; which I mention to you, as well to show that I covet any occasion of a grateful speaking of her favours, as that because I have thought the day is likely to bring you to London, I might tell you that my poor house is in your way and you shall there find such company, as (I think) you will not be loth to accompany to London.

"Your very true friend,

"*August* 6, 1608."   "J. DONNE.

---

[1] From the *Letters* of 1651.

"*To yourself* [George Gerrard?]."[1]

"Sir,—I send you here a translation; but it is not only to believe me, it is a great invention to have understood any piece of this book, whether the gravity of the matter or the poetical form give it his inclination and *principium motus;* you are his centre or his sphere, and to you as to his proper place he addresses himself. Besides that all my things, not only by obligation, but by custom, know that that is the way they should go. I spoke of this to my L[ady] of Bedford, thinking then I had had a copy which I made long since at sea, but because I find it not I have done that again: when you find it not unseasonable, let her see it; and if you can think it fit that a thing that hath either wearied or distasted you should receive so much favour, put it amongst her papers: when you have a new stomach to it, I will provide you quickly a new copy.—Your very true friend and servant and lover,

"J. Donne.

"At my Mitcham Hospital, *August* 10 [1608?]."

"*Probably to* Sir H. Goodyer.

"And the reason why I did not send an answer to your last week's letter was because it then found me under too great a sadness, and at present it is thus with me. There is no one person but myself well of my family; I have already lost half a child, and with that mischance of hers, my wife is fallen into such a discomposure as would afflict her too extremely, but that the sickness of all her other children stupefies her; of one of which, in good faith, I have not much hope; and these meet with a fortune so ill provided for physic and such relief, that if God should ease us with burials, I know not how to perform even that: but I flatter myself with this hope that I am dying too; for I cannot waste faster than by such griefs. As for ——

"From my Hospital at Mitcham,

"*August* 10." "John Donne.

---

[1] *Letters* of 1651.

To the next letter, which Walton quotes in a strangely garbled form, he gives the date September 7 :—

"*To* Sir H. Goodyer.[1]

"Sir,—Every Tuesday I make account that I turn a great hour-glass, and consider that a week's life is run out since I writ. But if I ask myself what I have done in the last watch, or would do in the next, I can say nothing; if I say that I have passed it without hurting any, so may the spider in my window. The primitive monks were excusable in their retirings and enclosures of themselves; for even of them every one cultivated his own garden and orchard, that is, his soul and body, by meditation and manufactures; and they ought [owed] the world no more since they consumed none of her sweetness, nor begot others to burden her. But for me, if I were able to husband all my time so thriftly, as not only not to wound my soul in any minute by actual sin, but not to rob and cozen her by giving any part to pleasure or business, but bestow it all upon her in meditation, yet even in that I should wound her more and contract another guiltiness. As the eagle were very unnatural if because she is able to do it, she should perch a whole day upon a tree, staring in contemplation of the majesty and glory of the sun, and let her young eaglets starve in the nest.

"Two of the most precious things which God hath afforded us here, for the agony and exercise of our sense and spirit, which are a thirst and inhiation after the next life, and a frequency of prayer and meditation in this, are often envenomed and putrified, and stray into a corrupt disease; for as God doth thus occasion, and positively concur to evil, that when a man is purposed to do a great sin, God infuses some good thoughts which make him choose a less sin, or leave out some circumstance which aggravated that; so the devil doth not only suffer but provoke us to some things naturally good, upon condition that we shall omit some other more necessary and more

[1] *Letters* of 1651.

obligatory. And this is his greatest subtlety, because herein we have the deceitful comfort of having done well, and can very hardly spy our error because it is but an insensible omission and no accusing act. With the first of these I have often suspected myself to be overtaken, which is with a desire of the next life; which though I know it is not merely out of a weariness of this, because I had the same desires when I went with the tide, and enjoyed fairer hopes than now; yet I doubt worldly encumbrances have increased it. I would not that death should take me asleep. I would not have him merely seize me, and only declare me to be dead, but win me and overcome me.

"When I must shipwreck, I would do it in a sea where mine impotency might have some excuse; not in a sullen weedy lake, where I could not have so much as exercise for my swimming. Therefore I would fain do something, but that I cannot tell what is no wonder. For to choose is to do; but to be no part of any body is to be nothing. At most, the greatest persons are but great wens and excrescences; men of wit and delightful conversation but as moles for ornament, except they be so incorporated into the body of the world that they contribute something to the sustentation of the whole.

"This I made account that I begun early, when I understood the study of our laws; but was diverted by the worst voluptuousness, which is an hydroptic, immoderate desire of human learning and languages—beautiful ornaments to great fortunes; but mine needed an occupation, and a course which I thought I entered well into when I submitted myself to such a service, as I thought might [have] employed those poor advantages which I had.

"And there I stumbled too, yet I would try again; for to this hour I am nothing, or so little, that I am scarce subject and argument good enough for one of mine own letters; yet I fear, that doth not ever proceed from a good root, that I am so well content to be less, that is dead. You, sir, are far enough from these descents, your virtue keeps you secure, and your natural disposition to mirth will preserve you; but lose none of these holds, a slip is often as dangerous as a bruise, and though you cannot fall to my lowness, yet in a much less distraction you may meet my sadness; for he is no safer which falls from an high tower into the leads, than he which falls from thence to the ground; make therefore to yourself some mark, and go towards it alegrement. Though I be in such a planetary and erratic fortune that I can do nothing constantly, yet you may find some constancy in my constant advising you to it.

"Your hearty true friend,
"J. Donne.

[*September* 1608.]

"I came this evening from Mr. Jones his house in Essex, where Mr. Martin hath been, and left a relation of Captain Whitlock's death, perchance it is no news to you, but it was to me; without doubt want broke him; for when Mr. Holland's company by reason of the plague broke, the Captain sought to be at Mrs. Jones' house, who in her husband's absence declining it, he went in the night, his boy carrying his cloak-bag, on foot to the Lord of Sussex, who going next day to hunt, the Captain not then sick, told him he would see him no more. A chaplain came up to him, to whom he delivered an account of his understanding, and I hope, of his belief, and soon after died; and my Lord hath buried him with his own ancestors. Perchance his life needed a longer sickness, but a man may go faster and safer when he enjoys that daylight of a clear and sound understanding, than in the night or twilight of an ague or other disease. And the grace of Almighty God doth everything suddenly and hastily, but depart from us, it enlightens us, warms us, heats us, ravishes us, at once. Such a medicine, I fear, his inconsideration needed; and I hope as confidently that he had it. As our soul is infused when it is created, and created when it is infused, so at her going out, God's mercy is had by asking, and that is asked by having. Lest your Polesworth carrier should cozen me, I send my man with this letter early to London, whither this Tuesday all the Court come to a christening at Arundel

House, and stay in town so that I will sup with the good Lady, and write again to-morrow to you if anything be occasioned there which concerns you, and I will tell her so; next day they are to return to Hampton, and upon Friday the King to Royston."

The "Lord of Sussex" mentioned in this postscript was Robert Ratcliffe, Earl of Sussex, who had succeeded to the title and to New Hall in 1593. He was probably within the circle of Donne's Twickenham acquaintances, for he afterwards married, in second nuptials, Mrs. Shute, who had been Frances Meautys. He was at this time Lord-Lieutenant of the county of Essex. Captain Whitlock (misprinted Whitcock by John Donne, junior) is Edmund Whitelocke, whose tragic death is described in a letter from Dudley Carleton, dated September 20, 1608. Henry Holland was a contributor, with Donne, to the collection of elegies called forth by the death of Prince Henry; his father, Philemon Holland, was a particular friend of Lord Harington.

"*To* Sir HENRY GOODYER.[1]

"SIR,—It is in our state ever held for a good sign to change prison, and, *nella signoria de mio*, I will think it so, that my sickness hath given me leave to come to my London prison. I made no doubt but my entrance pain (for it was so rather than a sickness, but that my sadness putrified and corrupted it to that name) affected you also; for nearer contracts than general Christianity had made us so much towards one [another], that one part cannot escape the distemper of the other.

"I was therefore very careful, as well to slack any sorrow which my danger might occasion in you, as to give you the comfort of having been heard in your prayers for me, to tell you as soon as my pain remitted what steps I made towards health, which I did last week. This Tuesday morning your man brought me a letter, which (if he had not found me at London) I see he had a hasty commandment to have brought to Mitcham.

[1] From *Letters* of 1651.

"Sir, though my fortune hath made me such as I am, rather a sickness and disease of the world than any part of it, yet I esteemed myself so far from being so to you, as I esteemed you to be far from being so of the world, as to measure men by fortune or events. I am now gone so far towards health, as there is not infirmity enough left in me for an assurance of so much nobleness and truth, as your last letter is to work upon, that might cure a greater indisposition than I am now in. And though if I had died, I had not gone without testimonies of such a disposition in you towards the reparation of my fortune, or preservation of my poor reputation; yet I would live, and be some such thing as you might not be ashamed to love. Your man must send away this hour in which he visits me; and I have not yet (for I came last night) offered to visit my Lady Bedford, and therefore have nothing to say which should make me grudge this straitness of time.

"He tells me he sends again upon Thursday, and therefore I will make an end of this letter, and perfect it then. I doubt my letters have not come duly to your hand, and that I writing in my dungeon of Mitcham without dating, have made the chronology and sequence of my letters perplexed to you; howsoever you shall not be rid of this ague of my letters, though perchance the fit change days. I have received in a narrow compass three of yours, one with the catalogue of your books, another I found here left last Saturday by your man, and this which he brought me this morning. Sir, I dare sit no longer in my waistcoat, nor have anything worth the danger of a relapse to write. I owe you so much of my health, as I would not mingle you in any occasion of repairing it, and therefore here ask leave to kiss your hands, and bid you goodmorrow and farewell.

"Your very true friend and servant,

"J. DONNE."

[1608?]

"*To* Sir H[ENRY] G[OODYER].¹

"SIR,—This letter hath more merit than one of more diligence, for I wrote it in my bed, and with much pain. I have occasion to sit late some nights in my study (which your books make a pretty library), and now I find that that room hath a wholesome emblematic use; for having under it a vault, I make that promise me, that I shall die reading, since my book and a grave are so near. But it hath another unwholesomeness, that by raw vapours rising from thence (for I can impute it to nothing else), I have contracted a sickness which I cannot name nor describe. For it hath so much of a continual cramp, that it wrests the sinews, so much of a tetane, that it withdraws and pulls the mouth, and so much of the gout (which they whose counsel I use, say it is) that it is not like to be cured, though I am too hasty in three days to pronounce it.

"If it be the gout, I am miserable; for that affects dangerous parts, as my neck and breast, and (I think fearfully) my stomach, but it will not kill me yet; I shall be in this world, like a porter in a great house, ever nearest the door, but seldomest abroad; I shall have many things to make me weary, and yet not get leave to be gone. If I go, I will provide by my best means that you suffer not for me in your bonds.

"The estate which I should leave behind me of any estimation, is my poor fame, in the memory of my friends, and therefore I would be curious of it, and provide that they repent not to have loved me.

"Since my imprisonment in my bed, I have made a meditation in verse, which I call a Litany; the word you know imports no other than supplication, but all Churches have one form of supplication by that name. Amongst ancient annals—I mean some eight hundred years—I have met two Litanies in Latin verse, which gave me not the reason of my meditations, for in good faith I thought not upon them then, but they give me a defence, if any man to a layman and a private impute it as a fault, to take

¹ *Letters* of 1651.

such divine and public names, to his own little thoughts. The first of these was made by Ratpertus, a monk of Suevia, and the other by St. Notker, of whom I will give you this note by the way, that he is a private saint for a few parishes; they were both but monks, and the Litanies poor and barbarous enough, yet Pope Nicolas the V. valued their devotion so much, that he canonised both their poems, and commanded them for public service in their Churches. Mine is for lesser chapels, which are my friends; and though a copy of it were due to you now, yet I am so unable to serve myself with writing it for you at this time (being some thirty staves of nine lines), that I must entreat you to take a promise that you shall have the first, for a testimony of that duty which I owe to your love and to myself, who am bound to cherish it by my best offices. That by which it will deserve best acceptation is, that neither the Roman Church need call it defective, because it abhors not the particular mention of the blessed triumphers in heaven, nor the Reformed can discreetly accuse it of attributing more than a rectified devotion ought to do.

"The day before I lay down I was at London, where I delivered your letter for Sir Ed. Conway, and received another for you, with the copy of my book, of which it is impossible for me to give you a copy so soon, for it is not of much less than three hundred pages. If I die, it shall come to you in that fashion that your letter desires it. If I warm again (as I have often seen such beggars as my indisposition is, end themselves soon, and the patient as soon), you and I shall speak together of that before it be too late to serve you in that commandment. At this time I only assure you, that I have not appointed it upon any person, nor ever purposed to print it, which, later, perchance you thought, and grounded your request thereupon.

"A gent. that visited me yesterday told me that our Church hath lost Mr. Hugh Broughton, who is gone to the Roman side. I have known before that Serarius the Jesuit was an instrument from Cardinal Baronius to draw him to Rome to accept a stipend, only to serve the Christian

Churches in controversies with the Jews, without endangering himself to change of his persuasion in particular deductions between these Christian Churches, or being inquired of, or tempted thereunto. And I hope he is no otherwise departed from us. If he be, we shall not escape scandal in it, because, though he be a man of many distempers, yet when he shall come to eat assured bread and to be removed from partialities, to which want drove him, to make himself a reputation and raise up favourers; you shall see in that course of opposing the Jews, he will produce worthy things: and our Church will perchance blush to have lost a soldier fit for that great battle, and to cherish only those single duellisms between Rome and England, or that more single, and almost self-homicide between the unconformed ministers and bishops. I writ to you last week that the plague increased, by which you may see that my letter's————————————————
————————opinion of the song; not that I make such trifles for praise, but because as long as you speak comparatively of it with my own, and not absolutely, so long I am of your opinion even at this time; when I humbly thank God, I ask and have His comfort of sadder meditations; I do not condemn in myself, that I have given my wit such evaporations as those, if they be free from profaneness or obscene provocations.

"Sir, you would pity me if you saw me write, and therefore will pardon me if I write no more: my pain hath drawn my head so much awry, and holds it so, that mine eye cannot follow mine hand. I receive you therefore into my prayers with mine own weary soul and commend myself to yours. I doubt not but next week I shall be good news to you, for I have mending or dying on my side, which is two to one. If I continue thus, I shall have comfort in this, that my B. Saviour, exercising His justice upon my two worldly parts, my fortune and body, reserves all His mercy for that which best tastes it and most needs it, my soul. I profess to you truly, that my loathness to give over now, seems to myself an ill sign that I shall write no more.—Your poor friend and God's poor patient,   Jo. DONNE."

The "book" referred to in the preceding letter is probably the *Biathanatos*, of which I shall presently give a particular account. The allusion to Hugh Broughton does not, unfortunately, supply us with an exact date. Broughton, the Cambrian divine and Hebrew scholar, was one of the curiosities of the age, and a centre round which gossip was always crystallising. He had travelled in Germany with Morton, but at this time he was residing at Middelburg as chaplain to the English colony there. Broughton was supposed to have leanings towards Rome; he had attacked Beza, and was accused of indulging the foibles of recusant disputants. He was a peppery, vain, and whimsical person, and there was incessant rumours that he was going over to the Catholics, tempted by the offer of a cardinal's hat. One of these had doubtless just reached Donne, but all were baseless, and Broughton died in 1612, a loyal member of the Church of England.

For the next letter the indications of date are numerous. Sir Geoffrey Fenton died in Dublin, October 19, 1608. The "Masque for Christmas," upon which the Queen was to meditate, slowly developed into the magnificent *Masque of Queens*, which Ben Jonson wrote, and which was at last performed at Whitehall on the 2nd of February 1609. In this famous pageant several of Donne's "great ladies" took a prominent part, particularly the Countesses of Derby, Huntingdon, and Bedford.

"*To* Sir H[ENRY] G[OODYER].[1]

"SIR,—This 14th of November last I received yours of the 9th, as I was in the street going to sup with my Lady Bedford. I found all that company sore possessed with a wonder why you came not last Saturday. I perceive that as your intermitting your letters to me gave me reason to hope for you, so some more direct address or conscience of your business here had imprinted in them an assurance of your coming; this letter shall but talk, not discourse; it shall but gossip, not consider, nor consult,

[1] *Letters* of 1651.

so it is made half with a prejudice of being lost by the way.

"The King is gone this day for Royston, and hath left with the Queen a commandment to meditate upon a masque for Christmas, so that they grow serious about that already; that will hasten my Lady Bedford's journey, who goes within ten days from hence to her Lord, but by reason of this can make no long stay there.

"Justinian the Venetian is gone hence, and one Carraw come in his place: that State hath taken a fresh offence at a friar who refused to absolve a gentleman, because he would not express in confession what books of Father Paul, and such, he knew to be in the hands of any others; the State commanded him out of that territory in three hours' warning, and he hath now submitted himself, and is returned as prisoner for Mantua, and so remains as yet. Sir H. Wotton, who writ hither, adds also that upon his knowledge there are 14,000 as good Protestants as he in that State.

"The Duke Joyeuse is dead, in Primont, returning from Rome, where M. Mole, who went with the L[ord] Rosse, is taken into the Inquisition, and I see small hope of his recovery (for he had in some translations of Plessis' books talked of Babylon and Antichrist), except it fall out that one Strange, a Jesuit in the Tower, may be accepted for him.

"To come a little nearer myself, Sir Geoffrey Fenton, one of his Majesty's secretaries in Ireland, is dead; and I have made some offer for the place, in preservation whereof, as I have had occasion to employ all my friends, so I have not found in them all (except Bedford) more haste and words (for when those two are together, there is much comfort even in the least) than in the L[ord] Hay. In good faith he promised so roundly, so abundantly, so profusely, as I suspected him, but performed whatever he undertook (and my requests were the measures of his undertakings) so readily and truly, that his compliments became obligations, and having spoke like a courtier, did like a friend.

"This I tell you, because being far under any ability of expressing my thankfulness to him by any proportional service, I do, as much as I can, thank him by thanking of you, who begot or nursed these good impressions of me in him. Sir, as my discretion would do, my fortune doth bring all my debts into one hand, for I owe you whatever Court friends do for me, yea, whatsoever I do for myself, because you almost importune me to awake and stare the Court in the face. I know not yet what conjecture to make of the event. But I am content to go forward a little more in the madness of missing rather than not pretend, and rather wear out than rust. It is extreme late; and as this letter is nothing, so if ever it come to you, you will know it without a name, and therefore I may end it here."

[*November* 1608.]

Such a letter as this would bear an annotation more lengthy than it is possible to give in a biography. "Justinian the Venetian," for instance, was Giustiniani, the ambassador of Venice; "Carraw" (I suppose), Noel de Carow; "M. Mole" may doubtless be identified with Mathieu Molé, the President; and "Primont" is an Italianated way of spelling Piedmont. These matters, however, are not within the scope of a life of Donne, except as remotely illustrating the gossip of his correspondence.

The reference to Lord Hay is particularly interesting, as the earliest to one of Donne's most ardent, intimate, and faithful friends. Later on in this history we shall be constantly meeting with his name. James Hay, the second son of Sir James Hay and godson of Sir Peter Hay of Megginch, Errol, Perthshire, was a young man of adventure who had accompanied James I. from Scotland. In 1603, being then about twenty years of age, he had started upon a career of extraordinary success by being appointed a Gentleman of the Bedchamber. In 1606 he had been created Lord Hay, and rose to be Viscount Doncaster, and Earl of Carlisle.

He was a jovial, harmless spendthrift of no great intellectual power, but of infinite good-nature and a sort of persuasive diplomatic charm which carried him far. He had been bred in France, and his manners were remarkable for their amenity and finish. Clarendon's picture of him is well known: "Lord Hay lived rather in a fair intelligence than any friendship with the favourites; having credit enough with his master to provide for his own interest, he troubled not himself for that of other men. In the excess of clothes and diet, he was surely a man of the greatest expense of any of the age in which he lived, and was the original of those inventions which others did but copy." We shall, much later, be brought to consider his monstrous style of expenditure, but at present it is not probable that the scion of an old Scotch family, and newly married to an English bride, the daughter of Lord Denny, afterwards Earl of Norwich, who had not yet come into her estates, was able to indulge his tastes for extravagant and ostentatious living. The approximate date of the first of the following letters, which are found in the Tobie Matthew collection, is marked by the fact that Donne speaks of his "disorderly proceedings" in marrying in his nonage, as having happened seven years before. That of the second, by the phrase, "If I be not fit for Ireland," Donne having requested the Irish post in November 1608:—

"*To* Lord Hay.[1]

"Noblest Lord,—The same conscience of mine own unworthiness, which kept me so long from daring to put myself into your Lordship's sight, provokes me to write now, we are ever justly more tender and jealous of those things, to which we have weakest title; and therefore finding how little pretence I have to your Lordship's favour, I am not only diligent, but curious, not to forfeit it. I have been told, that when your Lordship did me that extreme favour of presenting my name, his Majesty remembered me by the worst part of my history, which was my disorderly proceedings, seven years since, in my nonage. As your Lordship's earnestness and alacrity in

[1] From the Tobie Matthew Collection.

doing good, and almost unthriftiness in multiplying and heaping your favours, gave me scarce leisure to consider how great your first favour of promising was, because you overtook it presently with a greater, which was the performing it; so I humbly beseech your Lordship to add another to these, not to be too apprehensive of any suspicion, that there lies upon me any dishonourable stain, or can make my King have any prejudice against me, for that intemperate and hasty act of mine: for the Lord Chancellor and his brother-in-law, Sir G[eorge] M[ore], whose daughter I married, would both be likely, and will be ready to declare it, for his Majesty's satisfaction, or your Lordship's, that their displeasure, commenced so long since, should be thought to continue still, or interrupt any of my fortunes. This I say, lest I might have seemed to have betrayed your Lordship, and left my ill-fortune, by having got many victories upon myself, should dare to reach at your Lordship, and think to work upon your constancy, and perseverance in doing good, by making you repent your own act in favouring me.

"I am, my Lord, somewhat more worthy of your favour than I was at first; because every degree of your Lordship's favour is a great dignity. I am therefore in much confidence, that your Lordship, which disdained me not then, will at least allow your own work in me, and as you have laid a foundation, so you will by preferring me still, in your good opinion, build me up to such a capacity and worthiness, as may be fit for your Lordship to dwell in; to which I only bring an honest and entire devotion to do your Lordship service; all the rest is your Lordship's work, whose hand I humbly kiss, and beg a pardon for saluting your Lordship herein, by so bold a way as writing."

" *To* Lord Hay.[1]

"Noblest Lord,—Ever to good ends the way and passage is fair and delightful, of which no man can have had a better experience than I, who for my best end,

---
[1] From the Tobie Matthew Collection.

pretending to his Majesty's service, have by the way the honour to be received into your care; and though my fortune and my poor reputation importune me still not to forsake myself, but endeavour to be something, yet this descent of your Lordship, and your taking knowledge of so unuseful a servant as I am, gives me contentment and satisfaction enough, and so I may be sure to hold that room which your Lordship affords me in yourself, I care not to be anything else; it shall be my care that no fault make me unworthy of your Lordship's favour, since I feel already that it is your Lordship's care, to remove me from this darkness, in which my affection to do your Lordship service can no way appear.

"I perceive not yet any purpose to make any successor in that place in Ireland; if any be made, and not I, this would be the worst degree of the ill-fortune if that fail, that as I fear I should lose my hold in your Lordship, for it was but your affection that admitted me into you, but then your judgment would examine me, and conclude me to be very unfit for you if I be not fit for Ireland. Now your Lordship knows all my hopes and fears, and it is in your power to make my destiny, since to live in your memory is advancement enough, and I shall by your Lordship's favour be bold to refresh by my often Letters, not as diffident solicitors from me, but as your Lordship's auditors, to bring you in, the poor tribute of my thankfulness, who am, &c."

Donne did not succeed in stepping into Sir Geoffrey Fenton's shoes in Dublin, yet we end this chapter in a lighter key, and it is probable that when these last letters were written Donne's worst troubles were practically over.

TWICKENHAM

1608–1610

CHAPTER VII

TWICKENHAM

1608–1610

THE wretchedness of the household at Mitcham reached its climax of sickness and poverty in the autumn of 1608. At this time, or with the immediate memory of it upon him, Donne composed that extraordinary treatise of the *Biathanatos*, in which he defended the thesis that "self-homicide is not so naturally sin that it may never be otherwise." Lest we should suppose him to be a mere disinterested casuist, he admits that the notion of suicide was familiar to him, and that he grew accustomed more to entreat with it than to repel it. His confession has a singular poignancy. "Whensoever," he says in the preface to *Biathanatos*, " any affliction assails me, methinks I have the keys of my prison in my own hand, and no remedy presents itself so soon to my heart as mine own sword." He frankly tells us that the fascination which the idea of suicide has exercised over his own imagination has been the force which has led him to meditate over the amount of guilt involved in putting the delirious dream into action.

We shall examine the arguments which presented themselves to him when we come to deal with the *Biathanatos*. In the meantime it may be conjectured that when the fortunes of the Donnes had come to such a pass that suicide presented itself to the head of the household as the most natural way of solving the intolerable tangle, those who loved them best would feel that something practical must be done to help them. It is indicated that several things were in fact brought about in the autumn of 1608. Among these, by far the most important was the change achieved by Sir Francis Wooley. It would seem that this excellent friend had contrived, before the Donnes left his house in Pyrford, to reconcile them with Mrs. Donne's father. But this reconciliation had not proceeded so far as to make Sir George More willing to contribute to his daughter's maintenance. His own mode of life at Loseley continued to be magnificently expensive; he had many other children, who had married in accordance with his wishes, and whose docility contrasted with poor Anne's blind impulse of self-will. In short, he promised, and he put his promise by.

But Sir Francis Wooley now insisted that the question of Mrs. Donne's dower should be no longer postponed. Further delay might have resulted in the whole cluster of babes being thrown, without father or mother, on the charge of their unwilling grandparent. Sir George gave way at last, and the arrangement which he made was one which we cannot think ungenerous. We owe to Walton a knowledge of the particulars, "Sir George conditioning by bond to pay to Mr. Donne £800 at a certain day, as a portion with his wife, or £20 quarterly for their maintenance, as the interest for it, till the said portion was paid." It is notoriously difficult to decide what the comparative value of money is at two different periods. If, however, it may be roughly considered that, at the beginning of the reign of James I., money was ten times as valuable as it is now, Sir George More undertook to pay his daughter £8000 of our money, or an income of ten per cent. interest until it was convenient for him to produce the capital.

With a sudden increase of income equivalent to £800 a year of our money, Donne's worst misfortunes vanished like a cloud. The tone of his correspondence clears immediately. His wife and children were once more properly supplied with food and clothes, and we hear no more of their sufferings. He himself was released from his "hospital" and "prison" at Mitcham, and able to reappear in London. One cardinal result of poverty in the early seventeenth century is not sufficiently borne in upon us in this age of sartorial democracy. Rank and fashion were clearly defined, and the social distinctions defended by the expensiveness of dress. If a man became poor, retirement was forced upon him. He might retain the esteem of his friends at Court, but he could not visit them, except in ways that were informal and almost humiliating, because he could no longer dress with the magnificence which society imperatively demanded. Poverty, therefore, had meant, for Donne, the withdrawal from all those social exercises which were so essential to his entertainment; and that he had fashionable friends became of little value to him, since his wardrobe forbade him to circulate among them. Consequently, the very first symptom of the removal of indigence is that Donne re-enters that society with which, since his marriage, he had kept up but a shadowy connection.

In spite of the improvement in his fortunes he was still, as ever, anxious to obtain a regular appointment. A letter, dated February 14, 1609, tells us incidentally, "News is here none at all, but that John Donne seeks to be Secretary at Virginia." When, thirteen years afterwards, he preached before the Virginia Company at Merchant Taylors' Hall, this unsuccessful ambition of his youth may have flashed across his memory.

The great ladies now, once more, pass into Donne's life, those gracious and dignified women of quality whom he had charmed long ago in the Lord Keeper's household, and who had continued to have him in their minds. But a new figure had now entered the narrative of Donne's career, and a friendship was formed which was to be one of the most durable and the most intimate of his life. His letters begin to be filled with allusions to "the best Lady," "that dear Lady," "the happiest and worthiest Lady," "who only hath the power to cast the fetters of verse upon my free meditations." This was the incomparable Lucy Russell, Countess of Bedford. Her year of birth does not seem to be known, but she was little more than a child when, on the 12th of December 1594, she was married to Edward Russell, third Earl of Bedford. She was a daughter of

John Harington, first Baron Harington of Exton, who had been raised to the peerage on the accession of James I. Harington, who was an object of special suspicion and hatred to the Catholics, was put in charge of the infant Princess Elizabeth, and it seems to have been in remote consequence of this that the Countess of Bedford became Donne's patron.

After paying a short visit to Lord and Lady Harington in Rutland, the Princess Elizabeth was maintained at Combe Abbey, in Warwickshire, for five years; then, it being found necessary to provide her with a court of her own, arrangements were entered into for a fresh residence. It was determined that the Princess, now twelve years of age, should reside at Kew. Meanwhile Sir Henry Goodyer had passed into the service of the Earl of Bedford,—Donne speaks of the latter to his friend as "your Master,"—and some members of the family of the Woodwards, also highly sympathetic friends of Donne, appear to have acted for the Earl in a legal capacity. Accordingly, in 1607 the reversion of the lease of Twickenham Park, which had been the home of Francis Bacon, came into the hands of Sir Henry Goodyer and Edward Woodward, to be transferred in 1608 to George, Lord Carew and George Croke, in trust for Lucy, Countess of Bedford, who, when the Princess Elizabeth removed to Kew, took up her own residence close by at Twickenham, and lived there until 1618. There was later on a "Mistress Goodyer that served the Lady Bedford"; but whether this was the daughter or niece of Sir Henry Goodyer does not seem to be certain. At all events, it adds a touch to the sense of intimacy which we feel to have existed between the Twickenham people and Donne's closest friend.

Lady Bedford seems to have made Donne's acquaintance during the visit which we have already seen that she paid to Mitcham in the autumn of 1608. She was probably visiting either the hospitable and magnificent Sir Julius Cæsar or the Carews of Beddington. Sir Nicholas Throckmorton Carew was Donne's brother-in-law, having married Mary More; a little later he became lord of the manor and advowson of Mitcham. If Lady Bedford now, as I think likely, first became personally acquainted with Donne, the attractive character of his gifts and graces were certainly familiar to her from the Goodyers and Lady Huntingdon, if from no one else. But circumstances were now making her the centre of the principal group of Donne's friends, and for the rest of her life she was his patron, inspiration, and support. No friend of his lifetime, perhaps, did so much for Donne as Lady Bedford did. He found in her delightful company everything which he required to stimulate and develop him. She had a singular adroitness in making him express the noblest and brightest sides of his genius. "You have refined me, and to worthiest things," he bursts out in addressing her. His adoration pauses at no hyperbole in praising the beauty and virtue, the learning and piety, the sweetness and tender graciousness of Lady Bedford. "You are," he cries, "the first good angel that ever did in woman's shape appear." But, vast as are the terms of his celebration, the reader is induced to believe in their sincerity. The language of Donne in speaking of and to the Countess of Bedford is unique in his writings. He was never shy or put out of countenance by social obstacles. But in the presence of Lady Bedford there passes over him an unwonted reticence. He adores, and not from a distance, yet upon his knees. There is always the little touch of awe, of sacred wonder, which keeps his impassioned addresses dignified and pure. He worships her; his heart is beating in his hands; but he never forgets that this divine and crystal creature is not made for earthly love. She, on her side, is uniformly indulgent, gracious, noble. Her birth and beauty, as her poet says, are a balsam which keep her prestige always fresh and new, so that condescension bends in the most gracious extremes without yielding to familiarity for a moment; and her intrinsic serenity cannot be "injured by extrinsic blows." Such was the exquisite friend whom it was now Donne's privilege to make for life.

When Lady Bedford was at Mitcham, she stood god-

mother to Donne's second daughter, who was baptized
Lucy on the 8th of August 1608. There is an impression
that, at the same time, she relieved the poet's wants by
the gift of a sum of money. There was nothing, in the
ideas of the age, humiliating or surprising in such an act
of benevolence. The Countess was a wealthy woman, both
in her marriage and as co-heiress with her brother, John
Harington of Exton. She was just setting up at Twickenham Park a household maintained on so generous a footing,
that it seemed a small repetition of the Lady Elizabeth's
establishment, and was even compared with it. It was the
habit of those liberal and enlightened noblemen who were
able to maintain their rank in state, to think themselves privileged if they could attach a poet to their persons. Lady
Bedford, in this respect, outshone all her contemporaries.
She was known as the "Favourite of the Muses," and she
drew down to Twickenham the elderly Samuel Daniel, who
addressed to her, in *terza rima*, one of the most famous
of his epistles, Drayton, who had been in the household
of Sir Henry Goodyer's father at Polesworth, and many
other poets, rivals of whom Donne seems, in his proud
way, to have taken no sort of notice at any time. It was
her delight to have copies of verses addressed to her, and
it is to her deliberate stimulus that we owe the revival of
Donne's interest in his art. The Countess of Bedford was
herself a versifier, and she rewarded the efforts of her poets
by confiding to them her own effusions.

It is not probable that Donne began to visit Lady
Bedford at Twickenham until 1609. The group of letters
which now follow belong, I think, to the early part of that
year, and illustrate the growing hold which the Countess
took upon Donne's thoughts and aspirations, and the comfort which her generous kindness gave him. It may be
said, by way of elucidation, that Peckham was the dwelling
of Donne's "very worthy friend and kind brother-in-law,"
Sir Thomas Grymes, whose hospitalities were constant,
and that "Sir J. Harr." is more likely to be Sir John
Harington of Kelston, the poet and translator of the
Orlando Furioso, than one of the Exton family.

"*To* Sir H[enry] G[oodyer].[1]

"Sir,—I love to give you advantages upon me, therefore I put myself in need of another pardon from you, by not coming to you, yet I am scarce guilty enough to spend much of your virtue from you, because I knew not of your being come till this your letter told me so, in the midst of dinner at Peckham, this Monday.

"Sir, I am very truly yours; if you have overvalued me in any capacity, I will do what I can to overtake your hopes of me. I wish myself whatsoever you wish me, and so I do, whatever you wish yourself. I am prisoner and close, else I had not needed this pardon, for I long much, and much more by occasion of your letter, to see you: when you find that good lady emptiest of business and pleasure, present my humble thanks; you can do me no favour, which I need not, nor any which I cannot have some hope to deserve, but this, for I have made her opinion of me the balance by which I weigh myself.

"I will come soon enough to deliver my thanks to Sir J. Harr[ington] for your ease, whom I know I have pained with an ill-favoured letter, but my heart hath one style and character, and is yours in wishing and in thankfulness.

"J. Donne.

"Peckham, *Monday afternoon.*"

"*To my good friend* Sir H[enry] G[oodyer].[2]

"Sir,—The messenger who brought me your letter[s] presented me a just excuse, for I received them so late upon Thursday night, that I should have despatched before I could begin; yet I have obeyed you drowsily and coldly, as the night and my indisposition commanded: yet perchance those hindrances have done good, for so your letters are the less curious, in which men of much leisure may soon exceed when they write of business, they having but a little.

"You mention two more letters than I send. The

[1] From the *Letters* of 1651. [2] *Ibid.*

time was not too short for me to have written them (for I had an whole night), but it was too short to work a belief in me, that you could think it fit to go two so divers ways to one end. I see not (for I see not the reason) how those letters could well have concurred with these, nor how those would well have been drawn from them in a business wholly relating to this house. I was not lazy in disobeying you, but (I thought) only thrifty, and your request of those was not absolute but conditioned, if I had leisure. So, though that condition hinder them not, since another doth (and you forethought, that one might) I am not stubborn.

"The good Countess spoke somewhat of your desire of letters; but I am afraid she is not a proper mediatrix to those persons, but I counsel in the dark, and therefore return to that of which I have clear light, that I am always glad when I have any way to express my love, for in these commandments you feed my desires, and you give me means to pay some of my debts to you, the interest of which I pay in all my prayers for you, which, if it please not God to show here, I hope we shall find again together in heaven, whither they were sent. I came this morning to say thus much, and because the porter which came to Mitcham summoned me for this hour to London, from whence I am this minute returning to end a little course of physic.

"Yours very truly,

J. DONNE."

"Friday, 8 in the morning."

"*A V. Merced*.[1]

[Evidently to Sir HENRY GOODYER.]

"SIR,—I write not to you out of my poor library, where to cast mine eye upon good authors kindles or refreshes sometimes meditations not unfit to communicate to near friends; nor from the highway, where I am contracted and inverted into myself; which are my two ordinary forges of letters to you. But I write from the fireside in

---

[1] From *Letters* of 1651. *A Vuestra Merced*, "to your Worship," a playful use of the Spanish salutation.

my parlour, and in the noise of three gamesome children; and by the side of her, whom because I have transplanted into a wretched fortune, I must labour to disguise that from her by all such honest devices, as giving her my company and discourse; therefore I steal from her all the time which I give this letter, and it is therefore that I take so short a list, and gallop so fast over it. I have not been out of my house since I received your packet.

"As I have much quenched my senses and disused my body from pleasure, and so tried how I can endure to be mine own grave, so I try now how I can suffer a prison. And since it is but to build one wall more about our soul, she is still in her own centre, how many circumferences soever fortune or our own perverseness cast about her. I would I could as well entreat her to go out, as she knows whither to go.

"But if I melt into a melancholy whilst I write, I shall be taken in the manner: and I sit by one too tender towards these impressions, and it is so much our duty to avoid all occasions of giving them sad apprehensions, as S. Hierome accuses Adam of no other fault in eating the apple but that he did it *ne contristaretur delicias suas*. I am not careful what I write, because the enclosed letters may dignify this ill-favoured bark, and they need not grudge so coarse a countenance, because they are now to accompany themselves, my man fetched them, and therefore I can say no more of them than themselves say. Mistress Meautys entreated me by her letter to hasten hers; as I think, for by my troth I cannot read it. My Lady was despatching in so much haste for Twicknam, as she gave no word to a letter which I sent with yours; of Sir Thos. Bartlet I can say nothing, nor of the plague, though your letter bid me: but that he diminishes, the other increases, but in what proportion I am not clear. To them at Hammersmith and Mistress Herbert I will do your command. If I have been good in hope, or can promise any little offices in the future probably, it is comfortable, for I am the worst present man in the world; yet the instant, though it be nothing, joins times together, and therefore this unprofitableness, since I have been, and will still endeavour to be so, shall not interrupt me now from being

"Your servant and lover,

[1608.] "J. DONNE."

Dr. Jessopp identifies this Mistress Meautys (John Donne, the younger, misprinted the name Meauly) with Jane, daughter of Hercules Meautys, of West Ham. She was one of the ladies who "waited on" Lady Bedford. In the course of this year, 1608, she was married to Donne's old Oxford friend, Sir William Cornwallis of Brome.

The words about the plague give us the date of the preceding letter. By prerogative of Parliament the "city ditch was cleaned out," so unwholesome was the condition of London.

"*To my most worthy friend* Sir HENRY GOODYER.[1]

"SIR,—Because evenness conduces as much to strength and firmness as greatness doth, I would not discontinue my course of writing. It is a sacrifice which though friends need not, friendship doth; which hath in it so much divinity, that as we must be ever equally disposed inwardly so to do or suffer for it, so we must suppose some certain times for the outward service thereof, though it be but formal and testimonial: that time to me towards you is Tuesday, and my temple, the Rose in Smithfield.

"If I were by your appointment your referendary for news, I should write but short letters, because the times are barren, the Low Countries, which used to be the mart of news for this season, suffering also, or rather enjoying a vacation. Since, therefore, I am but mine own secretary (and what's that?) I were excusable if I writ nothing, since I am so: besides that, your much knowledge brings you this disadvantage, that as stomachs accustomed to delicacies find nothing new or pleasing to them when they are sick, so

[1] *Letters* of 1651.

you can hear nothing from me (though the country perchance make you hungry) which you know not.

"Therefore instead of a letter to you, I send you one to another, to the best Lady, who did me the honour to acknowledge the receipt of one of mine by one of hers; and who only hath power to cast the fetters of verse upon my free meditations: it should give you some delight, and some comfort, because you are the first which see it, and it is the last which you shall see of this kind from me.
"Your very affectionate lover and servant,
"J. DONNE.
"Mitcham, the 14*th August* [1609]."

The "vacation" in the Low Countries, to which Donne here refers, was the consequence of the Truce for twelve years, signed at Bergen, April 9, 1609, between the United Provinces and Philip III. This truce, and the happy emptiness that resulted from it, were the objects of a famous sonnet by the Dutch poet, Vondel.

"*To the* Countess of BEDFORD.

"HAPPIEST AND WORTHIEST LADY,—I do not remember that ever I have seen a petition in verse. I would not therefore be singular, nor add these to your other papers. I have yet adventured so near as to make a petition for verse, it is for those your Ladyship did me the honour to see in Twicknam garden, except you repent your making; and having mended your judgment by thinking worse, that is, better, because juster, of their subject. They must needs be an excellent exercise of your wit, which speak so well of so ill: I humbly beg them of your Ladyship, with two such promises, as to any other of your compositions were threatenings; that I will not show them, and that I will not believe them; and nothing should be so used that comes from your brain or breast. If I should confess a fault in the boldness of asking them, or make a fault by doing it in a longer letter, your Ladyship might use your style and old fashion of the court towards me, and pay me with a pardon. Here therefore I humbly kiss your Ladyship's fair learned hands, and wish you good wishes and speedy grants.—Your Ladyship's servant,

"J. DONNE."

The verses sent by Lady Bedford to Donne have not been preserved; but we possess several of his verse-epistles to her. The following lines belong to the beginning of their friendship, and to her visit to Mitcham:—

" MADAM—

"Reason is our soul's left hand, faith her right;
  By these we reach divinity, that's you;
Their loves, who have the blessing of your light,
  Grew from their reason; mine from fair faith grew.
. . . .
Therefore I study you first in your saints,
  Those friends whom your election glorifies;
Then in your deeds, accesses and restraints,
  And what you read, and what yourself devise.

But soon the reasons why you're loved by all,
  Grow infinite, and so pass reason's reach;
Then back again to implicit faith I fall,
  And rest on that the Catholic voice doth teach—

That you are good; and not one heretic
  Denies it; if he did, yet you are so.
. . . .
Since you are then God's masterpiece, and so
  His factor for our loves, do as you do;
Make your return home gracious, and bestow
  This life on that; so make one life of two.

For, so God help me, I'd not miss you there,
For all the good which you may do me here."

" *To* Sir H[ENRY] G[OODYER].[1]

"SIR,—It should be no interruption to your pleasures to hear me often say that I love you, and that you are as much my meditations as myself. I often compare not you and me, but the sphere in which your resolutions are

[1] From *Letters* of 1651.

and my wheel, both I hope concentric to God: for methinks the new astronomy is thus appliable well, that we which are a little earth should rather move towards God, than that He which is fulfilling, and can come no whither, should move towards us.

"To your life full of variety nothing is old, nor new to mine; and as to that life all stickings and hesitations seem stupid and stony, so to this, all fluid slipperinesses and transitory migrations seem giddy and feathery. In that life one is ever in the porch or postern, going in or out, never within his house himself: it is a garment made of remnants, a life ravelled out into ends, a line discontinued, and a number of small wretched points, useless, because they concur not: a life built of past and future, not proposing any constant present; they have more pleasures than we, but not more pleasure; they joy oftener, we longer; and no man but of so much understanding as may deliver him from being a fool, would change with a madman, which had a better proportion of wit in his often *lucidis*.

"You know they which dwell farthest from the sun, if in any convenient distance, have longer days, better appetites, better digestion, better growth, and longer life: and all these advantages have their minds who are well removed from the scorchings and dazzlings and exhalings of the world's glory: but neither of our lives are in such extremes; for you living at Court without ambition, which would burn you, or envy, which would divest others, live in the sun, not in the fire: and I which live in the country without stupefying, am not in darkness, but in shadow, which is not no light, but a pallid, waterish, and diluted one.

"As all shadows are of one colour, if you respect the body from which they are cast (for our shadows upon clay will be dirty, and in a garden green and flowery) so all retirings into a shadowy life are alike from all causes, and alike subject to the barbarousness and insipid dulness of the country: only the employments and that upon which you cast and bestow your pleasure, business, or books, gives it the tincture and beauty. But truly wheresoever we are, if we can but tell ourselves truly what and where we would be, we may make any state and place such; for we are so composed that if abundance or glory scorch and melt us, we have an earthly cave, our bodies, to go into by consideration and cool ourselves; and if we be frozen, and contracted with lower and dark fortunes, we have within us a torch, a soul, lighter and warmer than any without: we are therefore our own umbrellas and our own suns.

"These, sir, are the salads and onions of Mitcham, sent to you with as wholesome affection as your other friends send melons and quelque-choses from Court and London. If I present you not as good diet as they, I would yet say grace to theirs, and bid much good do it you.

"I send you, with this, a letter which I sent to the Countess. It is not my use nor duty to do so, but for your having of it there were but two consents, and I am sure you have mine, and you are sure you have hers. I also wrote to her Ladyship for the verses she showed in the garden, which I did not only to extort them, nor only to keep my promise of writing, for that I had done in the other letter, and perchance she hath forgotten the promise; nor only because I think my letters just good enough for a progress, but because I would write apace to her, whilst it is possible to express that which I yet know of her, for by this growth I see how soon she will be ineffable."

[1609.]

When we come to consider the *Ignatius his Conclave*, we shall see what prompt and excellent use Donne made of the "new astronomy" of Galileo.

There is ample evidence of the gravity of Donne's theological studies during these years at Mitcham. He was slowly, but steadily and definitely, coming into line with the doctrine of the Anglican communion. He now "often retired himself, and destined some days to a constant study of some points of controversy between the English and Roman Church, and especially those of Supremacy and Allegiance; and to that place and such studies he could willingly have wedded himself during his life." During the year 1609 this particular series of investigations led to the composition of his great controversial treatise, the *Pseudo-Martyr*, indications of the progress of which are to be found in the letters which it is now time to print. The first of these contain allusions to a work which attracted a great deal of contemporary attention, issued by William Barlow, who since 1608 had been Bishop of Lincoln. Barlow, who had been the chaplain and protégé of Whitgift, was a fiery controversialist, and, since the mind of Morton had been partly diverted to other matters, had come forward as the leading opponent of Rome. His book, which was entitled *An Answer to a Catholic Englishman* (1609), had been called forth by a treatise in which Parsons, the Jesuit, as "a banished Catholic Englishman," had in 1608 attacked James I.'s work, *An Apology for the Oath of Allegiance* (1607). Barlow was now nearing his end; he was to die in 1613.

"*To his honourable friend* Sir H[ENRY] G[OODYER].[1]

"SIR,—To you that are not easily scandalised, and in whom, I hope, neither my religion nor morality can suffer, I dare write my opinion of that book in whose bowels you left me. It hath refreshed, and given new justice to my ordinary complaint, that the divines of these times are become mere advocates, as though religion were a temporal inheritance; they plead for it with all sophistications, and illusions, and forgeries: and herein are they likest advocates, that though they be fed by the way with dignities and other recompenses, yet that for which they plead is none of theirs. They write for religion without it.

"In the main point in question, I think truly there is a perplexity (as far as I see yet), and both sides may be in justice and innocence; and the wounds which they inflict upon the adverse part are all *se defendendo*: for, clearly, our State cannot be safe without the Oath; since they profess that clergymen, though traitors, are no subjects, and that all the rest may be none to-morrow. And, as

[1] From the *Letters* of 1651.

clearly, the supremacy which the Roman Church pretend were diminished, if it were limited; and will as ill abide that, or disputation, as the prerogative of temporal kings, who being the only judges of their prerogative, why may not Roman bishops (so enlightened as they are presumed by them) be good witnesses of their own supremacy, which is now so much impugned?

"But for this particular author, I looked for more prudence and human wisdom in him in avoiding all miscitings, or misinterpretings, because at this time the watch is set, and everybody's hammer is upon that anvil; and to dare offend in that kind now is for a thief to leave the covert and meet a strong hue and cry in the teeth: and yet truly this man is extremely obnoxious in that kind; for, though he have answered many things fully (as no book ever gave more advantage than that which he undertook), and abound in delicate applications and ornaments from the divine and profane authors, yet being chiefly conversant about two points, he prevaricates in both.

"For, for the matter, which is the first, he refers it entirely and namely to that which D[ean] Morton hath said therein before, and so leaves it roundly. And for the person (which is the second) upon whom he amasses as many opprobries as any other could deserve, he pronounceth, that he will account any answer from his adversary slander, except he do (as he hath done) draw whatsoever he saith of him from authors of the same religion, and in print. And so, he having made use of all the quodlibetaries, imputations against the other, cannot be obnoxious himself in that kind, and so hath provided safely.

"It were no service to you to send you my notes upon the book, because they are sandy and incoherent rags, for my memory, not for your judgment; and to extend them to an easiness and perspicuity would make them a pamphlet, not a letter. I will therefore defer them till I see you; and in the meantime I will adventure to say to you, without inserting one unnecessary word, that the book is full of falsifications in words and in sense, and of falsehoods in matter of fact, and of inconsequent and unscholarlike arguings, and of relinquishing the King, in many points of defence, and of contradiction of himself, and of dangerous and suspected doctrine in divinity, and of silly ridiculous triflings, and of extreme flatteries, and of neglecting better and more obvious answers, and of letting slip some enormous advantages which the other gave and he spies not. I know (as I begun) I speak to you who cannot be scandalised, and that neither measure religion (as it is now called) by unity, nor suspect unity, for these interruptions.

"Sir, not only a mathematic point, which is the most indivisible and unique thing which art can present, flows into every line which is derived from the centre, but our soul which is but one, hath swallowed up a negative and feeling soul, which was in the body before it came, and exercises those faculties yet; and God Himself, who only is One, seems to have been eternally delighted with a disunion of persons. They whose active function it is, must endeavour this unity in religion; and we at our lay altars (which are our tables, or bedside, or stools, wheresoever we dare prostrate ourselves to God in prayer) must beg it of Him; but we must take heed of making misconclusions upon the want of it; for, whether the mayor and aldermen fall out (as with us and the Puritans; bishops against priests) or the commoners' voices differ who is mayor and who aldermen, or what their jurisdiction (as with the Bishop of Rome, or whosoever), yet it is still one corporation.

"Your very affectionate servant and lover,
"J. Donne.
" Mitcham, Thursday late.

"Never leave the remembrance of my poor service unmentioned when you see the good Lady."

"*To the Honourable Knight* Sir H[enry] Goodyer.[1]

"Because things be conserved by the same means which established them, I nurse that friendship by letters, which you

[1] From *Letters* of 1651.

begot so; though you have since strengthened it by more solid aliment and real offices. In these letters from the country there is this merit, that I do otherwise unwillingly turn mine eye or thoughts from my books, companions in whom there is no falsehood nor frowardness; which words I am glad to observe that the holy authors often join as expressers and relatives to one another, because else out of a natural descent to that unworthy fault of frowardness, furthered with that incommodity of a little thin house, I should have mistaken it to be a small thing, which now I see equalled with the worst.

"If you have laid my papers and books by, I pray let this messenger have them; I have determined upon them. If you have not, be content to do it in the next three or four days. So, sir, I kiss your hands; and deliver to you an entire and clear heart, which shall ever when I am with you be in my face and tongue, and when I am from you in my letters, for I will never draw curtain between you and it.

"Yours very affectionately,

"J. DONNE.

"From your house at
Mitcham, Friday morning.

"When you are sometimes at Mr. Sackville's, I pray ask if he have this book, *Baldvinus de Officio pii Hominis in Controversiis;* it was written at the conference at Poissy, where Beza was, and he answered it; I long for it."

Baldvinus was François (or Franciscus) Boudouin (or Baldwinus), Professor of Law in the University of Bruges. He died in 1573, the year that Donne was born.

"*To the Honourable Knight* Sir HENRY GOODYER.[1]

"SIR,—As you are a great part of my business when I come to London, so are you when I send. More than the office of a visitation brings this letter to you now; for I

[1] From *Letters* of 1651.

remember that about this time you purposed a journey to fetch, or meet the Lady Huntington. If you justly doubt any long absence, I pray send to my lodging my written books; and if you may stay very long, I pray send that letter in which I sent you certain heads which I purposed to enlarge, for I have them not in any other paper; and I may find time in your absence to do it, because I know no stronger argument to move you to love me; but because you have done so, do so still, to make my reason better, and I shall at last prescribe in you.—Yours,

"J. DONNE.

"Mitcham, Wednesday."

The next letter is almost without doubt addressed to Sir Henry Goodyer, with its references to the weekly letter which passed between them.

"*To* Sir H. R. [*sic*].[1]

"If a whole year be but *Annus ab Annulo*, because it returns into itself, what *Annulus* shall be diminutive enough to express our weekly revolutions? In chains the least links have most curiosity, but that can be no emblem of us; but they have also the most strength, and that may. The first sphere only which is resisted by nothing, absolves his course every day; and so doth true friendship well placed often iterate in act or purpose the same offices. But as the lower spheres, subject to the violence of that, and yet naturally encouraged to a reluctation against it, have therefore many distractions and eccentricities, and some trepidations, and so return but lamely and lately to the same place and office; so that friendship which is not moved primarily by the proper intelligence, discretion, and about the natural centre, virtue, doth perchance sometimes, some things, somewhat like true friendship; but hath many deviations, which are strayings into new loves (not of other men; for that is proper to true wise friendship, which is not a marrying; but of other things), and hath

[1] From *Letters* of 1651.

such trepidations as keep it from showing itself, where great persons do not love; and it returns to the true first station and place of friendship planetarily, which is uncertainly and seldom.

"I have ever seen in London and our Court, as some colours, and habits, and continuances, and motions, and phrases, and accents, and songs, so friends in fashion and in season; and I have seen them as suddenly abandoned altogether, though I see no change in them, nor know more why they were left than why they were chosen. To do things by example, and upon confidence of another's judgment, may be some kind of a second wisdom, but it is but writing by a copy: or, indeed, it is the hardest of all, and the issue of the first wisdom, for I cannot know that this example should be followed except I knew that it is good, and so I judge my Judge. Our assent, therefore, and arrest, must be upon things, not persons. And when we are sure we are in the right way for great persons, we may be glad of their company if they go our way; we may for them change our place, but not our end, nor our way, if there be but one, as in religion. In persevering in it, it concerns us much what our companions be, but very much what our friends. In which I know I speak not dangerously nor misappliably to you, as though I averted you from any of those friends, who are of other impressions than you or I in some great circumstances of religion.

"You know I never fettered nor imprisoned the word Religion, not straightening it friarly, *ad Religiones factitias* (as the Romans call well their orders of Religion), nor immuring it in a Rome, or a Wittemberg, or a Geneva; they are all virtual beams of one Sun, and wheresoever they find clay hearts, they harden them and moulder them into dust; and they entender and mollify waxen. They are not so contrary as the North and South Poles, and that [?] they are co-natural pieces of one circle. Religion is Christianity, which being too spiritual to be seen by us, doth therefore take an apparent body of good life and works, so salvation requires an honest Christian.

"These are the two elements, and he which elemented

from these hath the complexion of a good man and a fit friend. The diseases are, too much intention into indiscreet zeal, and too much remissness and negligence by giving scandal, for our condition and state in this, is as infirm as in our bodies; where physicians consider only two degrees, sickness and neutrality, for there is no health in us. This, sir, I used to say to you, rather to have so good a witness and corrector of my meditations, than to advise; and yet to do that too, since it is pardonable in a friend. Not to slack you towards those friends which are religious in other clothes than we (for *amici vitia si feras facis tua*, is true of such faults), but to keep you awake against such as the place where you must live will often obtrude, which are not only naked, without any fashion of such garments, but have neither the body of Religion, which is moral honesty and sociable faithfulness, nor the soul, Christianity.

"I know not how this paper escaped last week, which I send now; I was so sure that I enwrapped it then, that I should be so still, but that I had but one copy; forgive it as you use to do. From Mitcham in as much haste and with as ill pen and ink as the letter can accuse me of, but with the last and the next week's heart and affection.

"Yours very truly and affectionately,

"J. Donne."

"*To* Sir H[enry] G[oodyer].[1]

"I send not my letters as tribute, nor interest, nor recompense, nor for commerce, nor as testimonials of my love, nor provokers of yours, nor to justify my custom of writing, nor for a vent and utterance of my meditations, for my letters are either above or under all such offices; yet I write very affectionately, and I chide and accuse myself of diminishing that affection which sends them, when I ask myself why; only I am sure that I desire that you might have in your hands letters of mine of all kinds, as conveyances and deliverers of me to you, whether you

[1] From *Letters* of 1651.

accept me as a friend, or as a patient, or as a penitent, or as a beadsman, for I decline no jurisdiction, or refuse any tenure. I would not open any door upon you, but look in when you open it.

"Angels have not, nor affect not other knowledge of one another, than they list to reveal to one another. It is then in this only that friends are angels, that they are capable and fit for such revelations when they are offered. If at any time I seem to study you more inquisitively, it is for no other end but to know how to present you to God in my prayers, and what to ask of Him for you, for even that holy exercise may not be done inopportunely, no, nor importunely.

"I find little error in that Grecian's counsel, who says, If thou ask anything of God, offer no sacrifice, nor ask elegantly nor vehemently, but remember that thou wouldest not give to such an asker. Nor in his other countryman, who affirms sacrifice of blood to be so unproportionable to God, that perfumes, though much more spiritual, are too gross. Yea, words which are our subtlest and delicatest outward creatures, being composed of thoughts and breath, are so muddy, so thick, that our thoughts themselves are so, because (except at the first rising) they are ever leavened with passions and affections. And that advantage of nearer familiarity with God, which the act of incarnation gave us, is grounded upon God's assuming us, not our going to Him. And our accesses to His presence are but His descents into us; and when we get anything by prayer, He gave us beforehand the thing and the petition.

"For I scarce think any ineffectual prayer free from both sin and the punishment of sin; yet as God seposed a seventh of our time for His exterior worship, and as His Christian Church early presented Him a type of the whole year in a Lent, and after imposed the obligation of canonic hours, constituting thereby moral Sabbaths every day; I am far from dehorting those fixed devotions, but I had rather it were bestowed upon thanksgiving than petition, upon praise than prayer, not that God is endeared by that, or wearied by this; all is one in the receiver, but not in the sender, and thanks doth both offices, for nothing doth so innocently provoke new graces as gratitude. I would also rather make short prayers than extend them, though God can neither be surprised nor besieged, for long prayers have more of the man, as ambition of eloquence and a complacency in the work, and more of the devil by often distractions, for after in the beginning we have well entreated God to hearken, we speak no more to Him.

"Even this letter is some example of such infirmity, which, being intended for a letter, is extended and strayed into a homily. And whatsoever is not what it was purposed is worse, therefore it shall at last end like a letter by assuring you I am . . ."

The poet in attendance at a court was expected to exercise his talent on great occasions with an epithalamium or an epicede. Donne was called upon to illustrate the obsequies of those members of Lady Bedford's household whose prominence or beauty called for such a signal mark of distinction. Twice, at least, in 1609 he was thus occupied. Bridget, Lady Markham, was first cousin to the Countess of Bedford, being the daughter of Sir James Harington, younger brother of the first Lord Harington, by his first wife Frances, daughter of Robert Sapcotts of Elton. She was born in 1579, and in 1598 had married Sir Anthony Markham of Sedgebrook. This gentleman, who was knighted at Belvoir in April 1603, died at the age of twenty-seven, on the 10th of December 1604, leaving her with three infant sons. Lady Markham was appointed one of the Ladies of the Bedchamber to Anne of Denmark. She died at Twickenham Park on the 4th of May 1609. A monument to her memory was raised in Twickenham Church, and Francis Beaumont celebrated her virtues in verse. Donne wrote an elegy of more than sixty lines, in his most impressive manner, dwelling with harsh majesty on the horror and hopelessness of death, and illuminating the gloomy theme with violent and brilliant images:—

> "As men of China, after an age's stay,
> Do take up porcelain, where they buried clay;

> So at this grave, her limbeck—which refines
> The diamonds, rubies, sapphires, pearls and mines,
> Of which this flesh was—her soul shall inspire
> Flesh of such stuff, as God, when His last fire
> Annuls this world, to recompense it shall
> Make and name them the elixir of this all."

Our next letter, written at the close of July 1609, prepares us for a similar mournful occasion.

"*To* Sir H[ENRY] G[OODYER].[1]

"SIR,—I cannot yet serve you with those books of which your letter spake. In recompense I will tell you a story, which if I had had leisure to have told it you when it was fresh, which was upon Thursday last, might have had some grace for the rareness, and would have tried your love to me, how far you would adventure to believe an improbable thing for my sake who relates it. That day in the morning there was some end made by the Earl of Salisbury and others, who were arbitrators in some differences between Herford and Mountegle. Herford was ill-satisfied in it, and declared himself so far as to say he expected better usage in respect not only of his cause, but of his expense and service in his ambassage; to which Salisbury replied, that considered how things stood between his Majesty and Herford House at the King's entrance, the King had done him especial favour in that employment of honour and confidence, by declaring in so public and great an act and testimony that he had no ill affections toward him. Herford answered that he was then and ever an honest man to the King; and Salisbury said he denied not that, but yet solemnly repeated his first words again. So that Herford seemed not to make answer, but pursuing his own word, said that whosoever denied him to have been an honest man to the King lied. Salisbury asked him if he directed that upon him; Herford said, upon any who denied this. The earnestness of both was such, as Salisbury accepted it to himself, and made protestation before

[1] From *Letters* of 1651.

the Lords present, that he would do nothing else till he had honourably put off that lie. Within an hour after, Salisbury sent him a direct challenge, by his servant Mr. Knightley; Herford required only an hour's leisure of consideration (it is said it was only to inform himself of the special danger in dealing so with a Counsellor), but he returned his acceptation. And all circumstances were so clearly handled between them, that St. James was agreed for the place, and they were both come from their several lodgings, and upon the way to have met, when they were interrupted by such as from the King were sent to have care of it.

"So these two have escaped this great danger; but (by my troth) I fear earnestly that Mistress Bolstrod will not escape that sickness in which she labours at this time. I sent this morning to ask of her passage of this night; and the return is that she is as I left her yesternight, and then by the strength of her understanding and voice (proportionally to her fashion, which was ever remiss), by the evenness and life of her pulse, and by her temper, I could allow her long life, and impute all her sickness to her mind. But the history of her sickness makes me justly fear that she will scarce last so long as that you, when you receive this letter, may do her any good office in praying for her; for she hath not for many days received so much as a preserved barbery but it returns, and all accompanied with a fever, the mother, and an extreme ill spleen. Whilst I write this Tuesday morning from Bartlet House one brings me a packet to your master; he is gone; and that Lady and all the company is from town. I thought I might be pardoned, if I thought myself your man for that service to open it, which I did, and for the letters I will deliver them. What else you bid Foster do in his letter, bid him do it there, for (so God help me) I know not what it is. I must end now, else the carrier will be gone. God be with you. —Yours entirely.

[July 1609.]

"You know me without a name, and I know not how this letter goes."

Herford is "the little Lord Hertford," as Dudley Carleton calls him, who had been Ambassador-Extraordinary to Brussels, and was the surviving son of Edward Seymour, Duke of Somerset, "the Protector."

The "Mistress Bolstrod" here mentioned was Cecil Boulstrod or Bulstrode, daughter of Edward Boulstrod of Hedgerley Boulstrod, in Bucks. She was born in 1584, and died at Twickenham Park on the 4th of August 1609. She also, like Lady Markham, was a cousin of the Countess of Bedford, and a Lady of the Bedchamber to Queen Anne. Donne seems to have taken a personal interest in this lady, whom Ben Jonson, in an obscure passage of his *Conversations* with Drummond of Hawthornden, and in some worthless verses, presents in a much less favourable light. Donne certainly wrote two elegies on Cecil Boulstrod, and possibly a third, that beginning "Language, thou art too narrow and too weak"; these poems seem to be inspired by strong personal esteem, though the expression of it is no longer pathetic.

The following letter refers to the death of Lady Markham, for Roe was a friend of her family, and himself wrote an elegy on the death of Lord Harington.

"*To* Mr. GEORGE GERRARD.[1]

"SIR,—I have not received that letter, which by this I perceive you sent to London; if there were anything in that by which I might have taken occasion to have done you service before this time, I have a double reason of grief for the want of it. I came from thence upon Thursday, where I left Sir Thos. Roe so indulgent to his sorrow, as it had been an injury to have interrupted it with my unuseful company.

"I have done nothing of that kind, as your letter intimates, in the memory of that good gentlewoman; if I had, I should not find any better use of it than to put it into your hands. You teach me what I owe her memory; and if I pay that debt so, you have a part and

[1] From *Letters* of 1651.

interest in it, by doing me the honour of remembering it: and therefore it must come quickly to you.

"I hope not for your return from Court till I come thither; which if I can be master of myself or servant to myself, which I think is all one, I hope to do some ten days hence, making it my way to the Bath. If you find any there that have not forgot my name, continue me in their favour, and hold in yourself a firm assurance that I am,

"Your affectionate servant,
"J. DONNE."

When John Donne the younger edited, or rather flung to the world in complete disorder, the correspondence of his father in 1651, he dedicated the volume "to the most virtuous and excellent lady, Mrs. Bridget Dunch." This lady had "protected that part of [Donne's] soul that he left behind him, his Fame and his Reputation," and had conferred courtesies on him while he was living. It is therefore something more than a coincidence that the collection of letters should open with four trifling notes written, in or about the year 1609, to Mistress Bridget White. It seems obvious that the Bridget White of 1609 was in close relation with the Bridget Dunch of 1651. It is tempting to conjecture that they were the same person. The very young lady, addressed with so much gaiety in these trivial notes, had she been eighteen when they were written, would be but just sixty when they were printed. Bridget Dunch was the daughter of Sir Anthony Hungerford by his first marriage with Elizabeth, daughter of Sir Thomas Lucy, the father of Donne's friend. Sir Anthony did not die until 1637, when he must have attained a great age. His daughter and only child married Edmund Dunch of Wittenham, Berkshire, and thus the Down Ampney branch of the Hungerfords became extinct and passed to the Dunches. Bridget's son was Hungerford Dunch, who became a prominent man in the Commonwealth time. Tempting as it is, however, to identify this lady, to whom the *Letters* of 1651 were dedicated, as to an old friend of Donne, with Bridget White, I do not see how it can be done, except on the rather improbable supposition that she married, in brief first nuptials, some unrecorded Mr. White. I am myself inclined to identify Bridget White with that daughter of Thomas White, Esq., of Southwick, Hants, who about April 1612 married Sir Henry Kingsmill, son and heir of Sir William Kingsmill, and who in much later years was certainly a friend of Donne. Sir Henry died on the 26th of October 1624, but his widow survived at a very great age until 1672. The indications of internal evidence, except in one instance, the reference to Cleves, are slight. Sir Edward Herbert, who had been knighted on July 24, 1603, was in London between February 1609 and July 1610. His serious illness was nearer the former than the latter date.

"*To the Worthiest* Lady Mrs. BRIDGET WHITE.[1]

"MADAME,—I could make some guess whether souls that go to heaven retain any memory of us that stay behind, if I knew whether you ever thought of us, since you enjoyed your heaven, which is yourself, at home.

"Your going away hath made London a dead carcass. A Term and a Court do a little spice and embalm it and keep it from putrefaction, but the soul went away in you; and I think the only reason why the plague is somewhat slackened is because the place is dead already, and nobody left in it worth the killing.

"Wheresoever you are there is London enough; and it is a diminishing of you to say so, since you are more than the rest of the world. When you have a desire to work a miracle you will return hither, and both raise the place from the dead and the dead also who are in it; of which I were one, but that a hope that I have a place in your favour keeps me alive; which you shall abundantly confirm to me, if by one letter you vouchsafe to tell me that you have received my six, for now my letters are grown to that bulk, that I may divide them like Amadis

[1] From the Tobie Matthew Collection.

de Gaule's books, and tell you that this is the first letter of the second part of the first book.

"Your humblest and affectionate servant,
"J. D.

"Strand, St. Peter's Day
at nine, 29*th June.*"

"*To* BRIDGET WHITE.¹

"MADAME,—This letter which I send enclosed hath been yours many months, and hath languished upon my table for a passage so long, that as others send news in their letters, I send an antiquity in mine. I durst not tear it after it was yours: there is some sacrilege in defacing anything consecrated to you, and some impiety to despair that anything devoted to you should not be reserved to a good issue. I remember I should have sent it by a servant, of whose diligence I see I was too confident. I know not what it says; but I dare make this letter no longer, because being very sure that I always think the same thoughts of you, I am afraid I should fall upon the same words, and so send one letter twice together.—Your very affectionate servant, J. D.

"*November 8.*"

"*To the Worthiest Lady* Mrs. B. W.²

"MADAME,—I think the letters which I send to you single lose themselves by the way for want of a guide, or faint for want of company. Now, that on your part there be no excuse, after three single letters I send three together, that every one of them may have two witnesses of their delivery. They come also to wait upon another letter from Sir E. Herbert, of whose recovery from a fever you may apprehend a perfecter contentment than we, because you had none of the former sorrow. I am an heretic if it be found doctrine that pleasure tastes best after sorrow. For my part, I can love health well enough,

¹ From *Letters* of 1651.   ² *Ibid.*

though I be never sick; and I never needed my mistress' frowns and disfavours to make her favours acceptable to me. In States it is a weakness to stand upon a defensive war, and safer not to be invaded than to have overcome; so in our soul's health, an innocence is better than the heartiest repentance. And in the pleasures of this life, it is better that the variety of the pleasures give us the taste and appetite to it, than a sour and sad interruption quicken our stomach; for then we live by physic. I wish, therefore, all your happiness such as this entire, and without flaw or spot of discontentment; and such is the love and service of

"Your humblest and affectionatest servant,
"J. D.

" Strand, St. Peter's Day, at four."

" *To the Honourable Lady* Mrs. B. W.[1]

"MADAME,—I have but small comfort in this letter; the messenger comes too easily to me, and I am too sure that the letter shall be delivered. All adventures towards you should be of more difficulty and hazard. But perchance I need not lament this; it may be so many of my letters are lost already that it is time that one should come, like Job's servant, to bring word that the rest were lost. If you have had more before, this comes to ask how they were received; and if you have had none, it comes to try how they should have been received.

"It comes to you like a bashful servant, who, though he have an extreme desire to put himself in your presence, yet hath not much to say when he is come: yet hath it as much to say as you can think; because what degrees soever of honour, respect, and devotion you can imagine or believe to be in any, this letter tells you that all those are in me towards you.

"So that for this letter you are my secretary; for your worthiness and your opinion that I have a just estimation of them write it; so that it is as long and as good as you

[1] From *Letters* of 1651.

think it, and nothing is left to me, but as a witness, to subscribe the name of

"Your most humble servant,

[*July* 1610.] "J. D.

"Though this letter be yours, it will not misbecome or disproportion it that I mention your noble brother, who is gone to Cleve, not to return till towards Christmas, except the business deserve him not so long."

The reference here evidently is to the going of Mistress White's brother in the English force, under Sir Edward Cecil, to act with the Dutch in July 1610, under the general command of Christian of Anhalt. The death of Duke John William of Cleves, on the 25th of March 1609, led to the opening up of various important international questions connected with the Cleves-Juliers succession. The English and Dutch army sat down to the siege of Juliers on the 17th of July.

A friend whom Donne secured about this time, and retained for the remainder of his life, was Sir Robert Ker. This excellent and learned man, an enthusiast in letters and a most loyal and affectionate friend, was born in 1578. He came to England with James I., and in 1603 was made Groom of the Bedchamber to Prince Henry of Wales. About the time we have reached in this narrative, Ker had been appointed one of the prince's gentlemen-in-ordinary. Long afterwards, after the death of Donne in fact, he was created Earl of Ancrum.

On the 14th of February 1610 John Chamberlain writes to Dudley Carleton that John Donne again desires to be Secretary of Virginia. This was immediately after the "Starving Time," when the colony was only just saved from extermination by the relieving expedition from the Bermudas, which ultimately arrived under Sir Thomas Gates and Sir George Somers, on the 23rd of May. What Donne wished for was to be sent with Lord Delaware and Sir Ferdinando Werman on the expedition from England which arrived at Mulberry Point in Virginia on the 8th of June 1610. Lord Delaware administered the colony until ill-health drove him back to England in March 1611. This would have been a curious episode in Donne's life, although he seems fitted neither in constitution, nor aptitude, nor temperament for roughing it in so barbarous a commonwealth as Virginia was in those days of uncertain tenure. It will be seen later on that Donne never lost his interest in and sympathetic curiosity about Virginia.

The two letters now following may belong to the early part of this year 1610:—

" *To the Honourable Knight* Sir ROBERT KARRE [KER].[1]

" SIR,—Lest you should think yourself too much beholding to your fortune, and so rely too much upon her hereafter, I am bold to tell you that it is not only your good fortune that hath preserved you from the importunity of my visits all this time; for my ill-fortune, which is stronger than any man's good fortune, hath concurred in the plot to keep us asunder, by infecting one in my house with the measles.

" But all that is so safely overworn that I dare not only desire to put myself into your presence, but by your mediation a little farther. For, esteeming myself by so good a title as my Lord's own words, to be under his providence and care of my fortune, I make it the best part of my studies how I might ease his Lordship by finding out something for myself. Which, because I think I have done, as though I had done him a service therein, I adventure to desire to speak with him, which I beseech you to advance, in addition to your many favours and benefits to me.

"And if you have occasion to send any of your servants to this town to give me notice what times are fittest for me to wait to enjoy your favour herein, my business is of that nature, that loss of time may make it much more difficult, and may give courage to the ill fortune of
" Your humble servant,
" J. DONNE."

[1] From *Letters* of 1651.

"*To the Honourable Knight* Sir ROBERT KARRE [KER].[1]

"SIR,—I make account that it is a day of great distribution of honours at Court. I would not therefore lose my part and increase therein, since every letter admitted by you from me is a new stone in my best building, which is my room in your service, so much you add to me every time you give me leave thus to kiss your hands.

"But, sir, every addition pre-imagines a being, and the time of my being and creation is not yet come, which, I am sure, you will advance, because else I am no competent subject of your favours and additions. I know, by your forbearing to tell me so, that my L[ord] hath had no commodity to move the K[ing], and if this paper speak one word of difference or impatience in my name, by my troth it lies. Only give it leave to tell you that that L[ord], whom perchance the K[ing] may be pleased to hear in it, is an old and momentany [*sic*] man, and it may be late labouring for his assistance next winter.

"Besides, since it may be possible that the Master of the Rolls may a little resent this suit, there could be no fitter time than now to make him easy, as things stand with him at this time. If you stay in town this night, and no longer, I beseech you afford me a few of your late minutes at your own lodging, where I will wait upon you according to any directions, which by this gent. or otherwise I shall receive from you.

"Your humble servant,
"JOHN DONNE."

In the beginning of 1611 the Master of the Rolls was Sir Edward Phelips, of the famous house of Phelips of Montacute. He had had the reversion of this office for some months.

"*To* Sir H[ENRY] GOODYER.[2]

"SIR,—If this which I send you enclosed give me right intelligence, I present you a way by which you may

[1] From *Letters* of 1651.   [2] *Ibid.*

redeem all your former wastes, and recompense your ill fortunes, in having sometimes apprehended unsuccessful suits, and (that which I presume you affect most) ease yourself from all future inquisition of widows or such businesses as ask so over-industrious a pursuit, as divest a man from his best happiness of enjoying himself. I give you (I think) the first knowledge of two millions confiscated to the Crown of England, of which I dare assure myself the coffers have yet touched none, nor have the Commissioners for suits anything to oppose against a suit founded upon this confiscation, though they hold never so strictly to their instructions.

"After you have served yourself with a proportion, I pray make a petition in my name for as much as you think may be given me for my book out of this; for, but out of this, I have no imagination. And for a token of my desire to serve him, present Mr. Fowler with three or four thousand pounds of this, since he was so resolved never to leave his place without a suit of that value. I wish your cousin in the town better provided, but if he be not, here is enough for him. And since I am ever an affectionate servant to that journey, acquaint Mr. Martin from me how easy it will be to get a good part of this for Virginia.

"Upon the least petition that Mr. Brook can present, he may make himself whole again, of all which the King's servants, Mr. Lepton and Master Waterouse, have endamaged him. Give him leave to offer to Mr. Hakewill enough to please himself for his *Aurum Reginæ*. And if Mr. Gherard [Gerrard] have no present hopeful design upon a worthy widow, let him have so much of this as will provide him that house and coach which he promised to lend me at my return. If Mr. Inago Jones be not satisfied for his last masque (because I hear say it cannot come to much), here is enough to be had.

"This is but a copy, but if Sir Ro. Cotton have the original, he will not deny it you; if he hath it not, nobody else hath it, nor can prevent you; husband it well, which you may easily do, because I assure myself none of the children nor friends of the party condemned, will cross you or importune the King for any part. If I get no more by it, yet it hath made me a letter.

"And, sir (to depart from this mine), in what part of my letters soever you find the remembrance of my humble service to my Lord of Bedford, I beseech you ever think them intended for the first, and in that rank present them. I have yet received but one letter from you which was of the 10th of December, by Mr. Pory, but you see that as long as there is one egg left in the nest, I never leave laying, nor should, although you had sent none since; all at last will not amount to so good a testimony as I would fain give how much I am
"Your affectionate servant and lover,
"J. DONNE."

"SIR,—I write this letter in no very great degree of a convalescence from such storms of a stomach colic as kept me in a continual vomiting, so that I know not what I should have been able to do to despatch this wind, but that an honest fever came and was my physic. I tell you of it only lest some report should make it worse, for methinks that they who love to add to news should think it a masterpiece to be able to say no worse of any ill-fortune of mine than it deserves, since commonly it deserves worse than they can say, but they did not, and I am reprieved. I find dying to be like those facts which denying makes felony; when a sickness examines us, and we confess that we are willing to die, we cannot, but those who are—incur the penalty; and I may die yet, if talking idly be an ill sign. God be with you."

This curious outburst of jocose extravagance refers to persons and events now, in the main, hopelessly obscure to us. Some of the persons thus facetiously alluded to have already been mentioned in these pages. William Hakewill (1574-1655) was a legal antiquary of much industry, who at this time represented the little Cornish borough of Mitchell in Parliament. Of John Pory, whom we shall meet with again, there is more to be said. He was a useful, active cosmographer, who had worked assiduously for Hakluyt, and who now looked higher, and hoped to become a diplomatist. He was the intimate friend of Sir Robert Cotton, the antiquary, who is also the butt here of Donne's lively wit. Pory had entered Parliament in 1605, but in the autumn of 1607 he had gone travelling in the Low Countries trying to develop a scheme for introducing silk-loom stocking-weaving into England. We shall presently meet this industrious, energetic, and helpful man again.

Hakewill was Queen Anne's Solicitor-General. The *Aurum Reginæ*, or Queen-Gold, was a payment to a queen-consort due from all who give a fine to the king of ten marks or upward, being one-tenth of the offering or fine. This was an ancient right which had fallen into disuse in Tudor times, because after Henry VIII. there had been no queen-consort. Anne of Denmark claimed her "queen-gold," but did not exact it. The Chief Justice and Chief Baron reported against it, in spite of Hakewill's book. William Fowler was the Queen's Secretary. He was a poet in his way,[1] and was a maternal uncle of Drummond of Hawthornden; Drummond's interest in Donne is known, and was stimulated by the conversations of Ben Jonson. Mr. Martin was the son of that Sir Richard Martin, Lord Mayor of London in 1593, of whom mention has already been made. The younger Richard Martin became Recorder of London in 1618. Brook was the name of the member for St. Ives in the Parliament sitting in 1610.

It has been suggested to me by Dr. Jessopp that in the early part of this letter there is a series of far-fetched and obscure allusions to the debates in Parliament on the Great Contract of 1610. "It is at least deserving of notice," says my eminent friend, "that the names of Hakewill, Brook, Martin, and Sir Robert Cotton are those of prominent speakers in the debates" on that notable adventure in finance. I think there can be little question that Dr. Jessopp is right, and, if so, the date of Donne's letter is manifestly the summer or early autumn of 1610.

---

[1] His cycle of sonnets, *Love's Tarantula*, still remains, I believe, unpublished among the Hawthornden MSS.

CONTROVERSIAL WORKS

DIVINE POEMS

CHAPTER VIII

CONTROVERSIAL WORKS—DIVINE POEMS

THE close of Donne's residence at Mitcham was distinguished by a remarkable literary activity; this was indeed the moment of his life, from 1609 to 1611, at which his powers seem to have been most closely centred on literature. It is convenient to break off the record of his career at this point, to recapitulate and to review the various compositions of these months. We meet, first of all, with three curious books, each on the borderland of theology, and yet written by a man still resolutely determined to avoid the profession of divinity. These three works, *Pseudo-Martyr*, *Ignatius his Conclave*, and *Biathanatos*, are completely independent in intention and scope, but they have this one feature in common, they are the result of the peculiar mental discipline which Donne had gone through as the secretary and coadjutor of Morton in his controversy with the Roman Church. For years, now, Donne had been giving his most earnest attention to the points in dispute between the Church of England and the Papacy. He had been analysing and commentating, he had supplied Morton with an exact and copious précis of the arguments upon both sides. In the six volumes or tractates, which Morton had published, the mind of Donne had been ceaselessly active. Now, released from the service of the Dean, he continued to use his notes for his own purposes, reducing to order the spare material which remained at his hand.

It has been noted by Dr. Jessopp that "even if we had not been told that [Donne] gave Morton constant and valuable help, a comparison of the authorities quoted and referred to in Morton's *Catholic Appeal* with those set down in Donne's *Pseudo-Martyr*, would convince a careful reader of the fact. The curious and out-of-the-way books cited in both works are very numerous, and not to be found elsewhere." Donne himself speaks of his intense study of the religious controversies of the time, of his "cribrating and re-cribrating and post-cribrating" the various arguments of the Popish Recusants. Of the results of these meditations, so far as they were independent of the guidance of Morton, it may be convenient to take *Pseudo-Martyr* first as the earliest published, although the latest in order of composition. Walton states that "about this time there grew many disputes that concerned the Oath of Supremacy and Allegiance, in which the King had appeared, and engaged himself by his public writings now extant; and his Majesty discoursing [1] with Mr. Donne concerning many of the reasons which are usually urged against the taking of those oaths, apprehended such a validity and clearness in his stating the questions and his answers to them, that his Majesty commanded him to bestow some time in drawing the arguments into a method, and then to write his answers to them; and having done that, not to send but be his own messenger and bring them to him. To this he presently and diligently applied himself, and within six weeks brought them to him under his own handwriting as they be now printed; the book bearing the name of *Pseudo-Martyr*, printed anno 1610." [2]

This account has always been taken as correct, but it is necessary to point out difficulties in the way of its acceptance. In the work itself, and particularly in the epistle of dedication to James I., there is no trace of any such royal command as Walton suggests. If the King did urge the composition of such a work, the author is very careful to conceal the fact. It may be only a blind which makes him seem to recommend his treatise, somewhat anxiously, to the King's notice; but his exact words deserve quotation:—

"Of my boldness in this address, I most humbly beseech your Majesty to admit this excuse, that, having observed how much your Majesty had vouchsafed to de-

---

[1] "Occasionally talking," 1640. [2] Most of this was added in 1659.

scend to a conversation with your subjects by way of your books, I also conceived an ambition of ascending to your presence by the same way, and of participating, by this means, their happiness of whom that saying of the Queen of Sheba may be usurped, Happy are thy men, and happy are those thy servants, which stand before thee always and hear thy wisdom."

This ambition, by means of an erudite contribution to controversy in the Royal sense, to elevate himself and to stand before the King, is perhaps more intelligible than Walton's story of the Royal command. But again, although it may well be that six weeks sufficed in which to write the *Pseudo-Martyr*, there is internal evidence to show that the inception of the work was not so sudden. I do not know whether the curious fact has been noted that, while the "Table of the Chapters handled in this Book" promises fourteen sections, the volume itself contains only twelve. This "Table" is printed on a separate leaf, and from a passage in the "Advertisement" it may be concluded that it was circulated so freely, before the publication, or even composition, of the volume, that it fell into the hands of the adversaries of Donne. It would seem that it was sent about, as a syllabus of the forthcoming book, probably in order that before handling so extremely delicate a theme the best legal and theological opinion in the country might be obtained. "Some of the Roman profession, having only seen the heads and grounds handled in this book" (which proves that the circulation of the syllabus was far from being confidential), "have traduced me as an impious and profane undervaluer of martyrdom."

Moreover, the opinion of the legal authorities, and in particular of Sir Edward Coke, having proved adverse to the treatment of the subjects proposed by Donne for his thirteenth and fourteenth sections, those projected chapters were never written at all; Donne "chose to forbear the handling" of these themes for the present. But he allowed them to appear in his Table of Contents, and we may give the headings here as suggesting what it was still a little too hazardous for the most loyal and the most learned of James I.'s subjects to discuss in the year of grace 1610.

"CHAP. XIII.

"That all which his Majesty requires by this Oath [of Allegiance] is exhibited to the Kings of France, and not by virtue of any indult or concordat, but by the inherent right of the Crown.

"CHAP. XIV.

"Lastly: That no pretence, either of conversion at first, assistance in the conquest, or acceptation of any surrender from any of our Kings, can give the Pope any more right over the Kingdom of England than over any other free State whatsoever."

When it came to be published, *Pseudo-Martyr* was a handsome quarto of 392 pages, and its sub-title clearly defined its scope in the words, "wherein, out of certain propositions and gradations this conclusion is evicted, that those which are of the Roman Religion in this Kingdom may and ought to take the Oath of Allegiance." The author's name does not appear upon the title-page, but the Epistle Dedicatory is signed by "Your Majesty's most humble and loyal Subject, John Donne." The copy in my own library has the interesting feature that it was presented to Rowland Woodward, and bears the inscription— "Ex dono authoris Rou. Woodward: De juegos el mejor es con la hoja." This latter phrase, which seems to combine the double meaning: "The best of diversions is turning the page" [of a book] or the sword-blade [of a controversy], is an instance of Donne's fondness for using proverbial tags of Spanish. Walton's account of the haste with which the book was prepared is certainly borne out by the extremely formidable list of errata, which by no means exhausts the obvious misprints in the volume. Some of these deserve and account for Donne's irritation, as expressed "to the reader"; *inciting* for *aviling* and *dominium*

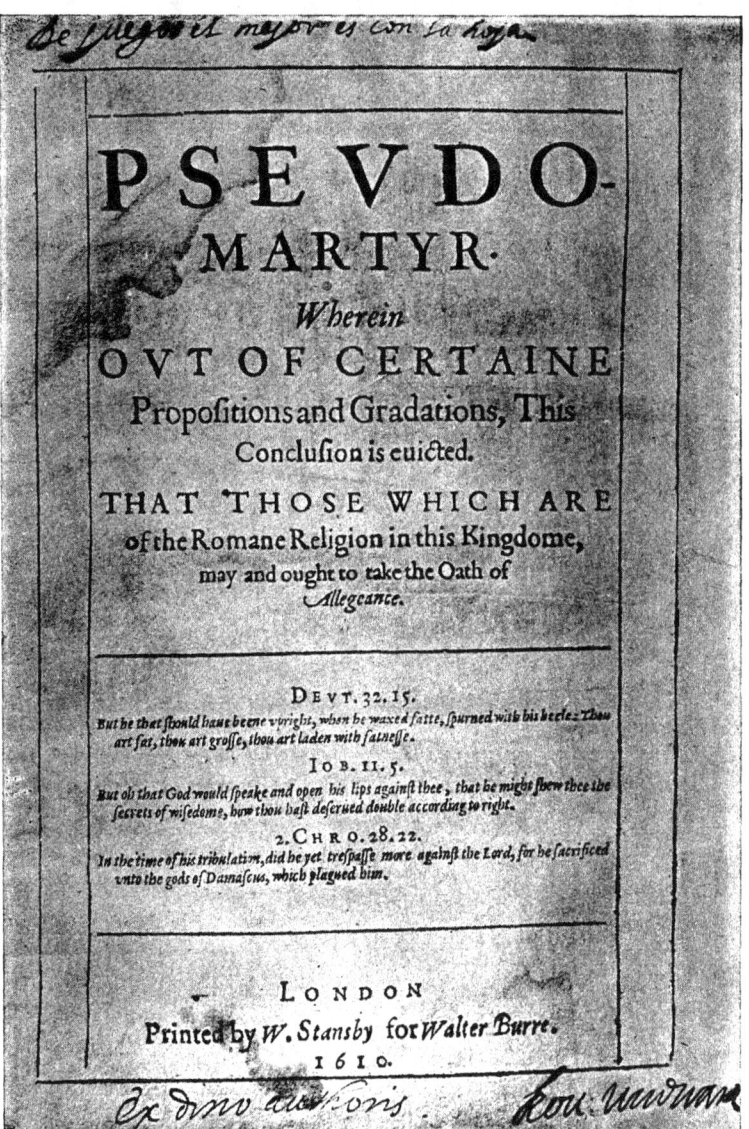

TITLE-PAGE OF *PSEUDO-MARTYR*
(REDUCED IN FACSIMILE)

From the Copy given by DONNE *to* ROWLAND WOODWARD

for *domicilium* would be enough to annoy a much meeker author than Donne ever was.

As was but due, *Pseudo-Martyr* is dedicated to that "most mighty and sacred sovereign," James I., whose personal contributions to the literary part of the controversy with Rome are eulogised in no measured terms. The Preface, addressed to "The Priests and Jesuits, and to their Disciples in this Kingdom," is of greater general value. The modern reader is to be excused if he examines these faded controversial works with a quicker interest in their author than in the dispute itself. Donne writes pathetically of his "infirmities," physical and mental, and we, who know that he enjoyed the reputation and displayed the results of an amazing application to a variety of learned studies, smile at this very modest report of his intellectual shortcomings.

"My natural impatience not to dig painfully in deep and stony and sullen learnings; my indulgence to my freedom and liberty, as in all indifferent things, so in my studies also, not to betroth or enthral myself to any one science, which should possess or denominate [? dominate] me; my easiness to afford a sweet and gentle interpretation to all professors of Christian Religion, if they shake not the foundation wherein I have in my ordinary communication and familiar writings often expressed and declared myself, hath opened me enough to their malice [who would disparage me], and put me into their danger, and given them advantage to impute to me whatsoever such degrees of laziness, of liberty, of irresolution, can produce."

A little further on we come to an apology for Donne's whole spiritual life up to 1610—an apology evidently written with the greatest sincerity and seriousness. It is well worthy of our close attention; and if what we know of the exterior of Donne's life up to this date does not coincide exactly with the solemn presentment of himself here given, we must not idly dismiss him, even in these early days, as guilty of any inconsistency. Doubtless, when he was alone, and when his mind, relieved from the stress of business and social pleasure, had leisure to commune with itself, this was its normal and profound condition.

"They who have descended so low, as to take knowledge of me and to admit me into their consideration, know well that I used no inordinate haste nor precipitation in binding my conscience to any local religion. I had a longer work to do than many other men, for I was first to blot out certain impressions of the Roman religion, and to wrestle both against the examples and against the reasons by which some hold was taken and some anticipations early laid upon my conscience, both by persons who by nature had a power and superiority over my will, and others who by their learning and good life seemed to me justly to claim an interest for the guiding and rectifying of mine understanding in these matters. And although I apprehended well enough that this irresolution not only retarded my fortune but also bred some scandal, and endangered my spiritual reputation by laying me open to many misinterpretations, yet all these respects did not transport me to any violent and sudden determination till I had, to the measure of my poor wit and judgment, surveyed and digested the whole body of Divinity controverted between ours and the Roman Church. In which search and disquisition, that God which awakened me then, and hath never forsaken me in that industry, as He is the author of that purpose, so is He a witness of this protestation, that I behaved myself, and proceeded therein with humility and diffidence in myself, and by that which by His grace I took to be the ordinary means, which is frequent prayer, and equal and indifferent affections."

In the composition of *Pseudo-Martyr*, Donne is punctiliously anxious to guard himself from misconstruction. He insists that he is "no professed Divine"; and it is not of Theology, as from within, but of temporal matters intimately connected with divinity, and from without, that he writes. His position is that the Catholic recusants, who complain so bitterly of the sufferings which come upon them for their resistance to the sovereignty of King James I., are unworthy of sympathy, as "pseudo-martyrs," who have no right to the honourable distinction of having suffered in the cause of religion. Whether the tenets of Rome are true or false is a question into which the author declines to go. In either case he denies that those who suffer for refusing to take the Oath of Allegiance are in any recognisable sense martyrs at all. To place himself in a position to form an opinion on this subject, he first examines the constitution and dignity of martyrdom in the abstract; and he claims that a needless suffering and a corrupt desire to be injured without cause lead to an inordinate and insane affectation of martyrdom. If there is an honest and inevitable self-sacrifice, so there may be that which is vicious and erroneous. This vain martyrdom, he argues, so far from being a virtue, is a sin, and, if pushed far enough, may develop into the crime of suicide. This consideration of the possible destruction of one's life, and its excuses and its palliations, was indeed never far from the desperate and melancholy mind of Donne.

He then proceeds to find the Jesuits particularly prone to foster in their disciples this vain affectation of martyrdom; and he denies the right of the Pope to warrant any justification of suicide thus adopted in defiance of the laws of England. Upon this depends, of course, what was the most difficult crux of all—a just definition of what distinguishes the obedience due to sovereign princes from the obedience due to the authorities of an alien church; and here Donne expatiates at great length, and with a vast show of authorities. He proceeds to argue that even if the Pope could salve the consciences of his recusant followers, which Donne does not think he can do, the obligations of the law of the land would still be paramount, and would deprive the sufferings of law-breakers of all moral and spiritual efficacy.

This takes him about half-way through his inquiry; and he then turns to examine the arguments of such doctors as Bellarmine, Baronius, and Serarius. Bellarmine was an old opponent of his, the three volumes of *Disputationes de controversiis fidei adversus hujus temporis Hæreticos* having for nearly twenty years been familiar to him—"about his nineteenth year," if we may believe Walton (but Bellarmine's book was not published until the twenty-first year of Donne's life)—he had been convinced that "Bellarmine was the best defender of the Roman cause." It was no doubt due to Donne's early and intimate acquaintance with the Catholics of his own family, and his knowledge of their sincere convictions, that throughout this volume he adopts a calm and reasonable tone which was rare in the controversies of that age. His moderation, perhaps, combined with the somewhat cold ingenuity of his line of reasoning in this instance, prevented *Pseudo-Martyr* from achieving what can be called a popular success. It did not reach a second edition, and has never been reprinted, although Dr. Jessopp thinks that "it was almost immediately recognised as the most solid and masterly contribution to the literature of a discussion which had already been taken part in by the ablest and most famous divines of the Church of England."

On the 17th of April 1610 the University of Oxford conferred upon John Donne, "armiger, olim ex Aula Cervina, optima de republica, litteris, et religione meritus," the honorary degree of Master of Arts, Convocation permitting him to receive the degree without exercises and without taking the preliminary B.A. The Grace pronounced "Causa est quod huic Academiæ maxime ornamento sit ut ejusmodi viri, optime de republica et ecclesia meriti, gradibus Academicis insigniantur,"—it was for the credit of the university that such men as he who had deserved so well of the Church and State should be distinguished by academic honours. Next day (April 18) Donne was given an *ad eundem* degree, as a M.A. of Cambridge, incorporated at Oxford, in company with his friend, John Pory.

In 1610 not many books had been published in England in prose so easy and eloquent as that which Donne uses for a theme which, it must frankly be admitted, offers little attraction to a modern reader. As *Pseudo-Mar.yr*, then, is rather a rare book, and not likely to be ever re-issued, it may not be amiss to quote here its most eloquent page. In it the future Dean of St. Paul's stand vividly revealed. Nowhere else, through the four hundred pages of *Pseudo-*

Martyr, does Donne forget that he is speaking as an advocate, as a legal adviser of the King in resisting the pretensions of the Roman Recusants. But here, for a moment, a gentler inspiration comes upon him, and his voice is softened and modulated to music; here he is, in his personal appeal, the poet that had been, and the glowing preacher that was to be:—

"I call to witness against you, those whose testimony God Himself hath accepted. Speak then and testify, O you glorious and triumphant Army of Martyrs, who enjoy now a permanent triumph in heaven, which knew the voice of your Shepherd, and stayed till He called, and went then with all alacrity: Is there any man received into your blessed Legion by title of such a death as sedition, scandal, or any human respect occasioned? Oh no, for they which are in possession of that laurel are such as have washed their garments, not in their own blood only (for so they might still remain red and stained), but in the blood of the Lamb which changes them to white. Saint Chrysostom writes well, that the Sinner in the Gospel bathed and washed herself in her tears, not in her blood; and of St. Peter he asks this question, When he had denied Christ, *numquid sanguinem fudit?* No, says he, but he poured forth tears and washed away his transgression. That which Christian religion hath added to old philosophy, which was to do no wrong, is in this point no more than this, to keep our mind in an habitual preparation of suffering wrong, but not to urge and provoke and importune affliction so much as to make those punishments just, which otherwise had been wrongfully inflicted upon us. We are not sent into this world *to suffer* but *to do*, and to perform the offices of society required by our several callings. . . . Thus much I was willing to premit, to awaken you, if it please you to hear it, to a just love of your own safety, of the peace of your country, of the honour and reputation of your countrymen, and of the integrity of that which you call the Catholic cause; and to acquaint you so far with my disposition and temper as that you need not be afraid to read my poor writings, who join you with mine own soul in my prayers, that your obedience here may prepare your admission into the heavenly Hierusalem, and that by the same obedience, *your days may be long in the land which the Lord your God hath given you.* Amen."

To the next of Donne's publications his critics and biographers have hitherto given less attention than it deserves. The *Conclave Ignatii*, of which only two copies are known to exist, has been treated as "a bookling of little merit," and has not been carefully enough examined for biographical matter. In the first place, even Dr. Jessopp has attributed it to the years when Donne was working with Morton; he says that "the date of composition can hardly be later than 1608." As we shall see, however, it cannot possibly be earlier or later than 1611. The Latin edition is without date, but an English version was published in the last-mentioned year; both were anonymous. The *Conclave Ignatii*, or, to give it its English title, *Ignatius his Conclave*, is a tract composed in a very different spirit from that of *Pseudo-Martyr;* this is a squib, or series of squibs, all composed of bitter jests and skirmishings. The two editions appear to be identically parallel, even the tags of verse in the Latin responding exactly to similar tags in the English. It has been suggested that these original editions were pirated; but of this I see no evidence whatever, and I conceive that the idea arose from a wish to excuse Donne for having published a work so frivolous. He seems himself to have felt that it was not quite a dignified thing to do, and he produces a pretended letter from a friend, who says that :—

"The author was unwilling to have this book published, thinking it unfit both for the matter, which in itself is weighty and serious, and for that gravity which himself had proposed and observed in another book [*Pseudo-Martyr*] formerly published, to descend to this kind of writing. But I, on the other side, mustered my forces against him, and produced reasons and examples." In the language of this apologetic friend it is Donne himself who masquerades.

The plan of *Ignatius his Conclave* has about it not a

little of the ingenuity of Swift, and even something of the splendour of Beckford. Donne, in consequence of having dazzled his imagination with the daring discoveries of the New Astronomy, falls asleep and dreams that he is at the gate of hell and sees all its rooms open to his sight. The lost souls crowd the vestibule, but a space is cleared from them and a throne set in the great central hall. Doors open at the back, and Lucifer appears, leaning on the arm of his obsequious favourite, Ignatius Loyola. The demon sinks into the throne and commands that the souls of the lost shall approach him to plead their causes. Copernicus (for Donne's mind is still full of astronomy and the new revolutionary discoveries) comes forward by Donne's side in the darkness and batters with his hands at the gates. He is admitted, and he holds a long conversation with the arch-fiend, who proves singularly timid, and would be foiled in argument were it not that Ignatius Loyola stands by the elbow of his throne and whispers to him insidious replies. Then Paracelsus advances in the guise of a cadaverous vulture, and then Macchiavelli, who, " having observed Ignatius' forwardness and sauciness, and how, uncalled, he had thrust himself into the office of King's Attorney, thought this stupid patience of Copernicus and Paracelsus (men which tasted too much of Germany) unfit for a Florentine, and therefore had provided some venomous darts out of his Italian arsenal to cast against this worn soldier of Pampeluna, this French-Spanish mongrel, Ignatius."

But finding from the expression of Lucifer's countenance that this would be highly impolitic, he veers round and assails Ignatius with every species of mollifaction and flattery. He goes so far, however, that the quick spirit of Ignatius takes fright, and fearing to arouse the demon's jealousy, the arch-Jesuit grovels at Lucifer's feet, protesting his idolatrous loyalty. At this point controversial rage gets the better of Donne's fancy; the vision fades in a scandalous diatribe against the Popes, and the author spares us not the crudity of that darkest and most mysterious of all the crimes of the Renaissance, the outrage on the Bishop of Fano. All this, and a great deal more, takes the incongruous form of a tirade from the mouth of Ignatius himself. "Truly," says the author, "I thought this oration very long." Macchiavelli, who has been impatiently listening, now vanishes; and gazing at Lucifer, the dreamer observes a change in his countenance. He no longer leers at the arch-Jesuit with a doting fondness, but a dark shade of jealousy has come over his face. "Lucifer now suffered a new hell, that is, the danger of a Popular Devil, vainglorious and inclined to innovations. Therefore he determined to withdraw himself into his inward chamber, and to admit none but Ignatius, for he could not exclude him who had deserved so well, neither did he think it safe to stay without and give him more occasions to amplify his own work."

Accordingly the monarch will retire, on the arm of the presumptuous favourite, but a crowd of fantastic inventors throng about them, praying for protection. Ignatius sweeps these paltry phantoms aside, especially wounding and offending the shade of Pietro Aretino, unjustly, the dreamer thinks, since that poet had surely deserved, by his obscene inventions, an eminent place in the Jesuit's triumphant church. The ghosts of Christopher Columbus and of Philip Neri then cumber the retreat of the august pair, and in the midst of a general skirmish of popes, embryos, and friars, the soul of Donne comes suddenly back to his body, and bursts into very pretty verse as follows :—

> "As a flower wet with last night's dew, and then
> Warmed with the new sun, doth shake off again
> All drowsiness, and raise his trembling crown,
> Which crookedly did languish and stoop down
> To kiss the earth, and panteth now to find
> Those beams returned, which had not long time shined,"

so the poet himself wakes on the sun-lighted world again. And so ends this rather unseemly, but very vivacious and original, piece of Lucianic satire.

The internal evidence with regard to the date of the tractate will be found, I think, to be conclusive. Ignatius Loyola had been beatified in Rome by Pope Paul V. in

1609, and the pretensions of the Jesuits had in consequence greatly advanced; it is the extent of these provocative incursions, which have now reached England, which has roused Donne to this stinging and rancorous attack. But what is exceedingly interesting, and has hitherto escaped notice, is that Donne is completely captivated by the recent epoch-making discoveries in the science of astronomy. The new light came in with Galileo's famous invention of the telescope, consisting of the two plano-convex and plano-concave lenses fitted into a leaden tube. Donne speaks with a kind of rapture of Galileo, "who of late hath summoned the other worlds, the stars, to come nearer to him, and to give him an account of themselves." This is a direct reference to the treatise, called *Sidereus Nuncius*, in which, early in 1610, Galileo gave the learned world the very first intimations of the working of his new telescope. But we can date the *Ignatius his Conclave* more exactly still, for the invention of Galileo made very slow way over the Alps, and Kepler himself did not contrive to obtain one of the new telescopes until August 1610. In the beginning of 1611 he announced his experiments with it, and his approbation of the statements of Galileo, in the tract called *Dissertatio cum Nuncio Sidereo*. This Donne had manifestly read, for he speaks of Kepler's having "received it into his care, that no new thing should be done in heaven without his knowledge." No less acquaintance is shown with the earlier researches of Copernicus and Tycho Brahé, and it is evident that Donne had been steeping himself in the sensational expansion of the New Astronomy. If the reader pushes on to the last few pages of *Ignatius his Conclave* he will be rewarded by a fresh outburst of astronomical enthusiasm, and by nothing less than a quotation from the *Sidereus Nuncius* itself. The following fantastic passage may be worth quoting as doubtless the earliest English tribute to the discoveries of the great Italian :—

"Galileo the Florentine by this time hath thoroughly instructed himself of all the hills, woods, and cities in the new world, the Moon. And since he effected so much with his first glasses that he saw the Moon in so near a distance that he gave himself satisfaction of all and the least parts in her, when now, being grown to more perfection in his art, he shall have made new glasses, and they have received a hallowing from the Pope, he may draw the Moon, like a boat floating upon the water, as near the Earth as he will."

It is worth noting, as an example of the plasticity of Donne's mind, that the astronomers whom he celebrates had yet hardly passed into their fame; Kepler was a young man of little more than Donne's own years, and even Galileo had been born in 1564. Whatever was new and strong and mysterious had an instant welcome from the intellect of Donne.

Earlier in date of composition than either *Ignatius his Conclave* or *Pseudo-Martyr* is the famous and very curious apology for the principle of suicide, called *Biathanatos*. This was, it appears, written in 1608, but was never printed in the author's lifetime. He "forbade both the press and the fire" to touch it, and although it would have been madness to publish a work which must have closed all promotion in the Church to Donne, as the *Tale of a Tub* afterwards closed it to Swift, yet Donne was very anxious that this supreme and highly characteristic specimen of his syllogistic cleverness should not disappear. In 1619 he presented one MS. copy to Lord Herbert of Cherbury, and this is now preserved in the Bodleian; another to Sir Robert Ker. He communicated it "to some particular friends in both universities then where I writ it"; they replied that they were sure that the reasoning could not be sound, yet that they could discover no flaw in it. His direct injunction was, "Preserve it for me if I live, and if I die . . . publish it not, but yet burn it not."

One copy came into the hands of John Donne the younger, and his memory has to bear the considerable responsibility of having published it although he was acquainted with his father's embargo. In 1644, at the very moment when Milton was appealing against the restrictive ordinance of June 14, 1643, for the Regulation of Printing, the younger Donne found an easy-going censor who licensed the little volume on the 20th of September. It appeared, at the price of three shillings, later in 1644, under the title, no part of which must be omitted.

ΒΙΑΘΑΝΑΤΟΣ.

A

DECLARATION

of that

PARADOXE,

OR

THESIS, that

Selfe-Homicide is not so Naturally
Sinne, that it may never be otherwise.

WHEREIN

The Nature, and the extent of all these Lawes,
Which seem to be violated by this Act,
are diligently surveyed.

Written by JOHN DONNE, *who afterwards received
Orders from the Church of* England, *and dyed
Deane of Saint* Pauls, London.

It is a small quarto of 218 pages, bound in sheepskin. In order, doubtless, to deprecate criticism of his own act, the younger Donne has dedicated it to Philip, Lord Herbert. A comparison of the 1644 edition with the MS. in the Bodleian shows, by the trifling nature of the variations it introduces, that the younger Donne did not knowingly tamper with his father's text. There is prefixed an enormous list of nearly a hundred authorities quoted in the body of the work, among them being such names as those of Schlusselburgius and Pruckmannus, at which the modern eye gazes with respectful awe.

Donne starts on the perilous path of his inquiry by

frankly admitting that, like Beza, he has a natural tendency towards suicide. Beza, it appears, once nearly threw himself off a bridge in Paris to escape from pain, and Donne admits that he too has "often such a sickly inclination." His confession in this respect has been referred to in an earlier chapter, but may here be cited in full.

"Whether it be because I had my first breeding and conversation with men of a suppressed and afflicted religion, accustomed to the despite of death, and hungry of an imagined martyrdom; or that the common Enemy finds that door worst locked against him in me; or that there be a perplexity and flexibility in the doctrine itself; or because my conscience ever assures me that no rebellious grudging at God's gifts, nor other sinful concurrence accompanies these thoughts in me, or that a brave scorn, or that a faint cowardliness beget it—whensoever any affliction assails me, methinks I have the keys of my prison in mine own hand, and no remedy presents itself so soon to my heart as mine own sword. Often meditation of this hath won me to a charitable interpretation of their action who die so; and provoked me a little to watch and exagitate their reasons who pronounce so peremptory judgments upon them."

It needed no little intellectual courage to take up so perilous a thesis. Donne was well aware of the danger he ran of being pronounced a scandalous dreamer, a defender of immoral propositions. But his conscience was healthy if his nerves were not, and he had no idea of shrinking from the logical consideration of a problem because its terms were a little startling. "I abstained not," he proudly says, "for fear of misinterpretation from this undertaking. Our stomachs are not now so tender and queasy, after so long feeding upon solid divinity, nor we so umbrageous and startling, having been so long enlightened in God's paths, that we should think any truth strange to us."

Donne approaches his delicate and thorny theme through a consideration of the state of martyrdom. From the history of the church itself he argues that Man, as though he were a buried angel, labours to be discharged of that earthly sepulchre, his body. Martyrdom, examined closely, is but a sanctified self-homicide. A man is required to blaspheme God or to sin a deadly sin, and is told that if he refuses he will sacrifice his life. He does refuse and dies; he dies, therefore, by his own hand, since to have made another choice would have been to live. Yet, by the universal voice of Christendom his contempt of life is counted to him as righteousness. Nor is it in Christian annals only that the preference for death over shame is considered honourable; and Donne proceeds to draw up a martyrology of glorious suicides, beginning with Petronius Arbiter. One feels sorry that he never heard of the philosophy of the Kangakusha of Japan; the theory of the necessity of practising *hari-kiri* would have fascinated the imagination of Donne.

He is now bold enough to include John the Baptist, and all who have sealed their faith with their blood, in the category of self-homicided; and he claims that those who speak so glibly of "the scandalous disease of headlong dying," the sinful infirmity of despising life, should have the courage to include Cyprian and Germanus in their condemnation. And so he leads up, with a myriad of instances and arguments, to his central question, Is Suicide necessarily and essentially sin? This is the crux of the whole situation, and Donne proceeds to examine this from every possible point of view.

First of all, he finds nothing positively condemning it in Civil Law, and then, turning to Canon Law, he declares this to be governed by an apparatus so vague and so vast, that it is impossible to say what any remote corner of it may affirm or deny. It is plain, however, that we are permitted, under certain conditions, to long for the release of the spirit in death, and he argues that what we may lawfully wish for we may lawfully further. His method may here be exemplified by a very curious passage, which lends itself to our purpose, moreover, by being, less than almost any other in the body of the book, a string of cited instances. Thus he sums up the arguments in favour of permitting that species of passive self-homicide which is *mors negativa*, an irresponsible death :—

"Since I may without flying, or eating, when I have means, attend an executioner, or famine; since I may offer my life, even for another's temporal good; since I must do it for his spiritual; since I may give another my board [plank] in a shipwreck, and so drown; since I may hasten my arrival to heaven by consuming penances,—it is a wayward and unnoble stubbornness in argument to say, still, I must not kill myself, but I may let myself die; since, of affirmations and denials, of omissions and committings, of enjoining and prohibitory commands, ever the one implies and enwraps the other. And if the matter shall be resolved and governed only by an outward act, and ever by that; if I forbear to swim [when thrown into] a river, and so perish, because there is no act, I shall not be guilty; and yet I shall be guilty if I discharge a pistol upon myself, which I know not to be charged, nor intended harm, because there is an act."

He is very severe on those who quote against suicide the text about our bodies being the "temples of the Holy Ghost," and assert that it is sinful to demolish or to deface those temples. The sin against the body is to diminish its dignity, which only defilement does. But in the case of the self-slayer there is no defilement:—

"When he withdraws and purges [his body] from all corruptions [by killing himself], he delivers it from all the inquinations and venom and malign machinations of his and God's adversaries, and prepares it by God's insinuation and concurrence to that glory, which, without death, cannot be attained."

In the face of these and similar passages, it does not seem possible to say that Donne approached what has been excellently styled "this the greatest and most hazardous of all cases of conscience" from a purely dialectical standpoint. I cannot admit that Donne attacked his paradoxical thesis as "an idealist and an idealist only." It seems quite certain that he preserved, at all events in early middle life, a very faint hold upon vitality, and that he suffered, in his moments of depression, from an intense desire to free himself from the burden of it by poison, pistol, or flood. He knew that the wish was a morbid one, but he was conscious of its strength, and the fear was always present with him that he might some day succumb to it. But he was a man of unquestioning faith and of intense religious convictions. The ideas of mental disease, of neurosis, of irresistible and irresponsible impulse, which prevail to-day, and are so great a comfort to the weak, had not been propounded in Donne's day, although it is plain that some of them had faintly suggested themselves to him. It was, therefore, of extreme importance to Donne to persuade himself, with all the casuistry of which his ingenious brain was capable, that if he did some day yield to his weakness, and in a moment of despair throw off the intolerable load of life, he would yet have not committed a mortal sin. If this is not the purpose and the aim of *Biathanatos*, then it appears to me the idlest trifling with the dry bones of disputation that was ever committed. I am willing to believe that Donne was sick in soul, but not that he was a fantastic trifler, and I regard this curious little book as one of the most poignant relics of his intellectual career. Happily he resisted his sinister demon; he lived to praise God and fight his enemies; and we are therefore able to read *Biathanatos* without anguish, though never without deep and awestruck sympathy.

The Divine Poems of Donne offer considerable difficulty to his biographer. A few of them already are, or can approximately be, dated, but the majority are subject to conjecture founded upon internal evidence. They are of two orders; there are hymns and spiritual poems of Donne's which, however rugged their form, breathe a fervid spirit of faith and a genuine humility. In others the intellectual element outweighs the religious. These verses are rather extremely ingenious exercises in metrical theology than bursts of impulsive piety. It may be broadly suggested that the latter belong to the second, and the former to the third or final, division of Donne's career. That is to say, the more metaphysical pieces are the outcome of the years when religious inquiry formed one of his prominent studies, but when no exclusive call had summoned him to the ministry. In form all the sacred poetry of Donne suffers from his determination to introduce Spanish effects into English prosody, and Spanish ingenuities into the expression of English thought. If Donne's early hymns and litanies do not move us, it is largely due to the fact that they did not move himself. They are frigid, they are stiffened with legal and medical phraseology, the heart of a sinner saved does not beat beneath their "cross and correct concupiscence of wit."

An excess of ingenuity is peculiarly fatal to the unction of religious poetry. Unless it is spontaneous, unless it palpitates with ecstasy or moans with aspiration, unless it is the outpouring of a contrite spirit, it leaves upon the listener a sense of painful artificiality. The dogmatic verses of Donne do not escape from this disability. We admit their cleverness, and are sure that it is misplaced. The solemn mystery of Christ's three days' sojourn in the tomb is not, for instance, illuminated when Donne speaks of Him as one

> " Whose body, having walk'd on earth, and now
> Hasting to heaven, would—that He might allow
> Himself unto all stations and fill all—
> For those three days become a mineral.
> He was all gold when He lay down, but rose
> All tincture, and doth not alone dispose
> Leaden and iron wills to good, but is
> Of power to make e'en sinful flesh like His."

Here Donne's intellectual arrogance stood him in evil stead. He would not continue and intensify the tradition of such gentle Catholic singers of the Elizabethan age as Southwell and Constable; the hymns of Wither he had probably never seen, and would have despised; he shows not the slightest sign of having read the noblest religious poem written between the *Vision of Piers Plowman* and *Paradise Lost*, that *Christ's Victory and Triumph* which Giles Fletcher published just when Donne was moving to Drury House in 1610. He had doubtless read, without advantage to his style, Sylvester's popular version of the *Divine Weeks and Works*. But he disdained all that was purely English. His sympathy with Elizabethan verse, good or bad, was a negative quantity, and we can scarcely trace that he allowed himself to be even conscious of the existence of Spenser or Shakespeare. Among his English contemporaries he admired but one poet, Ben Jonson, and to him he was attracted by the very qualities which we now recognise as being anti-Elizabethan. Hence, in the history of literature, the sacred poetry of Donne is interesting mainly for its resolute independence of all existing English types, and for its effect in starting a new and efficient school of religious verse in which many of the disciples far exceeded the master. Donne prophesied, while those poets were not born or were but children, of George Herbert, of Crashaw, of the Vaughans, of Herrick in the *Noble Numbers*, of Cowley in the *Davideis*; and when we come to consider his posthumous glory we shall have to return to his crabbed and litigious early sacred poetry.

Of Donne's spiritual poems the most important, if we omit the two cycles of "Holy Sonnets," which belong to a later period, is that which he called "A Litany." He composed it in his bed, during his tedious illness at Mitcham in 1609, and he sent it to Sir Henry Goodyer with a learned note on the Litaneia, or public form of chanted prayer to God, and on its use in the Primitive Church. His own specimen is composed in a curious measure of his invention, in grave lines with an odd singing break in the middle of each stanza, an artifice from which, it is only fair to say, he rarely extracts so much charm as we might reasonably expect. The "Litany" is burdened with ingenuity. From a dogmatic point of view it shows Donne still imperfectly divorced from the tenets of Rome. He still proclaims the efficacy of the Virgin Mary's prayers to God the Father for souls on earth. Donne, who was much occupied at this time with the principle of martyrdom, dedicates these stanzas to the martyrs and confessors—

> " And since Thou so desirously
> Didst long to die, that long before thou could'st
> And long since Thou no more could'st die,
> Thou in thy scatter'd mystic body would'st

> In Abel die; and ever since
> In Thine; let their blood come
> To beg for us a discreet patiënce
> Of death, or of worse life; for O, to some
> Not to be martyrs is a martyrdom.
>
> Therefore with thee triumpheth there
> A virgin squadron of white cónfessors,
> Whose bloods betroth'd, not married, were,
> Tender'd, not taken, by those ravishers.
> They know, and pray that we may know,
> In every Christian
> Hourly tempestuous persecutions grow;
> Temptations martyr us alive; a man
> Is to himself a Diocletian."

The ingenious darkness of Donne's poetical expression never went further or achieved a richer gloom than it does in some of his Sacred Poems. The "Litany" is certainly not for use by the poor of the flock. The intellectual dangers so strangely petitioned against in the following stanza do not certainly afflict many humble-minded Christians, although they were real enough to Donne—

> "That learning, Thine ambassador,
> From Thine allegiänce we never tempt;
> That beauty, paradise's flower,—
> For physic made,—from poison be exempt;
> That wit—born apt high good to do—
> By dwelling lazily
> On Nature's nothing be not nothing too;
> That our affections kill us not, nor die;
> Hear us, weak echoes, O Thou Ear and Eye."

One more stanza may be given from this highly metaphysical poem, in which a considerable flower of beauty is choked by the weeds of pedantry and misplaced intelligence—

> "From being anxious, or secure,
> Dead clods of sadness, or light squibs of mirth,
> From thinking that great courts immure
> All, or no happiness, or that this earth
> Is only for our prison fram'd;
> Or that Thou'rt covetous
> To them whom Thou lovest, or that they are maim'd
> From reaching this world's sweet who seek Thee thus,
> With all Thy might, Good Lord, deliver us."

A poem which we can exactly date is that written for Good Friday 1613. Donne had been staying at Polesworth, in Warwickshire, with Sir Henry Goodyer, and he set forth on horseback to visit Magdalen Herbert and her son, Sir Edward, at Montgomery Castle. Six years earlier he had sent to this beloved lady "holy hymns and sonnets," of which but one survives, the quatorzain beginning—

> " Her of your name, whose fair inheritance
> Bethina was, and jointure Magdalo."

He now, looking forward to the joys of high spiritual converse with these elected friends, sends to him whom he leaves at Polesworth a meditation on the day. He is more direct and less tortured than usual—

> " I am carried towards the west,
> This day, when my soul's form bows to the East;
> There I should see a Sun by rising set,
> And by that setting endless day beget;
> But that Christ on His cross did rise and fall,
> Sin had eternally benighted all.
> Yet dare I almost be glad, I do not see
> That spectacle of too much weight for me;
> Who sees God's face, that is self-life, must die,—
> What a death were it then to see God die!"

That is impressive, and comparatively simple; but a spasm of his disease of style catches him, and he proceeds—

> " It made His own lieutenant, Nature, shrink,
> It made His footstool crack, and the sun wink.
> Could I behold those hands, which span the poles
> And tune all spheres at once, pierced with those holes?
> Could I behold that endless height, which is
> Zenith to us and our antipodes,
> Humbled below us?"

Nothing could be more odious; yet, such was the taste of the day that, no doubt, when he read these verses that evening in Montgomery Castle, the noble Herberts were not merely astonished, but charmed and edified.

We may confidently attribute "The Cross" to the Mitcham period. It shows Donne still more indignant at the obstinacy of political recusants than convinced with regard to the dogmas which separate Rome from the Reformed Churches. He writes here precisely as any fervent Italian or Spanish monk might do—

> " From me no pulpit, nor misgrounded law,
> Nor scandal taken, shall this cross withdraw,"

and he rejoices to see its emblem in every manifestation of natural force—

> " Look down, thou spiest out crosses in small things;
> Look up, thou seest birds rais'd on cross'd wings;
> All the globe's frame, and spheres, is nothing else
> But the meridian's crossing parallels."

In composing these early sacred poems, although he was at the very time fighting with Morton for the Anglicans, he could not but look back to Rome as the real arbiter, and had no warmer excuse to make for his odes and litanies than that the Roman Church herself need not call them defective.

It is to be observed that the early and amatory writings of Donne contain no single example of the sonnet, and that with the exception of one or two unimportant epistles in the quatorzain form, all his work in this class is to be found among his divine poems. He disdained the softness and vagueness of the Petrarchists, and had no ambition to compete with Drayton or Daniel in their addresses to a dimly-outlined Idea or Delia. The form he ultimately adopted for his sonnets is neither purely Italian, nor purely Elizabethan. He had not Milton's courage in recurring to the splendid fulness of the sonnet of Petrarch, but he eschewed the laxity of the English writers of his age; and though we have to regret that he adopted the final couplet, his octett is of perfect arrangement, and boasts but two rhymes. It is strange that he did not perceive how much his sonnets lose in grandeur by this concession to triviality in the sestett. It is part, however, of Donne's irremediable imperfection as an artist, that he has produced much noble poetry in his divine sonnets, and yet not one sonnet that can be considered faultless.

The style of this section of his poetry is extremely characteristic of himself and of certain exotic influences of his time. When he was in Italy, he must have been familiar with Tansillo and Molza, the polished Petrarchists of the age, who celebrated love and religion with an equal refinement. But he is not more touched by their manner of writing than by that of Spenser. Underneath the graceful accomplishment of the Cinque Cento, however, there ran hidden the vehement stream of speculative philosophic style, rugged and bold, and it was this which attracted Donne. With Galileo we know that he had a close sympathy. Did he dip with curiosity into the forbidden writings of Galileo's fellow-martyr, Giordano Bruno? We know not; yet here at least was an Italian with whom Donne had not a little fellowship in the construction of his mind. He had still more with that of a Dominican monk who was more exactly his contemporary, and of whose misfortunes he cannot fail to have heard. The Sonnets of Campanella have more kinship with "La Corona" and the Ecclesiastical Sonnets of Donne than with any other English writings. Yet neither poet can well have read the work of the other, and it is even a stretch of probability to hope that Donne may have seen the obscure volume of Campanella's poems which the German, Tobias Adami, published in 1622. The similarity is accidental, and is founded upon a certain double sympathy with the obscurity and with the heterodoxy of the strange Italian pantheists of the age. Had Donne been born south of the Alps, his work might probably have taken a less tormented form than it actually adopted, but his body would almost certainly have been tortured with Campanella's, if by a happy fate it escaped the stake with Vanini's.

The influence of Hooker has been observed on the writings of Donne, but the name of the author of the *Ecclesiastical Polity* is nowhere mentioned in print by the younger divine. Hooker died in 1600, and there is nothing to suggest that the two men ever came into personal relations. A scrap of information, hitherto unpublished, is not without interest in this connection. A copy of Dr.

William Covell's *A Just and Temperate Defence of the Five Books of Ecclesiastical Polity, written by Mr. Richard Hooker*, 1603, exists, on the fly-leaf of which was written the following distich—

"AD AUTHOREM.
Non eget Hookerus tanto tutamine; tanto
Tutus qui impugnet sed foret Auxilio.
J. DONNE."

I do not doubt the authenticity of this couplet, and we see Donne, like Dr. Johnson of Mrs. Montagu, inquiring of Covell whether he had estimated the value of his help before he proffered it.

DRURY HOUSE AND PARIS
1610–1612

PORTRAIT OF ELIZABETH DRURY

From the Original Painting, now in the possession of G. Milner-Gibson-Cullam, Esq.

CHAPTER IX

DRURY HOUSE AND PARIS

1610–1612

IN the year 1610, and shortly after the death of his faithful patron and kinsman, Sir Francis Wolley, Donne formed an acquaintance which gave an entirely new colour to his life and a new channel to his thoughts. Sir Robert Drury, of Hawsted, in Suffolk, who was one of the wealthiest men in England, had a daughter, Elizabeth, for whom he nourished the loftiest ambitions.[1] It is said that he dreamed of preparing her, as the consort of Prince Henry, for the throne itself. This girl, his sole heiress and hope, died in her fifteenth year, early in 1610, and was commemorated by the erection of an almshouse for widows at Hawsted. The despairing grief of Sir Robert Drury, who was a man of extravagant passions, was widely reported, and came to the ears of Donne. The poet, although he had never seen the young lady, set about to compose in her honour a little "funeral elegy" of 106 lines, which he forwarded to her sorrowing father. The tone he took was exalted enough—

"We may well allow
Verse to live so long as the world will now,
For her death wounded it. The world contains
Princes for arms, and counsellors for brains,
Lawyers for tongues, divines for hearts, and more,
The rich for stomachs, and for backs the poor;
The officers for hands, merchants for feet,
By which remote and distant countries meet;

---

[1] Through the courtesy of Mr. G. Milner-Gibson-Cullum, I am enabled to reproduce for the first time the interesting portrait of Elizabeth Drury which is in his possession.

> But those fine spirits, which do tune and set
> This organ, are those pieces which beget
> Wonder and love; and these were she; and she
> Being spent, the world must needs decrepit be."

With extreme hyperbole of praise and lamentation there are mingled some personal touches, such as of the smallness of Elizabeth Drury's stature, and of her delicacy, like "a lamp of balsamum"—

> "One, whose clear body was so pure and thin,
> Because it need disguise no thought within,"

and we are left with a suspicion that Donne was supplied with information, if not actually approached with a suggestion. However this may be, no poem was ever more lucky in securing the fortunes of a poet. Sir Robert Drury accepted with rapturous pleasure an elegy which informed the world that Death, having slain his poor little daughter,

> "can find nothing, after her, to kill,
> Except the world itself, so great as she."

He was "a gentleman of a very noble estate and a more liberal mind," and having formed Donne's personal acquaintance, he determined to attach him to his person. He "assigned him and his wife a useful apartment in his own large house in Drury Lane, and not only rent-free, but was also a cherisher of his studies, and such a friend as sympathised with him and his in all their joy and sorrows." Drury Place, in which the Donnes now settled under such pleasant auspices, was a mansion surrounded by gardens on the road north-west of Temple Bar. It was afterwards shorn of part of its demesne and became known as Craven House, its last remnants being destroyed in 1809. The Olympic Theatre is said to be built on a portion of its site.

When a year had elapsed since the death of Elizabeth Drury, Donne gratified his patron by the composition of the very curious and fantastical gnomic poem called *An Anatomy of the World*. By this time a monument had been placed in Hawsted Church, in which the child was represented, as in so many similar memorials, supporting her head with her hand. This gave rise to a foolish legend that her death was due to her father's having boxed her ears. Donne's poem was published in 1611, with the original Funeral Elegy appended to it. This was the earliest of his publications in verse, and it was against his will that it appeared. His opinion, and almost his conscience, was opposed to so much publicity, but the amiable vanity of Sir Robert Drury overpowered him. Of this original edition only two copies are known to exist. In *An Anatomy of the World*, the extravagance of hyperbole, which the taste of the age permitted to such compositions, reaches a height unparalleled elsewhere. It is difficult to understand how the desire to please and the intoxication of his own ingenuity can have so blinded Donne to the claims of self-respect, as to permit him to use language which is positively preposterous. The death of Elizabeth Drury has so wounded and tamed "the sick world" that it has thrown the globe into a lethargy. Her life was so precious that we might

"have better spared the Sun, or Man."

All light has left the earth except a ghostly glimmer, "the twilight of her memory." But a longer extract from this catalogue of superlatives will give a juster impression both of the reckless absurdity of Donne's extravagance, and of the technical beauty of the verse which he dedicated to such servile ends—

"She whose rich eyes and breast
Gilt the West Indies, and perfumed the East;
Whose having breathed in this world did bestow
Spice on those isles, and bade them still smell so;
And that rich India, which doth gold inter,
Is but as single money coin'd from her;
She to whom this world must itself refer,
As suburbs, or the microcosm of her;
She, she is dead; she's dead; when thou know'st this,
Thou know'st how lame a cripple this world is."

The *Anatomy of the World* is an astonishing constellation of absurdities and beauties, of profound thoughts and maddening conceits. Nothing could be lovelier than some of its incidental passages, as, for instance, this reminiscence of the Canary Islands, seen by Donne in his youth upon the Azores Expedition—

> "Doth not a Teneriffe or higher hill
> Rise so high like a rock, *that one might think
> The floating moon would shipwreck there, and sink?*"

or than this transcendental glorification of the delicate beauty of girlhood—

> "she, in whom all white and red and blue,
> Beauty's ingredients, voluntary grew,
> As in an unvex'd paradise; from whom
> Did all things' verdure, and their lustre come;
> Whose composition was miraculous,
> Being all colour, all diaphanous,
> For air and fire but thick gross bodies were,
> And liveliest stones but drowsy and pale to her;
> She, she is dead; she's dead; when thou know'st this,
> Thou know'st how wan a ghost this our world is."

These beauties, however, are rare and transitory; they are soon eclipsed by the scholastic obscurity of the cold, extravagant eulogy. At the end Donne is almost cynical, for, addressing the "blessed Maid," he begs her to

> "Accept this tribute, and his first year's rent,
> Who till his dark short taper's end be spent,
> As oft as thy feast sees this widow'd earth,
> Will yearly celebrate thy second birth."

Accordingly, early in 1612 Donne paid "rent" again in a "second Anniversary," called *Of the Progress of the Soul*. This was a still longer metaphysical celebration of poor little Elizabeth Drury, whom the barest decency might by this time have left to sleep under her monument in Hawsted Church. In this Donne announces that his Muse's

> "chaste ambition is
> Yearly to bring forth such a child as this."

This threat filled his friends with justifiable alarm, for even in the age of James I. the *Second Anniversary* was not a poem to be generally appreciated, in spite of the sustained learning and cleverness of its reflections upon man's mortality. It was added in 1612 to a reprint of *An Anatomy of the World*, and the collection of elegiacal pieces so formed was again republished twice, in 1621 and 1625, before being merged in Donne's poems from 1633 onwards. All these separate editions were anonymous, but the authorship was well known. John Davies of Hereford, in one of the earliest allusions to Donne which has come down to us, starts the pun on the poet's name which was to be so frequent. In *The Muse's Sacrifice* of 1612 Davies evidently alludes to the 1611 pamphlet when he says—

> " I must confess a priest of Phœbus late
> Upon like text so well did meditate,
> That with a sinless envy I do run
> In his *Soul's Progress*, till it all be DONNE,"

the subject of Davies' elegy being Mrs. Dutton, the eldest daughter of Lord Keeper Egerton.

A letter to George Gerrard, which we shall presently print, shows that various animadversions were made on the hyperbolic praise lavished by Donne on his new patron's daughter. The ladies at Twickenham and at Peckham seem to have expressed their resentment, and when Donne was in France he heard "from England of many censures of my book," the completed *Anatomy*. That Ben Jonson was among those who objected appears from his conversations with William Drummond, who records that Jonson said that "Donne's *Anniversary* was profane and full of blasphemies; that he told Mr. Donne, if it had been written of the Virgin Mary it had been something; which he answered, that he described the Idea of a Woman, and not as she [Elizabeth Drury] was." Each *Anniversary* is introduced by a poem, apparently by another hand, and the second of those is entitled "The Harbinger to the Progress." As Ben Jonson is reported to have made to Drummond the cryptic remark, "Joseph Hall the Harbinger to Donne's *Anniversary*," it has been supposed that these pieces, which are of trifling merit, and contrast with the sinewy vigour of

Donne's own versification, were written by the Satirist, afterwards Bishop of Norwich. Mr. E. K. Chambers, in editing the *Second Anniversary*, notes that Donne has the Aristotelian conception of a series of grades or stages of spiritual development, the life of sense absorbed by the life of motion, and that in turn by the still higher life of reason.

We can but regard this elaborate and repeated celebration of Elizabeth Drury as an eccentric and, on the whole, unfortunate episode in Donne's career as a poet. It is plain that he undertook and conducted it as a perfectly straightforward piece of business; he saw no reason why he should not expend his art on the eulogy of a young lady whom he had never seen, but whose father was generously expending upon him all the evidences of a princely hospitality. In return for house and home, for comforts to Donne's wife and food to his children, Sir Robert Drury asked a small expenditure of extravagantly laudatory verse, and Donne, no doubt, saw no shame in supplying what was asked for. He would probably have seemed to himself niggardly and ungrateful if he had refused to give it. But poetry composed under such conditions must needs be void and frigid, and if Donne thought to escape these faults by a strenuous exercise of intellect and fancy, he was disappointed. The expressions in his letters show that he was conscious of failure, and vexed at the sacrifice of his own dignity. At all events, we may be thankful that he did not carry out his dreadful threat of inditing a long poem upon each anniversary of Elizabeth Drury's death. He, like Sir Robert and Lady Drury, was presently to find distraction elsewhere.

On the 2nd of September 1611, Tom Coryat of the *Crudities* wrote a copy of Latin rhymes, which still remain unpublished, describing a "philosophical feast" which had lately taken place at Brasenose College, Oxford, in which Donne and Christopher Brooke took part. This was the year of the great efflorescence and self-glorification of Coryat, who had come back from his five months' travel on the Continent, and had "newly digested" his "Crambe" and various other "macaronic dishes" in "that hungry air of Odcombe, in the county of Somerset." Donne seems to have been amused by this preposterous being, and in this year, 1611, he wrote several copies of "commendatory" (or rather ironical) verses to be prefixed with those of many other writers to the *Crudities*.

Among the MSS. of the Duke of Rutland at Belvoir Castle there exists a Latin poem of perhaps 1612, in thirty-eight stanzas, celebrating a banquet to be held at the Mitre, in Fleet Street, on the day after the Feast of St. Giles (Sept. 1). The author is styled Dr. Rodolfus Calfaber. Among those who will attend are Sir Henry Goodyer, Inigo Jones, John Donne, Sir Henry Neville, and Coryat, "without whom the party would be incomplete"; others are expected to be present. It is curious that on the few occasions of gregarious jollification at which we detect the presence of Donne, Tom Coryat is almost always of the party.

On the 4th of December 1611, J. Chamberlain, writing to his faithful correspondent, Sir Dudley Carleton, says: "I cannot tell whether you have heard that Sir Robert Drury and his lady have leave to travel for three years, and are already settled at Amiens, and with them John Donne." Walton has told us that the cause of this journey was a desire on the part of Sir Robert Drury to accompany Lord Hay upon "a glorious embassy to the then French King, Henry the Fourth." This, however, is manifestly incorrect, since that monarch had been assassinated by Ravaillac more than a year earlier, namely, on the 14th of May 1610. Nor was Lord Hay engaged on any embassy of this kind until, in July 1616, he was appointed Ambassador Extraordinary to Paris. It is not likely that the Drurys were attached to any embassy, but rather that they went for their own pleasure; we are twice told that it was "a sudden resolution" which led to their journey. The proposal to start was certainly made to Donne with great abruptness, and led to an incident which Walton has related in eloquent and touching terms:—" Sir Robert put on a sudden resolution to solicit Mr. Donne to be his companion in that journey. And this desire was suddenly made known to his wife, who was then with child, and otherwise under so dangerous a habit of body as to her health, that she professed an unwillingness to allow him any absence from her, saying, 'Her divining soul boded her some ill in his absence,' and therefore desired him not to leave her. This made Mr. Donne lay aside all thoughts of the journey, and really to resolve against it. But Sir Robert became restless in his persuasions for it, and Mr. Donne was so generous as to think he had sold his liberty when he received so many charitable kindnesses from him, and told his wife so; who did therefore, with an unwilling willingness, give a faint consent to the journey, which was proposed to be but for two months; for about that time they determined their return.

"Within a few days after this resolve, the ambassador, Sir Robert, and Mr. Donne left London, and were the twelfth day got all safe to Paris. Two days after their arrival there, Mr. Donne was left alone in that room in which Sir Robert and he and some other friends had dined together. To this place Sir Robert returned within half-an-hour; and as he left, so he found, Mr. Donne alone, but in such an ecstasy, and so altered as to his looks, as amazed Sir Robert to behold him; insomuch that he earnestly desired Mr. Donne to declare what had befallen him in the short time of his absence. To which Mr. Donne was not able to make a present answer; but, after a long and perplexed pause, did at last say: 'I have seen a dreadful vision since I saw you; I have seen my dear wife pass twice by me through this room, with her hair hanging about her shoulders, and a dead child in her arms: this I have seen since I saw you.' To which Sir Robert replied, 'Sure, sir, you have slept since I saw you; and this is the result of some melancholy dream, which I desire you to forget, for you are now awake.' To which Mr. Donne's reply was: 'I cannot be surer that I now live than that I have not slept since I saw you; and am as sure that at her second appearing she stopped and looked me in the face and vanished.'

"Rest and sleep had not altered Mr. Donne's opinion the next day; for he then affirmed this vision with a more deliberate and so confirmed a confidence that he inclined

Sir Robert to a faint belief that the vision was true. It is truly said that desire and doubt have no rest, and it proved so with Sir Robert; for he immediately sent a servant to Drury House, with a charge to hasten back and bring him word whether Mrs. Donne were alive, and, if alive, in what condition she was as to her health. The twelfth day the messenger returned with this account: that he found and left Mrs. Donne very sad and sick in her bed; and that, after a long and dangerous labour, she had been delivered of a dead child. And, upon examination, the abortion proved to be the same day and about the very hour that Mr. Donne affirmed he saw her pass by him in his chamber.

"This is a relation that will beget some wonder, and it well may; for most of our world are at present possessed with an opinion that visions and miracles are ceased. And, though it is most certain that two lutes, being both strung and tuned to an equal pitch, and then one played upon, the other that is not touched being laid upon a table at a fit distance, will, like an echo to a trumpet, warble a faint audible harmony in answer to the same tune, yet many will not believe there is any such thing as a sympathy of souls; and I am well pleased that every reader do enjoy his own opinion."[1]

Several circumstances confirm the truth of this very charming and affecting story. Mrs. Donne was delivered of her eighth child in January 1612, and it died at birth; while the phrase which Walton quotes as spoken by her recurs in what is perhaps the most faultless of all her husband's poems. The common idea that Donne's poetical genius entirely left him in early youth is belied by the fact that he was in his fortieth year when he wrote these exquisite stanzas—

"Sweetest love, I do not go
  For weariness of thee,
Nor in hope the world can show
  A fitter love for me,
    But since that I
At the last must part, 'tis best,
Thus to use myself in jest
    By feignèd deaths to die.

---

[1] Walton, 1659; there is nothing answering to this story in the *Life* of 1640.

> Yesternight the sun went hence,
>   And yet is here to-day;
> He hath no desire nor sense,
>   Nor half so short a way;
>   Then fear not me,
> But believe that I shall make
> Speedier journeys, since I take
>   More wings and spurs than he.
>
> O how feeble is man's power,
>   That if good fortune fall,
> Cannot add another hour,
>   Nor a lost hour recall;
>   But come bad chance,
> And we join to it our strength,
> And we teach it art and length,
>   Itself o'er us to advance.
>
> When thou sigh'st, thou sigh'st not wind,
>   But sigh'st my soul away;
> When thou weep'st, unkindly kind,
>   My life's blood doth decay.
>   It cannot be
> That thou lov'st me as thou say'st,
> If in thine my life thou waste,
>   That art the best of me.
>
> Let not thy divining heart
>   Forethink me any ill;
> Destiny may take thy part,
>   And may thy fears fulfil.
>   But think that we
> Are but turn'd aside to sleep;
> They who one another keep
>   Alive, ne'er parted be."

In a hitherto unpublished note written in 1811, S. T. Coleridge says of this lyric :—

"This beautiful and perfect poem proves by its title '*Song*,' that *all* Donne's Poems are equally *metrical* (misprints allowed for), tho' *smoothness*, that is to say, the metre necessitating the proper reading, be deemed appropriate to *Songs;* but, in Poems where the Author *thinks*, and expects the Reader to do so, the sense must be understood in order to ascertain the metre."

This is a consideration of essential importance in all criticism of Donne's versification.

If Walton is to be credited, the famous "Valediction, forbidding to mourn," beginning—

> "As virtuous men pass mildly away,
> And whisper to their souls to go,
> Whilst some of their sad friends do say
> 'The breath goes now!' and some say 'No!'"

was written on the same occasion; but I confess that this appears to me to belong to an earlier period of the poet's life.

Walton, writing from Donne's report after many years, has fallen into some slight inaccuracy about the journey. The party probably left London at the end of November 1611, and, so far from reaching Paris on the twelfth day, were still at Amiens in the middle of February 1612. The incident of the thought-transference probably took place soon after Donne's arrival in Paris at the end of February, but, even at the beginning of April, he says, "I have received no syllable, neither from herself nor by any other, how my wife hath passed her danger; nor do I know whether I am increased by the birth of a child, or diminished by the loss of a wife."

Donne's absence from England is illustrated by a variety of interesting letters, hitherto dispersed in the irregular publication of 1651; these, arranged in chronological order, and increased by several which have not hitherto been printed, will be found to throw a considerable light upon his acts and movements at this period.

To whom the first of these letters was addressed I do not know, unless to George Hastings, who, however, had since 1595 been fourth Earl of Huntingdon.

"*To my* Lord G. H.[1]

"SIR,—I am near the execution of that purpose for France; though I may have other ends, yet if it do but keep me awake, it recompenses me well. I am now in the afternoon of my life, and then it is unwholesome to sleep. It is ill to look back, or give over in a course; but worse never to set out.

[1] From the *Letters* of 1651.

"I speak to you at this time of departing, as I should do at my last upon my deathbed; and I desire to deliver into your hands a heart and affections as innocent towards you, as I shall to deliver my soul into God's hands then. I say not this out of diffidence, as though you doubted it, or that this should look like such an excuse as implied an accusation; but because my fortune hath burdened you so, as I could not rectify it before my going, my conscience and interpretation (severer I hope than yours towards myself) calls that a kind of demerit, but God who hath not only afforded us a way to be delivered from our great many debts, contracted by our executorship to Adam, but also another for our particular debts after, hath not left poor men unprovided for discharge of moral and civil debts; in which acknowledgment and thankfulness is the same as repentance and contrition is in spiritual debts; and though the value and dignity of all these be not perchance in the things, but in the acceptation, yet I cannot doubt of it, either in God, or you.

"But, sir, because there is some degree of thankfulness in asking more (for that confesses all former obligations, and a desire to be still in the same dependency) I must entreat you to continue that wherein you have most expressed your love to me, which is, to maintain me in the same room in my Lady Bedford's opinion, in the which you placed me. I profess to you that I am too much bound to her for expressing every way her care of my fortune, that I am weary before she is; and out of a loathness, that so good works should be bestowed upon so ill stuff, or that so much ill-fortune should be mingled with hers, as that she should miss anything that she desired, though it were but for me; I am willing to depart from further exercising her endeavours in that kind. I shall be bold to deliver my poor letters to her ladyship's hands, through yours, whilst I am abroad, though I shall ever account myself at home whilst I am in your memory.

"Your affectionate servant and lover,
"J. DONNE."

[*November* 1611.]

The earliest letter which Donne sent from France was addressed in December 1611 from Amiens, to George Gerrard (or Garrard, or Garrat). This gentleman was the second son of Sir William Gerrard of Dorney, Bucks. To him Donne addressed the letters which are headed "To Yourself," and, after Sir Henry Goodyer, he was, perhaps, the most intimate of Donne's friends. Gerrard became Master of the Charterhouse, and survived the poet, who mentions him with affection in his Will.

"*To my honoured friend* Mr. GEORGE GERRARD.[1]

"SIR,—I would I were so good an alchemist to persuade you that all the virtue of the best affections that one could express in a sheet were in this rag of paper. It becomes my fortune to deal thus in single money; and I may hit better with this hail-shot of little letters (because they may come thick) than with great bullets; and trouble my friends less. I confess it were not long enough if it came to present my thanks for all the favours you have done me; but since it comes to beg more, perchance it may be long enough, because I know not how short you will be with an absent friend.

"If you will but write that you give me leave to keep that name still, it shall be the gold of your letter; and for alloy, put in as much news as you will. We are in a place where scarce any money appears but base; as, I confess, all matters of letters is in respect of the testimonies of friendship; but obey the corruption of this place, and fill your letters with worse stuff than your own.

"Present my service to all those gentlemen whom I had the honour to serve at our lodging; I cannot fly an higher pitch than to say that I am so much their servant as you can say I am. At the Queen's Arms in Cheapside, which is a mercer's, you may hear of one Mr. John Brewer, who will convey any letters directed to me at Sir Rob. Drury's at Amiens, though he know not me; and I should

[1] From the *Letters* of 1651.

be glad to hear that this first that I sent into England had the fortune to find you.

"Yours,

"Amiens [*December* 1611]."

"J. DONNE.

John Pory, who is mentioned in several preceding letters, was a useful and active cosmographer, who had worked long for Hakluyt on his geographical compilations, and who now looked to rise in the world as a diplomatist. He had perhaps become known to Donne through his intimate friendship with Sir Robert Cotton, and we have seen that they met at Oxford in 1610. Pory had entered Parliament in 1605, and in the autumn of 1607 had travelled in the Low Countries that he might elaborate a scheme for the introduction into England of silk-loom stocking-weaving. His diplomatic ambition had at last been gratified, for he had accompanied Lord Carew on a mission to Paris in 1611, and there Donne found him. Pory was an industrious, active, and helpful man. His business in France now was to carry a treatise from James I. to Cardinal Perron.

"*To Yourself.*[1]

[GEORGE GERRARD.]

"SIR,—All your other letters, which came to me by more hazardous ways, had therefore much merit in them; but for your letter by Mr. Pory, it was but a little degree of favour, because the messenger was so obvious and so certain that you could not choose but write by him. But since he brought me as much letter as all the rest, I must accept that as well as the rest.

"By this time, Mr. Garret [Gerrard], when you know in your conscience that you have sent no letter, you begin to look upon the superscription, and doubt that you have broken up some other body's letter; but whosesoever it were it must speak the same language, for I have heard from nobody.

"Sir, if there be a proclamation in England against

[1] From the *Letters* of 1651.

writing to me, yet since it is thereby become a matter of State, you might have told Mr. Pory so. And you might have told him what became of Sir Thomas Lucy's letter in my first packet (for any letter to him makes any paper a packet and any piece of single money a medal), and what became of my Lady Kingsmel's in my second, and of hers in my third, whom I will not name to you in hope that it is perished, and you lost the honour of giving it.

"Sir, mine own desire of being your servant hath sealed me a patent of that place during my life, and therefore it shall not be in the power of your forbidding (to which your stiff silence amounts) to make me leave being

"Your very affectionate servant,
"J. DONNE."

[Amiens, *Feb.* 1612.]

The next letter[1] is now, I believe, for the first time printed. It was evidently written to one of his brothers-in-law :—

"SIR,—This is my second letter to you, that is my second fault, for letters from this barren place are well enough accepted, if they be pardoned. We hear from Paris (but I think scarce so soon as you do) that the extreme great confluence of all the princes and great persons thither, with so great trains as have not been in use before, breed general jealousies and suspicions, though it appear not yet where the sore will break. But one resultance out of all is easily discovered, that the Religion is like to suffer in France, for the Duke of Bouillon is so united to the great ones, especially to the Regent and her purposes, as he neglects that party which used to receive favour and heart from his good disposition toward them.

"The Duke of Sully is desperate of return to any greatness, and for his son, the Marquis of Rosny, he is yet under the affliction of an importunity and solicitation to resign his great office of Great Master of the Artillery, and very like to lose it. And his grandfather, l'Esdiguires (by a marriage), receives

[1] Loseley MSS.

but ill satisfaction, being come brave and strong to Paris to give countenance to the young Marquis his pursuit of his right, for retaining that office. So that I cannot perceive but they are very willing, that those of the Religion should be discontent: that so it might either appear how much they are able to do and where their strength consists, or that some act of discontent from them might occasion and justify severe proceedings against them; for in the last assembly which was afforded them, when they presented petitions only for the ratifying and due executing of things granted unto them by former Edicts, they found the passages so dull and dilatory, as their time expired before they had any particular answer: and now when they send deputies to the court to solicit a new assembly, they find the same difficulties.

"And that which affects them as much, as any of these affronts done to the swordmen, is a danger, Servin, the King's Attorney. He is a Catholic, but a French Catholic, and, Sir, French papistry is but like French velvet—a pretty slack Religion, that would soon wear out, and not of the three-piled papistry of Italy and Spain. As he doth in all such occasions, so in this last arrest which concerned the Jesuits, he used much vehemency against them. And though upon the Jesuit Cotton his importunity, Servin and the Judge (that is the President), being converted by the Queen Regent, gave so good a justification of all that they had done in that pleading, and that arrest, against the Jesuits, that she then seemed to desist from moving any modification of the arrest, yet a Cardinal hath since that time told Servin, that his best way is to despatch himself of that place, which he understands for a liberty to sell it, or a warning that otherwise he may lose all.

"So that, Sir, as I said at first, all that directly or obliquely might succour the Religion, suffer great diminutions. The Edict against duels hath been lately infringed much, and will be oftener if the Queen be not severe in the observing of it, by reason of the very many and very different sorts of people at this time at Paris. Two or three have been committed for the breach of it, and remain so, but as yet I have heard of no severer prosecution.

"I beseech you present my humble thanks and services where you know they are due. I should not have forborne to have written to Sir Th. Grymes, if this place gave anything which he desired to know. To him and to his Lady I am bound to do better offices than words or letters are, if my fortune could express it.

"When there is any way open to you to send unto Wight, I may give this letter a passage. If one could not get to that isle but by the north-west discovery, I could not think the returns so difficult and dilatory, for yet I have had no return from thence of any letter since my coming out of England, and this silence, especially at this time when I make account that your sister is near her painful and dangerous passage, doth somewhat more affect me than I had thought anything of this world could have done.

"Good Sir, if perchance any letter come to you from thence, do me the favour to send it to Mr. John Brewer, at the Queen's Arms, a mercer in Cheapside, from whence anything will safely be brought to

"Your affectionate friend and servant,
"J. Donne.
"Amiens, 7 *Febr.* here, 1611[2]."

From this it would appear that Mrs. Donne had been taken by some members of her family to await her delivery in the Isle of Wight, which would have the effect of still further delaying the passage of correspondence between husband and wife.

Cotton, the Jesuit Father, who is mentioned in this and a succeeding letter, had been the confessor to Henri IV.

"*To the* Lady G[rymes ?]."[1]

"Madam,—I am not come out of England, if I remain in the noblest part of it, your mind; yet I confess it is too much diminution to call your mind any part of England,

[1] *Letters* of 1651.

or of this world, since every part even of your body deserves titles of higher dignity. No prince would be loth to die that were assured of so fair a tomb to preserve his memory: but I have a greater advantage than so; for since there is a Religion in friendship, and a death in absence, to make up an entire frame, there must be a heaven too: and there can be no heaven so proportional to that Religion and that death, as your favour. And I am gladder that it is a heaven, than that it were a court, or any other high place of this world, because I am likelier to have a room there than here; and better cheap.

"Madam, my best treasure is time; and my best employment of that is to study good wishes for you, in which I am by continual meditation so learned, that your own good angel, when it would do you most good, might be content to come and take instructions from

"Your humble and affectionate servant,
"J. DONNE.
"Amiens, *Feb.* 7, 1612."

The next letter, addressed to Sir Henry Wotton on one of his rare visits to England, presents considerable difficulty as to its exact date. We must, however, place it in 1612, and probably in February of that year. Donne had plainly not arrived in Paris; the references to Constantinople are definite. Sir Dudley Carleton had written from Venice on the 28th of February, "I have news from Constantinople of the safe arrival thither of Mr. Paul Pindar, who, having a happy passage of nineteen days, surprised Sir Thos. Glover before he was aware." I think that Donne's letter was written from Amiens about the same time as Carleton's from Venice.

"*To* Sir H. WOTTON.[1]

"SIR,—That which is at first but a visitation and a civil office, come quickly to be a haunting and an uncivil importunity: my often writing might be subject to such a misinterpretation, if it were not to you, who as you know

[1] From *Letters* of 1651.

that the affection which suggests and dictates them is ever one and continual and uninterrupted; may be pleased to think my letters so too, and that all the pieces make but one long letter, and so I know you would not grudge to read any entire book of mine at that pace as you do my letters, which is a leaf a week; especially such letters as mine, which (perchance out of the dulness of the place) are so empty of any relations, as that they oppress not your meditations, nor discourse, nor memory.

"You know that for air we are sure we apprehend and enjoy it, but when this air is rarified into fire, we begin to dispute whether it be an element or no: so when letters have a convenient handsome body of news, they are letters; but when they are spun out of nothing, they are nothing, or but apparitions and ghosts, with such hollow sounds, as he that hears them knows not what they said.

"You (I think) and I am [are] much of one sect in the philosophy of love; which, though it be directed upon the mind, doth inhere in the body, and find plenty entertainment there: so have letters for their principal office to be seals and testimonies of mutual affection, but the materials and fuel of them should be a confident and mutual communicating of those things which we know.

"How shall I then, who know nothing, write letters? Sir, I learn knowledge enough out of yours to me. I learn that there is truth and firmness and an earnestness of doing good alive in the world; and therefore, since there is so good company in it, I have not so much desire to go out of it as I had if my fortune would afford me any room in it. You know I have been no coward, nor unindustrious in attempting that; nor will I give it over yet. If at last I must confess that I died ten years ago, yet as the Primitive Church admitted some of the Jews' ceremonies, not for perpetual use, but because they would bury the synagogue honourably, though I died at a blow then when my courses were diverted, yet it will please me a little to have had a long funeral, and to have kept myself so long above ground without putrefaction. But this is melancholic discourse.

"To change, therefore, from this metaphorical death to

the true, and that with a little more relish of mirth, let me tell you the good-nature of the executioner of Paris; who, when Vatan was beheaded (who, dying in the profession of the religion, had made his peace with God in the prison, and so said nothing at the place of execution), swore he had rather execute forty Huguenots than one Catholic, because the Huguenot used so few words and troubled him so little in respect of the dilatory ceremonies of the others in dying.

"Cotton, the great Court Jesuit, hath so importuned the Queen to give some modifications to the late interlocutory arrest against the Jesuits, that in his presence, the Count Soissons, who had been present in the court at the time of the arrest, and Servin, the King's Advocate, who urged it, and the Premier president, were sent for. They came so well provided with their books, out of which they assigned to the Queen so many, so evident places of seditious doctrine, that the Queen was well satisfied that it was fit by all means to provide against the teaching of the like doctrine in France.

"The Duke of Espernon is come to Paris with (they say) 600 horse in his train; all which company came with him into the court: which is an insolency remarkable here. They say that scarce any of the Princes appear in the streets, but with very great trains. No one enemy could waste the treasures of France so much as so many friends do; for the Queen dares scarce deny any that so she may have the better leave to make haste to advance her Marquis of Ancre, of whose greatness for matter of command or danger they have no great fear, he being no very capable nor stirring man; and then for his drawing of great benefits from the Queen they make that use of it, that their suits pass with less opposition. I believe the treasure is scattered because I see the future receipt charged with so very many and great pensions.

"The Queen hath adventured a little to stop this rage of the Princes' importunity, by denying a late suit of Soissons; which, though the other Princes grudge not that Soissons should fail, for he hath drawn infinite sums already, yet they resent it somewhat tenderly, that any of them should be denied when the Marquis obtains.

"That which was much observed in the King's more childish age, when I was last here, by those whom his father appointed to judge by an assiduous observation, his natural inclination is more and more confirmed, that his inclinations are cruel and tyrannous; and when he is any way affected, his stammering is so extreme as he can utter nothing. They cannot draw him to look upon a son of the Marquis, whom they have put into his service. And he was so extremely affectionate towards the younger son of Beaufort, that they have removed him to a charge which he hath, as he is made Prior of Malta; but yet there pass such letters between them, by stealth and practice, as (though it be between children) it is become a matter of State, and much diligence used to prevent the letters. For the young Marquis of Vervueil the King speaks often of transplanting him into the Church, and once this Christmas delighted himself to see his young brother in a cardinal's habit.

"Sir, it is time to take up, for I know that anything from this place, as soon as it is certain, is stale. I have been a great while more mannerly towards my Lady Bedford than to trouble her with any of mine own verses, but having found these French verses accompanied with a great deal of reputation here, I could not forbear to ask her leave to send them. I wrote to you by Mr. Pory, the 17th of January, here, and he carried that letter to Paris, to gather news, like a snowball. He told me that Pindar is gone to Constantinople with commission to remove and succeed Glover: I am afraid you have neglected that business. Continue me in Mr. Martin's good opinion: I know I shall never fall from it by any demerit of mine, and I know I need not fear it out of any slackness or slipperiness in him, but much business may strangle me in him. When it shall not trouble you to write to me, I pray do me the favour to tell me how many you have received from me, for I have now much just reason to imagine that some of my packets have had more honour than I wished them: which is to be delivered into the hands of greater personages than I addressed them unto.

"Hold me still in your own love, and proceed in that noble testimony of it, of which your letter by Mr. Pory spoke (which is the only letter that I have received since I came away), and believe me that I shall ever with much affection and much devotion join both your fortune and your last best happiness, with the desire of mine own, in all my civil and divine wishes, as the only retribution in the power of

"Your affectionate servant,

"Jo. Donne."

[Amiens, *Feb.* 1612.]

It is to be noted here that Donne speaks of what "was much observed in the King's more childish age, when I was last here." This, then, is an allusion to a visit of Donne's to France not recorded elsewhere. Louis XIII. was born in 1601; Donne's reference is to a time when Henri IV. was still alive, because he speaks of "those whom his father appointed to judge." These tutors noted the Prince's tendency to a cruel and tyrannous disposition. This would not be observable in a child of less than seven or eight years, and Henri IV. died on the 14th of May 1610. The date of Donne's unrecorded visit to Paris, therefore, seems narrowed down to a period from 1608 to 1610.

"*To my very worthy friend* Mr. George Gerrard.

"Sir,—This is the 4th of this month, and I receive your packet so late that I have scarce waking time enough to tell you so, or to write anything but dreams. I have both your letters, mother and daughter, and am gladder of them than if I had the mother and daughter here in our neighbourhood; you know I mean Sir H. Goodyer's parties.

"Sir, you do me double honour when my name passes through you to that noble lady in whose presence you are. It is a better end and a better way to that than I am worth.

I can give you nothing in recompense of that favour but good counsel: which is to speak sparingly of any ability in me, lest you endanger your own reputation by overvaluing me. If I shall at any time take courage by your letter to express my meditations of that lady in writing, I shall scarce think less time to be due to that employment than to be all my life in making those verses, and so take them with me and sing them amongst her fellow angels in heaven.

"I should be loath that in anything of mine composed of her she should not appear much better than some of those of whom I have written. And yet I cannot hope for better expressings than I have given of them. So you see how much I should wrong her by making her but equal to others. I would I could be believed when I say that all that is written of them is but prophecy of her.

"I must use your favour in getting her pardon for having brought her into so narrow and low-roofed a room as my consideration, or for adventuring to give any estimation of her; and when I see how much she can pardon, I shall the better discern how far farther I may dare to offend in that kind.

"My noble neighbour is well, and makes me the steward of his service to you. Before this letter reaches you I presume you will be gathering towards these parts, and then all news will meet you so fast, as that out of your abundance you will impart some to
"Your affectionate friend to serve you,
"J. Donne."

[*March?* 4, 1612: Paris.]

A very remarkable political news-letter now follows, addressed to Goodyer, a letter which would lend itself to elaborate historical annotation, if that were within the scope of this biography.

"*To the Honourable Knight* Sir H. Goodyer.

"Sir,—If I would go out of my way for excuses, or if I did not go out of my way from them, I might avoid writing now because I cannot choose but know that you have in this town abler servants, and better understanding the persons and passages of this court. But my hope is not in the application of other men's merits to me, however abundant. Besides, this town hath since our coming hither afforded enough for all to say.

"That which was done here the 25th of March, and which was so long called a publication of the marriages, was no otherwise public than that the Spanish ambassador, having that day an audience, delivered to the Queen that his master was well pleased with all those particulars which had been formerly treated. And the French ambassador in Spain is said to have had instruction to do the same office in that court the same day. Since that, that is to say, these four last days, it hath been solemnised with more outward bravery than this court is remembered to have appeared in. The main bravery was the number of horses, which were above 800 caparisoned. Before the days the town was full of the five challengers' cartels, full of rodomontades; but in the execution there were no personal rencounters, nor other trial of any ability, than running at the quintain and the ring.

"Other particulars of this you cannot choose but hear too much, since at this time there come to you so many Frenchmen. But lest you should believe too much, I present you these two precautions, that for their gendarmerie there was no other trial than I told you, and for their bravery no true stuff. You must of necessity have heard often of a book written against the Pope's jurisdiction, about three months since, by one Richer, a doctor and syndic of the Sorbonists, which book hath now been censured by an assembly of the clergy of this archbishopric, promoved with so much diligence by the Cardinal Peroun, that for this business he hath intermitted his reply to the King's answer, which now he retires to intend seriously.

"I have not yet had the honour to kiss his Grace's hand, though I have received some half invitations to do it. Richer was first accused to the Parliament, but when it was there required of his delators to insist upon some propositions in his book, which were either against Scripture or the Gallican Church, they desisted in that pursuit. But in the censure which the clergy hath made, though it be full of modifications and reservations of the rights of the King and the Gallican churches, there is this iniquity, that being to be published by commandment of the Assembly in all the churches of Paris which is within that diocese, and almost all the curates of the parishes of Paris being Sorbonists, there is by this means a strong party of the Sorbonists themselves raised against Richer; yet against this censure, and against three or four which have opposed Richer in print, he meditates an answer.

"Before it should come forth I desired to speak with him, for I had said to some of the Sorbonists of his party that there was no proposition in his book which I could not show in Catholic authors of 300 years: I had from him an assignation to meet, and at the hour he sent me his excuse, which was that he had been traduced to have had conference with the ambassadors of England and the States, and with the Duke of Bouillon, and that he had accepted a pension of the King of England; and withal, that it had been very well testified to him that day that the Jesuits had offered to corrupt men with rewards to kill him. Which I doubt not but he apprehended for true, because a messenger whom I sent to fix another time of meeting with him, found him in an extreme trembling and irresolutions; so that I had no more but an entreaty to forbear coming to his house, or drawing him out of it, till it might be without danger or observation.

"They of the Religion hold a Synod at this time in this town, in which the principal business is to rectify, or at least to mature, against their Provincial Synod, which shall be held in May, certain opinions of Tilenus, a divine of Sedan, with which the churches of France are scandalised. The chief point is whether our salvation be to be attributed to the passive merit of Christ, which is His death, or to His active also, which is His fulfilling of the law. But I doubt not but that will be well composed, if Tilenus, who is here in person with two other assistants, bring any disposition to submit himself to the Synod, and not only to dispute.

"I do (I thank God) naturally and heartily abhor all schism in religion so much, as, I protest, I am sorry to find this appearance of schism amongst our adversaries the Sorbonists; for I had rather they had held together, to have made a head against the usurpations of the Roman Church, than that their disuniting should so enfeeble them, as that the Parliament should be left alone to stand against those tyrannies.

"Sir, you will pardon my extravagances in these relations. I look upon nothing so intentively as these things, nor falls there anything within my knowledge which I would conceal from you. Though it concern not you to know it, yet methinks it concerns me to tell it.

"That cook of which you writ to me is come hither, and hath brought me other letters, but not those of which you writ to me, which packet, he says, you received again of him; whether by his falsehood, or by your diligence in seeking a worthier messenger, I know not, but I am sure I never lost anything with more sorrow, because I am thereby left still in uncertainties and irresolutions of that which I desire much to know in women's businesses. If you write this way any more, choose no other means than by Mr. Bruer [Brewer], at the Queen's Arms, a mercer in Cheapside: he shall always know where we are, and we are yet in a purpose to go from hence within a fortnight, and dispose ourselves to be at Frankfort the 25th of May, when the election of the Emperor shall be there.

"Though I be merely passive in all this pilgrimage, yet I shall be willing to advance that design, because upon my promise that I would do so, Sir Rob. Rich gave me his, that he would divert from his way to Italy so much as to be there then. When I came to this town I found Mr. Matthew diligent to find a means to write to you; so that at this time, when there go so many, I cannot doubt but he provides himself, therefore I did not ask his commandment, nor offer him the service of this packet.

"Sir, you are not evener to yourself in your most general

wishes of your own good than I am in my particular, of which none rises in me that is not bent upon your enjoying of peace and reposedness in your fortunes, in your affections, and in your conscience, more than which I know not how to wish to

"Your very affectionate servant and lover,
"J. DONNE.
"Paris, the 9 *Apr.* 1612 here."

Donne has an exasperating way of being silent exactly when we wish him to speak. We are almost indignant that a great English theologian should be in Paris in 1612, and have nothing to tell us of the evolution of French theology. This was the turning-point at which the Protestants ceased to have all the talent on their side, and at which the Gallican divines took up the tale of eloquence. Can we believe that Donne heard nothing said of St. François de Sales, now at the very height of his influence in Paris? Nothing of the *Traité de l'Amour de Dieu*, which, in this year, 1612, first saw the light in its imperfect form? The picturesqueness and humour of St. François de Sales, so different from the pomp and studied simplicity of later French theologians, should have interested Donne. The two leading Catholic writers of the moment in Paris, both of them followers of St. François, were the Cardinal du Perron (whom Donne means by *Peroun*) and Coëffeteau, each of whom was engaged in fitful controversy with the English Protestants, and chiefly with James I. In the absence of St. François in his diocese of Geneva—and even in his presence, for the Saint was no great master of delivery—Coëffeteau was in 1612 the first religious orator of France. With St. François de Sales, at this moment the ruling influence among French divines, Donne had a good deal in common, even to the admiration they both felt for that mundane work, the *Diana Enamorada* of Montemôr. At this moment, however, if the truth be told, Donne's interest in theology was at its nadir, and if he had read the *Traité*, it would have been merely to criticise the mysticism and the style of it.

"*To Yourself.*[1]

[*i.e.* GEORGE GERRARD.]

"SIR,—The first of this month I received a letter from you—no letter comes so late, but that it brings fresh news hither. Though I presume, Mr. Pory, and since Sir Rob. Rich came after the writing of that letter, yet it was good news to me, that you thought me worthy of so good a testimony. And you were subtile in the disguise; for you shut up your letter thus, Lond. 22, in our style, but I am not so good a Cabalist as to find in what month it was written.

"But, sir, in the offices of so spiritual a thing as friendship, so momentary a thing as time must have no consideration. I keep it therefore to read every day, as newly written: to which vexation it must be subject, till you relieve it with another. If I owed you not a great many thanks for every particular part of it, I should yet thank you for the length; and love it as my mistress's face, every line and feature, but best all together.

"All that I can do towards retribution is (as other bankrupts do in prison) to make means by commissioners, that a great debt may be accepted by small sums weekly. And in that proportion I have paid my tribute to you almost ever since I came, and shall still do so. You know that they say those are the strongest and the firmest and most precious things which are composed of the most and smallest parts.

"I will flatter myself therefore that the number of my letters may at last make a strong argument of my desire to serve you, but because I remember, out of this philosophy, that they should be little, as well as many, lest this letter should not get into the building, it shall be no bigger; thus much addition will not much disfigure it, that it swear to you that I am

"Your affectionate servant,

"J. DONNE.

[Paris, *April* 9, 1612.]

[1] *Letters* of 1651.

"Sir, I cry you mercy for sealing your sister's letter, but I deliver you up my authority, and I remember you, that you have hers to open it again. You will the easier forgive me that I write no news, when you observe by this transgression that I live in a place which hath quenched in me even the remembrance of good manners. By naming her, I have made my postscript the worthiest place of my letter; and therefore I choose that place to present my service to all the company at our lodging; in which house, if I cannot get room for a pallet at my return, my comfort is, that I can ever hope to be so near them as the Spittle in the Savoy, where they receive travellers."

[*To* GEORGE GERRARD?]

"SIR,—It is one ill affection of a desperate debtor that he dares not come to an account, nor take knowledge how much he owes; this makes me that I dare not tell you how many letters I have received from you since I came to this town; I had three the first by the cook, who brought none but yours, nor ever came to me to let me know what became of the rest: the two other of the 7th and 8th of March came in a letter which Sir H. Wotton wrote to me from Amiens; there is not a size of paper in the palace large enough to tell you how much I esteem myself honoured in your remembrances; nor strong enough to wrap up a heart so full of good affections towards you, as mine is. When anything passes between Sir Thomas Roe and you, tell him I am not the less his servant, for not saying so by often letters; for by my troth, I am that so much as he could desire I should be, when he began to love me. Sir Thomas Lucy's business, and perchance sadness, forbid me writing now.

"I have written to him (whilst I lived in darkness, whether my letters came to you or no) by another way; and if my poor letters were any degree of service, I should do it often, and rather be mine own post, than leave anything undone, to which he would give such an interpretation, as that it were an argument of my devotion to him.

"For my purpose of proceeding in the profession of the law, so far as to a title, you may be pleased to correct that imagination where you find it. I ever thought the study of it my best entertainment and pastime, but I have no ambition nor design upon the style.

"Of my *Anniversaries*, the fault which I acknowledge in myself is to have descended to print anything in verse, which, though it have excuse, even in our times, by example of men, which one would think should as little have done it, as I; yet I confess I wonder how I declined to it, and do not pardon myself. But for the other part of the imputation of having said so much, my defence is, that my purpose was to say as well as I could; for since I never saw the gentlewoman, I cannot be understood to have bound myself to have spoken just truth; but I would not be thought to have gone about to praise anybody in rhyme, except I took such a person, as might be capable of all that I could say. If any of those ladies think that Mistress Drury was not so, let that lady make herself fit for all those praises in the book, and it shall be hers.

"Nothing is farther from colour or ground of truth, than that which you write of Sir Robert Drury's going to mass. No man of our nation hath been more forward to apply himself to the church of the Religion where he hath come, nor to relieve their wants, where that demonstration hath been needful.

"I know not yet whether Sir John Brooke's purpose of being very shortly here, be not a just reason to make me forbear writing to him. I am sure that I would fainest do that in writing or abstaining which should be most acceptable to him.

"It were in vain to put into this letter any relation of the magnificence which have been here at publication of these marriages; for at this time there come into England so many Frenchmen, as I am sure you shall hear all at least. If they speak not of above eight hundred horse well caparisoned, you may believe it; and you may believe that no court in Christendom had been able to have appeared so brave in that kind. But if they tell you of any other stuff than copper, or any other exercise of arms than running at the quintain and the ring, you may be bold to say *pardonnez-moi*.

"Sir, this messenger makes so much haste that I cry you mercy for spending any time of this letter, in other employment than thanking you for yours, and promising you more before my remove from hence. I pray venture no letter to me by any other way than Mr. John Bruer, at the Queen's Arms, a mercer in Cheapside, who is always like to know where we are. And make me by loving me still, worthy to be

"Your friend and servant,
"J. Donne."

[Paris, *April* 14, 1612.]

"*To my honoured friend* G. G., Esquire.[1]

[George Gerrard.]

"Sir,—Neither your letters nor silence needs excuse; your friendship is to me an abundant possession, though you remember me but twice in a year: he that could have two harvests in that time might justly value his land at a high rate; but, sir, as we do not only then thank our land when we gather the fruit, but acknowledge that all the year she doth many motherly offices in preparing it; so is not friendship then only to be esteemed when she is delivered of a letter, or any other real office, but in her continual propenseness and inclination to do it.

"This hath made me easy in pardoning my long silences, and in promising myself your forgiveness for not answering your letter sooner. For my purpose of proceeding in the profession of the law so far as to a title, you may be pleased to correct that imagination wheresoever you find it. I ever thought the study of it my best entertainment and pastime, but I have no ambition nor design upon the style.

"Of my *Anniversaries*, the fault that I acknowledge in myself is to have descended to print anything in verse, which though it have excuse even in our times by men who profess and practice much gravity; yet I confess I

[1] *Letters* of 1651.

wonder how I declined to it, and do not pardon myself: but for the other part of the imputation of having said too much, my defence is that my purpose was to say as well as I could; for since I never saw the gentlewoman, I cannot be understood to have bound myself to have spoken just truths, but I would not be thought to have gone about to praise her or any other in rhyme; except I took such a person as might be capable of all that I could say.

"If any of those ladies think that Mistress Drury was not so, let that lady make herself fit for all those praises in the book, and they shall be hers. Sir, this messenger makes so much haste that I cry you mercy for spending any time of this letter in other employment than thanking you for yours. I hope before Christmas to see England, and kiss your hand, which shall ever (if it disdain not that office) hold all the keys of the liberty and affection, and all the faculties of

"Your most affectionate servant,
"J. D.

"Paris, the 14 of *April*, here, 1612."

The coincidence of many expressions in the two foregoing letters will strike every reader. I see no reason to doubt that they are mutilated copies of the same letter.

In connection with what Donne here says to Gerrard with regard to his studying the law, it may be of interest to quote, from R. B.'s *Life of Bishop Morton*, 1669, the following statement, which belongs to those early months of 1612:—

"And long after, the said Mr. Donne, having grappled with many extremities at home, he passed over into France, where he gave himself to study of the laws. And from Amiens (as I remember) he wrote a letter to his always true friend Dean Morton, wherein he requested his advice whether the taking of the degree of a doctor in that profession of the laws, it might be conducible and advantageous unto him to practise at home in the Arches, London."[1]

---

[1] "Life of Dr. Tho. Morton, Bishop of Duresme," by R[ichard] B[addiley], 1669; pp. 3-5. In the official "Life of Morton," by John Barwick, D.D., 1660, the name of Donne does not once occur.

JOHN DONNE

From a Drawing made by G. CLINT, A.R.A., *after an Original Painting*

DRURY HOUSE AND PARIS

It is much to be noted that, on accepting Sir Robert Drury's hospitality, Donne seems to have abandoned, for the time being, any study of theology and any solicitude about it. Nowhere is he so little of a divine as in these years immediately preceding his sudden resolution to enter the Church.

"*To* Sir G. F.[1]

"SIR,—I writ to you once this week before; yet I write again, both because it seems a kind of resisting of grace to omit any commodity of sending into England, and because any packet from me into England should go not only without just freight, but without ballast, if it had not a letter to you.

"In letters that I received from Sir H. Wotton yesterday from Amiens, I had one of the 8th March from you, and with it one from Mrs. Danterey, of the 28th of January: which is a strange disproportion. But, sir, if our letters come not in due order, and so make not a certain and concurrent chain, yet if they come as atoms, and so meet at last by any crooked and casual application, they make up and they nourish bodies of friendship; and in that fashion, I mean one way or other, first or last, I hope all the letters which have been addressed to us by one another are safely arrived, except perchance that packet by the cook be not, of which before this time you are clear; for I received (as I told you) a letter by Mr. Nat. Rich,[2] and if you sent none by him, then it was that letter which the cook tells you he delivered to Mr. Rich; which, with all my criticisms, I cannot reconcile; because in your last letter I find mention of things formerly written which I have not found.

"However, I am yet in the same perplexity which I mentioned before, which is, that I have received no syllable, neither from herself nor by any other, how my wife hath passed her danger, nor do I know whether I be increased by a child or diminished by the loss of a wife.

"I hear from England of many censures of my book

[1] From *Letters* of 1651.   [2] Afterwards Sir Nathaniel Rich (1585-1636).

of Mistress Drury; if any of those censures do but pardon me my descent in printing anything in verse (which if they do they are more charitable than myself; for I do not pardon myself, but confess that I did it against my conscience, that is, against my own opinion, that I should not have done so), I doubt not but they will soon give over that other part of that indictment, which is that I have said so much; for nobody can imagine that I who never saw her, could have any other purpose in that, than that when I had received so very good testimony of her worthiness, and was gone down to print verses, it became me to say, not what I was sure was just truth, but the best that I could conceive; for that had been a new weakness in me, to have praised anybody in printed verses, that had not been capable of the best praise that I could give.

"Presently after Easter we shall (I think) go to Frankfort to be there at the election, where we shall meet Sir H. Wotton and Sir Ro. Rich,[1] and after that we are determined to pass some time in the Palatinate. I go thither with a great deal of devotion; for methinks it is a new kind of piety, that as pilgrims went heretofore to places which had been holy and happy, so I go to a place now which shall be so and more, by the presence of the worthiest princess of the world, if that marriage proceed.

"I have no greater errand to the place than that at my return into England I may be the fitter to stand in her presence, and that after I have seen a rich and abundant country in his best seasons, I may see that sun which shall always keep it in that height. Howsoever we stray, if you have leisure to write at any time, adventure by no other way than Mr. Bruer, at the Queen's Arms, a mercer in Cheapside.

"I shall omit no opportunity, of which I doubt not to find more than one before we go from Paris. Therefore give me leave to end this, in which if you did not find the remembrance of my humblest services to my Lady Bedford, your love and faith ought to try all the experiments of powders and dryings and waterings to discover some lines

---

[1] Later, Lord Rich, and ultimately famous as the admiral Earl of Warwick (1587-1658).

which appeared not; because it is impossible that a letter should come from me with such an ungrateful silence.
"Your very true poor friend and servant and lover,
"J. DONNE.
[*April* 1612.]

"This day begins a history, of which I doubt not but I shall write more to you before I leave this town. Monsieur de Rohan, a person for birth, next heir to the Kingdom of Navarre, after the King's children (if the King of Spain were weary of it), and for alliance, son-in-law to D. Sally, and for breeding in the wars and estate the most remarkable man of the Religion, being Governor of S. Jean d'Angeli, one of the most important towns which they of the Religion hold for their security, finding that some distastes between the Lieutenant and the Mayor of the town and him were dangerously fomented by great persons, stole from Court, rode post to the town, and removed these two persons.

"He sent his secretary and another dependant of his to give the Queen satisfaction, who is so far from receiving it, that his messengers are committed to the Bastile, likely to be presently tortured; all his friends here commanded to their houses, and the Queen's companies of light horse sent already thitherward, and foot companies preparing, which troops being sent against a place, so much concerning those of the Religion to keep, and where they abound in number and strength, cannot choose but produce effects worthy your hearing in the next letter."

Sir Robert and Lady Drury, with Donne in attendance, spent April and part of May in Paris, where Donne suffered from fever and dysentery. Before he had wholly recovered, they all started for Spa. I have no hesitation in venturing to insert here a curious fragmentary letter of Donne's which has not hitherto been printed. Much of it is quite unintelligible, but "Mr. Matthew" is certainly Tobie Matthew, the eccentric and recusant son of Tobias Matthew, Archbishop of York. This oddity, of whom we shall hear more, is said to have been visited by Donne and Morton, who were anxious to extract Roman gossip from him, while he was detained in the Fleet Prison in 1607–8. He had been allowed to leave England in the latter year, and since then had lived a strange, marauding life on the Continent, the subject of a good deal of wild gossip. In 1611 Tobie Matthew was in Venice with Thomas Gage the traveller, who is here mentioned. In 1612 Gage left Italy, to be a Dominican monk in Spain, and, long after Donne's death, became notorious for extraordinary adventures in Mexico and Guatemala. Tobie Matthew remained in Italy, and a report was spread that he was dead; Sir Dudley Carleton, just about the time of Donne's stay at Spa, denied this rumour, but justified it by describing Matthew as "so broken with travel," that the Italians called him *Il Vecchio*, although he was only in his thirty-fifth year. So far from dying, he was forgiven by the King, knighted on the 20th of October 1623, and lived on until 1655.

Sir Tobie Matthew has been spoken of as the "friend" of Donne. That he never was. Donne was interested in his wit and learning, but the two men were utterly opposed in interests, and when Matthew protested his goodwill, Donne, as we shall see in a future letter, received his protestations with a sarcasm which was hardly civil. Yet it is to the fortunate circumstance that Sir Tobie Matthew was a collector of autographs, and amassed a large number of Donne's manuscript letters after his death, that we owe some of the most valuable illustrative documents contained in this biography.

The Lord Chandos mentioned here was Grey Brydges, fifth Lord Chandos of Sudeley. He was in Donne's circle through having married Anne, eldest of the three daughters of Lady Ellesmere, the Lord Keeper's third wife. The younger sister of Lady Chandos was Donne's particular friend, Lady Huntingdon. Lord Chandos was at Spa on the 23rd of July 1612, but Donne missed him by two hours. If they met, it was elsewhere in the Low Countries. The person to whom the letter was addressed would seem, by a special despatch, to have warned Donne of Lord

Chandos' arrival. The fragment itself[1] must have been written at Spa before the close of the month of July. The talk about elegies and epithalamia is doubtless a reflection of the chat of Lord Chandos, who was exceedingly interested in all such things, and liked nothing better than to arrange a masque or to propose an epicede.

"SIR,—I have received your letter by Mr. Lakeryte with more diligence in excusing the not-delivery of it with his own hands than I am worthy. But I lose also the honour of kissing his hand by going to him, because his messenger tells me that he goes this day out of this town. Such ambitions, especially in so slow a paced fortune as mine, have ever delays. But I am abundantly recompensed by having had occasion, by receipt of another packet from you some hours after your former letter, to present my service to my Lord Chandos, from whom I received a promise that he would send letters to me time enough to make my acceptable by ushering them [?], and I hope they come with this.

"By his favour, I say, your elegy, at least I see not how your absence from home can be excusable otherwise than by an epithalamium. I speak in as much earnest as if it were matter of prose. If Mademoiselle Isabelle will make one, the first [poem?] I make in heaven shall be of her sister Clifton. I am sorry my muse was past children before this occasion.

"Before we depart far from the consideration of this dead lady, who begins but now to live in me by this celebration, I must tell you that you have lost again, a second time, a very worthy friend, who had so much worthiness to be lost all at once; a gentleman, whom, in good faith, I ever loved well, out of those things which were within my comprehension which were his wit and appliableness; but, since his death, I hear of one exercise of his judgment which I knew not before, which is that he loved not me. This is Mr. Mathew, of whose death I had knowledge enough to make me think him

[1] MS. in the possession of J. H. Anderdon, Esq.

dead some weeks since. But because I find that my
Lord Chandos hath received from gentlemen interested in
Mr. Mathew's friendship other assurances thereof, I dare
now tell it you. He is said to have given all his estate
to Mr. Gage, and that is said to be £7000, which gentleman hath since lost one of his eyes, which I mention as
a loss of which I am sensible and compassionate.

"Mr. Gerrard, if he had had more warning, would have
wrote to you this week. Next week he will tell you that
one Swinburne, a clerk, appertaining to Sir H. Ffanshaw,
upon Wednesday last, past, put on a resolution to play,
and pursued it three or four days, and upon Saturday, in
three hours, lost at the Tunns £1000, and went home to
bed and died. I spoke with some that were present at his
opening, and the physician pronounced him poisoned, but
they think it to be received before his loss. No near——"

At Spa the party seem to have spent June, and in
July to have passed on to Maastricht, with the intention
of traversing what they called Holland, and we now call
the province of Limburg, for the purpose of travelling
up the Rhine to Nassau. But "the lowness and slackness"
of the river Maas turned them back. Returning through
Spa, they seem to have made a dash at Cleves and the
Palatinate, where, as we learn from other sources, Drury
was greatly disappointed by his reception and entertainment.
They made their way north and west again, through Spa
and Louvain, and on the 16th of August Donne writes
from a town which must be Brussels. In September we
know that the Drurys were settled in London again, and
Donne was doubtless with them. The following letters
belong to his journeyings in the Spanish Netherlands.

"*To Yourself.*[1]

[*i.e.* GEORGE GERRARD.]

"SIR,—Age becomes nothing better than friendship;
therefore your letters, which are ever good effects of

[1] From *Letters* of 1651.

friendship, delight to be old before I receive them; for it is but a fortnight since those letters which you sent by Captain Peter found me at Spa; presently upon the receipt I adventured by your leave to bestow the first minutes upon this letter to your fair, noble sister; and because I found no voice at Spa of any messenger, I respited my writing to you till I came thus much nearer.

"Upon the way hither another letter from you overtook me, which, by my Lord Chandos' love to me for your sake, was sent after me to Maastricht: he came to Spa within two hours after I went away; which I tell you to let you see that my fortune hath still that spiteful constancy to bring me near my desires, and intercept me. If I should write to you any news from this place, I should forestall mine own market, by telling you beforehand that which must make me acceptable to you at my coming.

"I shall sneak into London about the end of August. In my remotest distances I did not more need your letters than I shall then. Therefore, if you shall not be then in London, I beseech you to think me at Constantinople, and write one large letter to be left at my Lady Bartlet's, my lodging; for I shall come in extreme darkness and ignorance, except you give me light. If Sir John Brooke be within your reach, present my humble service and thankfulness to him; if he be not, I am glad, that to my conscience, which is a thousand witnesses, I have added you for one more, that I came as near as I could to do it.

"I shall run so fast from this place, through Antwerp and some parts of Holland, that all that love which you could perchance be content to express by letters if I lay still, may be more thriftily bestowed upon that one letter, which is by your favour, to meet me, and to welcome to London

"Your unworthy, but very true friend,
[*July* 1612.] "J. DONNE."

" *To your fair Sister.*[1]

"MADAM,—The dignity and the good fortune due to your letter hath preserved a packet so well, that through

[1] From the *Letters* of 1651.

France and Germany it is at last come to me at Spa. This good experience makes me in despite of contrary appearances hope that I shall find some messenger for this before I remove, though it be but two days. For, even miracles are but little and slight things, when anything which either concerns your worthiness is in consideration or my valuation of it. If I fail in this hope of a messenger, I shall not grudge to do myself this service of bringing it into England, that you may hear me say there that I have thus much profited by the honour of your conversation and contemplation, that I am, as your virtues are, everywhere equal; and that, that which I shall say then at London I thought and subscribed at Spa, which is, that I will never be anything else than—Your very humble and affectionate servant,
"J. DONNE."

[*July* 1612.]

The death of Lord Salisbury took place on the 24th of May 1612.

"*To Yourself* [GEORGE GERRARD].[1]

"SIR,—If this letter find you in a progress, or at Bath, or at any place of equal leisure to our Spa, you will perchance descend to read so low meditations as these. Nothing in my Lord of Salisbury's death exercised my poor considerations so much as the multitude of libels. It was easily discerned, some years before his death, that he was at a defensive war both for his honour and health, and (as we then thought) for his estate, and I thought that had removed much of the envy. Besides, I have just reasons to think that in the chiefest businesses between the nations he was a very good patriot.

"But I meant to speak of nothing but the libels, of which all which are brought into these parts are so tasteless and flat, that I protest to you I think they were made by his friends. It is not the first time that our age hath seen that art practised, that when there are witty and sharp libels made which not only for the liberty of speaking, but for

[1] From the *Letters* of 1651.

the elegancy and composition would take deep root, and
make durable impressions in the memory, no other way
hath been thought so fit to suppress them as to divulge
some coarse and railing one; for when the noise is risen
that libels are abroad, men's curiosity must be served with
something, and it is better for the honour of the person
traduced that some blunt, downright railings be vented, of
which everybody is soon weary, than other pieces which
entertain us long with a delight and love to the things
themselves. I doubt not but he smothered some libels
against him in his lifetime. But I would all these (or
better) had been made then, for they might then have
wrought upon him; and they might have testified that the
authors had meant to mend him, but now they can have no
honest pretence. I dare say to you, where I am not easily
misinterpreted, that there may be cases where one may do
his country good service by libelling against a live man;
for where a man is either too great, or his vices too general
to be brought under a judiciary accusation, there is no way
but this extraordinary accusing, which we call libelling,
and I have heard that nothing hath soupled and allayed the
Duke of Lerma in his violent greatness so much as the
often libels made upon him. But after death it is in all
cases unexcusable. I know that Lucifer, and one or two
more of the Fathers who writ libellous books against the
emperors of their times, are excused by our writers because
they writ not in the lives of those emperors. I am glad
for them that they writ not in their lives, for that must
have occasioned tumult and contempt against so high and
sovereign persons. But that doth not enough excuse them
to me for writing so after their death, for that was ignoble
and useless, though they did a little escape the nature of
libels by being subscribed and avowed; which excuse would
not have served in the Star Chamber, where sealed letters
have been judged libels; but these of which we speak at
this present are capable of no excuse, no amolishment, and
therefore I cry you mercy, and myself too, for disliking
them with so much diligence, for they deserve not that.

"But, Sir, you see by this, and by my letter of last

week, from hence the peremptory barrenness of this place, from whence we can write nothing into England but of that which comes from thence. Till the Lady Worcester came hither I had never heard anything to make me imagine that Sir Rob. Rich was in England; the first hour that I had knowledge of it I kiss his hands by this letter. I make account to be in London transitorily about the end of August. You shall do me much favour if I may find a letter from you (if you shall not then be there) at the Lady Bartlet's.

"I shall come home in much ignorance, nor would I discern home by a better light or any other than you. I can glory of nothing in this voyage but that I have afflicted my Lady Bedford with few letters. I protest earnestly to you, it troubles me much more to despatch a packet into England without a letter to her than it would to put in three. But I have been heretofore too immodest towards her, and I suffer this purgatory for it.

"We make account to leave this place within eight or ten days, and hence to make our best haste to the Count Maurice, where we think to find again the young Palatine. All this I tell you only because when you know that we shall run too fast to write any more letters, you may easily pardon the importunities and impertinences of this, and cast into no lower place of your love

"Your very true friend and servant,
"J. DONNE.

"Spa, 26 *July* here [*i.e.* 16 *July*], 1612."

It may be remembered that the Countess of Worcester was Elizabeth Hastings, the fourth daughter of Francis, Earl of Huntingdon.

" *To my much honoured friend* Sir T. LUCY.[1]

"SIR,—I have scarce had at any time anything so like news to write to you, as that I am at this town; we came from Spa with so much resolution of passing by Holland.

[1] From *Letters* of 1651.

But at Maastricht we found that the lowness and slackness of the river would incommodate us so much, as we charged our whole gests, and came hither by land. In the way at Louvain we met the Earl of Arundel, to recompense the loss we had of missing my Lord Chandos and his company, who came to Spa within a few hours after we came away. Sir Edward Conway, by occasion of his body's indisposition, was gone home before: he told me he had some hope of you about Bartholomewtide; but because I half understood by a letter from you that you were determined upon the country till Michaelmas, I am not so earnest in endeavouring to prolong our stay in these parts as otherwise I should. If I could join with him in that hope of seeing you on this side the water, and if you should hold that purpose of coming at that time, I should repent extremely my laying of our journeys; for (if we should by miracle hold any resolution) we should be in England about that time, so that I might miss you both here, and there. Sir, our greatest business is more in our power than the least, and we may be surer to meet in heaven than in any place upon earth; and whilst we are distant here, we may meet as often as we list in God's presence, by soliciting in our prayers for one another.

"I received four letters from you at Spa by long circuits. In the last, one from my Lord Dorset: I, who had a conscience of mine own unworthiness of any favour from him, could not choose, but present my thanks for the least. I do not therefore repent my forwardness in that office; and I beseech you not to repent your part therein.

"Since we came to this town there arrived an Extraordinary from Spain, with a reconfirmation of the Duke d'Aumale's pension, which is thereby £2400 a year, and he brings the title of Count to Rodrigo de Calderon, who, from a very low place, having grown to be Secretary to Lerma, is now Ambassador here, and in great opinion of wisdom: they say yet he goes to Prague with the Marquis Spinola and the G[raf?] Buqoy, to congratulate the Emperor; but we all conclude here that persons of such quality, being great in matter of war, are not sent for so small an employment: we believe certainly that they deliberate a war, and that the reduction of Aix being not worthy this diligence, their intentions must be upon Cleves, for the new town which the two Princes make by Cologne, despites them much.

"The Elector of Mainz hath lately been here upon pretence of coming in devotion to Sichem, and shortly the Electors of Cologne and Saxony are to be here severally: all concurs to a disposition of such a war, and the Landgrave of Hesse (who is as yet in the Union) is much solicited and caressed by this party, and I doubt will prove a frail and corruptible man. I durst think confidently that they will at least proceed so far towards a war as to try how France will dispose itself in the business; for it is conceived that the Duke of Bouillon brought to our King good assurances from the Queen Regent that she would pursue all her husband's purposes in advancing the designs of those Princes who are in possession of Cleves, and in the Union. If she declare herself to do so, when they stir, they are like to divert their purposes; but if she stand but neutral (as it is likely, considering how Spanish the Court is at this time), I see not that the Princes of the Union are much likely to retard them.

"Sir, you see what unconcerning things I am fain to write of, lest I should write of myself, who am so little a history or tale, that I should not hold out to make a letter long enough to send over a sea to you; for I should despatch myself in this one word that I am

"Your affectionate servant and lover,
"J. DONNE.
"[Brussels], *Aug.* 16, here, 1622."

A new patron of Donne's appears for the first time in the preceding letter. This was Richard Sackville, third Earl of Dorset, grandson of the illustrious poet of *Gorbuduc* and the *Induction*. Born in 1590, he had succeeded to the title in the nineteenth year of his age. Much less is known about him than about his brilliant brother Edward, who became the fourth Earl, and was also a friend of Donne; Richard took little or no part in public affairs.

From the expressions at the close of the last letter but one, it seems clear that the Drurys were now engaged on some embassy, perhaps connected with arrangements for a marriage between the Palsgrave and the Princess Elizabeth. The young Palatine arrived in England about a month after the return of Donne and his party in September. The travellers, who had started with the intention of a three years' absence, had been out of England about ten months.

While he was abroad, Donne wrote not inconsiderably in verse. The indignation felt by his own group of noble ladies at the somewhat venal laudation of that Mistress Elizabeth Drury on whom he had never set eyes, was appeased by epistles in which the poet laid himself out to pay delicate and appropriate compliments. From Amiens he sent a long paper of terzets to two daughters of Robert, Lord Rich, namely, to Lettice, Lady Carey, afterwards Lady Lake, and to Essex, Lady Cheke; their mother had been Penelope, the Stella of Sir Philip Sidney. This is a composition in Donne's harshest and most scholastic manner, and was evidently intended to flatter the charming young ladies by the assumption that they could rapidly comprehend such subtleties as—

> " Spiritual choleric critics, which in all
> Religions find faults, and forgive no fall,
> Have through their zeal virtue but in their gall.
>
> We're thus but parcel-gilt; to gold we're grown
> When virtue is our soul's complexion;
> Who knows his virtue's name or place, hath none.
>
> Virtue's but aguish, when 'tis several,
> By occasion wak'd, and circumstantial;
> True virtue's soul, always in all deeds all."

This is Donne in his very quiddity, and it would be difficult to find a more uncompromising specimen of the peculiar eccentricity of his style. An epistle to Lady Bedford, begun in France but never finished, is sweeter and more personal. He confesses an overwhelming debt to this the most exquisite of all his friends—

> "I confess I have to others lent
> Your stock, and over-prodigally spent
> Your treasure, for, since I had never known
> Virtue or beauty, but as they are grown
> In you, I should not think or say they shine—
> So as I have—in any other mine."

These last words are a direct and a humble apology for all the vain raptures over Elizabeth Drury.

To this period, moreover, belong, in my judgment, the poetical addresses to the Woodwards, which are so tantalising to us. R. W., T. W., and J. W. were doubtless all members of this family, but of Rowland alone have we so much as the Christian name. To him in 1610 Donne had presented a copy of *Pseudo-Martyr*, and a little later there was copied for him the Westmoreland MS. of the *Poems*. To Rowland Woodward was addressed the noble epistle beginning, "Like one who in her third widowhood doth profess." A short verse-letter to him has never until now been printed:[1]—

> "Zealously my Muse doth salute all thee,
> Enquiring of that mystic trinity
> Whereof thou, and all to whom heavens do infuse
> Like fire, are made,—thy body, mind and Muse.
> Dost thou recover sickness, or prevent?
> Or is thy mind travail'd with discontent?
> Or art thou parted from the world and me,
> In a good scorn of the world's vanity?
> Or is thy devout Muse retir'd to sing
> Upon her tender elegiac string?
> Our minds part not; join then thy Muse with mine,
> For mine is barren thus divorc'd from thine."

There is none of Donne's friends of whom we would more gladly know more than of Rowland Woodward.

[1] From the Westmoreland MS.

www.ingramcontent.com/pod-product-compliance
Lightning Source LLC
Chambersburg PA
CBHW051627230426
43669CB00013B/2210